SIX
YEARS
A
HOSTAGE

SIX
YEARS
A
HOSTAGE

THE STEPHEN MCGOWN STORY
AS TOLD TO TUDOR CARADOC-DAVIES

ROBINSON

ROBINSON

First published in South Africa in 2020 by MAVERICK 451,
a division of The Daily Maverick (Pty) Ltd

First published in Great Britain in 2021 by Robinson

13 5 7 9 10 8 6 4 2

Text copyright © Stephen McGown, 2020

Photography copyright © Stephen McGown, Maverick 451

The moral right of the author has been asserted.

A CIP catalogue record for this book
is available from the British Library.

ISBN: 978-1-47214-666-3 (hardcover)
ISBN: 978-1-47214-665-6 (trade paperback)

Printed and bound in Great Britain by Clays Ltd, Elcograf S.p.A.

MIX
Paper from
responsible sources
FSC® C104740

Robinson
An imprint of
Little, Brown Book Group
Carmelite House
50 Victoria Embankment
London EC4Y 0DZ

An Hachette UK Company
www.hachette.co.uk

www.littlebrown.co.uk

Dedicated to my mom

I would like to dedicate this book to the
memory of my mom, Bev McGown, who was
a beautiful lady inside and out.

You were an incredible mother and role model,
putting your children first before anything.
I thank you for the privileged life you gave me,
filled with the unconditional giving of love,
warmth and an amazing family environment,
far beyond what any money can buy.

Contents

PART ONE
Abduction

CHAPTER ONE

Adam

The First Mujahideen, Friday, 25 November 2011

I wasn't the first to see him – Tilly was. I was sitting at a table with the Dutch mother hen of our recently formed clutch of travellers, her husband Sjaak, and a German guy called Martin, on the porch of our Timbuktu *auberge*, when Adam walked in.

We weren't supposed to be staying there. The previous night, as we rolled into town from Douentza, our ragtag crew of bikers and over-landers got lost in the dusty warren of streets that make up the out-skirts of Timbuktu. We couldn't find the backpackers we'd planned to stay at, and decided the Alafia would do.

Designed for shade, security and livestock, the run-down *auberge* was a typical compound-style, rectangular building with high walls and a central dirt courtyard. There was an entrance onto the street, a shaded patio along one side of the ground-level rooms, and a staircase that took you upstairs to the roof and a view of the Sahara. The big steel gates, which closed the compound up at night, were open.

I was sitting with my back to the street. Next to me, on my left, was Sjaak. Across the table was Tilly, with Martin on her right. Both Tilly and Martin were facing the street. The only other person around was Johan, one of two Swedish bikers. He had returned with us from that morning's excursion to town, but while we hung out on the patio he had gone inside for a nap.

In the way that overland tourists share information, form loose alli-ances and part ways again, we were discussing what our next moves would be after Timbuktu. Everyone had different regions, countries and sights they wanted to see. I had my head down, updating my notes from the last few days of travel from Bamako to Timbuktu on my Samsung Mini. Tilly was flipping through a guidebook.

I wanted to see the famous Dogon cliff dwellings of Bandiagara and spend time along the mighty Niger River before leaving Mali and making my way south into Burkina Faso. Sjaak and Tilly were still weighing up their options. Martin didn't say much. Every few minutes Tilly would make a suggestion, but save for the odd polite response no one was particularly engaged. We were all feeling lethargic after lunch, and the heat left us flattened.

It was an absolute scorcher. After a few weeks riding down to Mali from London, I was growing more comfortable with living on and off my motorbike, but I still had the pink, easily-sunburned pallor of a UK office worker, and I was feeling the temperature that day. Timbuktu seemed to have slowed right down to handle the heat. Save for the odd stray, the streets were deserted as everyone attended 2pm prayers. Even the security guard who was normally at the gate had buggered off – and anyway, I doubt a skinny guy with a stick could have done anything with what fate dished up next.

When Tilly screamed, I turned to follow her line of sight over my shoulder and saw a man at the entrance gate. Later, I would come to know him as Adam, a fisherman from Nouakchott, the capital of Mauritania. He didn't look like a mujahid, which I suspect was the point. He wore dark jeans, a golf shirt and white sneakers. He had short hair and was clean-shaven, which in a region that prizes facial hair was a little unusual. In fact, he had a proper baby face. He looked off, because in a dusty, desert town, not many people look that polished. That and the fact that he had a pistol, which he was holding up in the air, his arm bent at the elbow, like he was in a buddy cop movie. We were just 12 metres from him, but he was not looking at us.

It's funny how your brain tries to make sense of a situation. Here was a clean-cut guy who looked like he should have been running a disco, except that he had a gun. Who carries guns and wears civilian clothes? Undercover policemen. Therefore, he must be a cop and he must be looking for a criminal in the compound. Right?

Wrong.

For some reason, probably to make sense of the nonsensical, I looked at my watch. It was 3pm. Adam walked in the gate, went left and scanned down the side of the building. By this stage I had almost convinced myself he was a cop. I was watching his every move but starting to relax just a little. That all changed seconds later when two gunmen came through the entrance armed with AK-47s. Wrapped in full Arab gear from their matching *suruwal kameez* (trouser and tunic combo) to their *imamah* (turban), they were completely covered except for one little slit for their eyes. One of the gunmen stood guard at the gate while the other came to stand in the middle of the courtyard. His gun was pointed directly at us. These were not cops.

One at the gate, Adam in the middle and one in the courtyard – all with guns. The four of us at the table. Johan inside. The gunman at the gate appeared a little nervous, but Adam looked calm. Satisfied that he had scoped out the compound sufficiently, he started walking directly towards us. Tilly screamed, 'Get under the table! Get under the table!'

I couldn't make sense of it. Why? What the hell were we going to do under the table? I could understand putting our hands in the air – Hollywood has taught us how to surrender to bad guys with guns. Still in all this chaos, it was the only bit of direction coming from anywhere that we could understand, so we all climbed under the table. It was dirty down there, a cement floor coated with dust and sand. I lay on my stomach, head to head with Tilly, trying not to look at Adam's approaching sneakers.

Adam started shouting and dragging Sjaak from under the table by one foot. Sjaak groaned as he put up resistance and tried to grab hold of the table legs, so Adam took his belt off and started beating Sjaak. Eventually Sjaak gave up and stood up, his body stiff as a rod. Over my shoulder I saw him get pushed out towards the street. I was doing a lot of looking, backwards and forwards from Tilly, who was less than a metre from my face, to Sjaak who was being bundled off outside. It was bizarre to see this incredibly tall guy in a tank top, shorts and flip-flops, who looked like he had just walked off the beach, getting marched away at gunpoint. Tilly was making all sorts of panicked sounds. She had a look of absolute horror on her face as she said under her breath, 'They are taking Sjaak. They are taking my husband.' It was almost like she was thinking out loud.

As we watched Sjaak getting dragged out into the street, I remember my own running commentary, midway between apology and explanation, 'But what can I do? What can I do? I can't do anything. These guys have got guns. We're lying under the table here. These guys are taking him out.'

The next thought I had, which in retrospect is quite embarrassing, was, 'Shit, I hope they don't come back, because if they come back they're going to take the rest of us.' For quite some time afterwards I thought about how selfish that was. What happens when your life is on the line does not follow your pre-imagined script.

They were gone for maybe 20 seconds, and in that time I lay there, mind racing, looking for a way out. The front gate was blocked by a guy with a gun, as was the yard. I thought about running and jumping over the wall of the compound and disappearing into the dirty streets of Timbuktu. Maybe I could make it up the stairs and jump off the roof, but it was a six or seven-metre drop; I'd probably break my leg and they would likely catch me in the street. All I knew was that I had to get away from these people. But while I was running through all the variables, only seconds had passed. Adam walked back into the yard and came up to the table. It was my turn.

He pulled me out by my left leg. Once he had dragged me out on my stomach, I stood up without a fight. He had my left flip-flop in his hand and was hitting me with it to get me to move. I put my hands in the air and everything seemed to go into slow motion as I began walking.

Action movies give you a false sense of what real-life situations are like. It's always binary – fight or flight, bravery or cowardice. There's no grey area, no description of the paralysis of panic. When you've got people shouting at you, pointing guns at you, dragging, pushing and pulling you, it's fucking terrifying. How you react is beyond your control.

I remember walking. Every movement was very deliberate. I could feel each muscle moving, my foot placed where it was supposed to be placed as my knee lifted up my other leg for the next step. My body awash with adrenaline, it felt like I was wearing a heavily padded jacket and there was this tiny version of me right in the middle. I was aware of everything, from Adam hitting me with the flip-flop to the contrast of the shade and the sun as I walked out into the street, but I didn't truly feel it. The jacket muted all sounds and sensations. My visual memory of what I saw in those moments is not a high-definition single-take video, but a slideshow of skits. The Table Skit. The March to the Street Skit. The Being Bundled into the Land Cruiser Skit.

The initial shock overwhelms you. There is so much new data rushing at your brain and your body; from the guys with guns to escape options, to the whereabouts of the others, the warp speed of what had just happened to our baking-hot Friday afternoon as tourists in Timbuktu, and even thoughts about the afterlife. It was as if I had been hacked by a supercomputer, spitting out the unbelievable questions that I did not have the mental capacity to process and to which there were no answers anyway.

Where are they taking me? What will they do with me? What do they want with me? How will my family find out? Am I going to die? Will I feel pain? Will I hear the gun? What happens then? Where do I go? At this stage, heaven and hell become quite real considerations.

We all know we are going to die, but most of us are pretty confident it is not going to happen today. We envisage it as some future point, with ever-shifting goalposts the older we get. If it's something out of our control, like getting hit by a car, well, that's just really bad luck, but at least that kind of thing will happen quickly. Standing there with a gun against me and a guy screaming at me in a language I did not understand was like getting the spoiler for how a film ends.

I thought: this gun could go off in 10 seconds. Maybe that's all I've got. A countdown of 10. Nine, eight, seven, I've got seven seconds of life left. It's like running a 100-metre race. You spend all your life charging into the wind with all your might, but now there's a finish line coming up on you very quickly. That final line is zero. When you cross it, it's all over, lights out.

Six, five, four seconds of life.

We walked out into the street. On the left was a beige Toyota Land Cruiser, idling. The tailgate was down and the gunmen were putting Sjaak, now handcuffed, in the back, lying down next to the spare wheels. I was waiting in the street as if in a queue, with my hands up, looking confused. Once they had Sjaak how they wanted him, they handcuffed me. This was even more terrifying. I had never been handcuffed before and these things took on their own personality; the metal deliberate and uncompromising, their intent submission and control. I climbed onto the back of the vehicle and lay down immediately behind Sjaak. I felt more vulnerable and at the mercy of fate than ever before. Instead of lying from front to back across the bed of the truck, they had made Sjaak lie from left to right in front of the wheel arch. I was lying awkwardly squeezed between the two wheel arches. Then they brought out Johan.

When Johan heard Tilly screaming he came out to investigate. He left his bedroom, walked down the passage, turned the corner to the patio, and came face-first into the business end of a Kalashnikov. Like Sjaak and me he was marched out, down the stairs, across the sand and out to the Land Cruiser. He was handcuffed and forced to lie down in the back of the vehicle. There was some jostling for feet position – to fit between those wheel arches you would need to be four foot tall, and I had nowhere to put my feet. Both Johan and Sjaak were lying on their left side facing the cab, but I was lying more on my back, looking upwards at the sky. I could not see the compound at that angle, but out of the corner of my eye I could see part of the street. By now I had figured out there were three gunmen and one driver.

Three seconds. Two seconds.

The next thing I saw were gunmen dragging Martin out of the Alafia. Martin was completely out of control. Three mujahideen were pulling at him and he was fighting them every step of the way, hitting their hands off him, pushing them away and walking backwards. He wasn't saying anything but he was making a lot of grunting sounds. The mujahideen were grappling with him while trying to control their AK-47s, which were slung over their shoulders. I could see they were getting irritated because their guns, swinging around like unruly handbags, were getting in the way of their attempts to control Martin, who by now was about three metres from me. He was up against the side wall of the compound when I saw him stumble backwards into the street and disappear just below the tailgate flap of the truck. I lost sight of him, but he was right there, almost within touching distance.

One second.

At the exact moment Martin fell, the tallest of the three, whose name I later learnt was Ghanda Hari, had had enough. As the two other gunmen stepped forward as if to pick Martin up, Ghanda Hari simply stopped fighting the momentum of the AK-47's sling, allowed the gun to swing up into his hands and fired three shots.

Zero.

I couldn't see what they saw, but the finality with which all three mujahideen turned and walked to the vehicle told me that Martin was dead. One of them gave the 'A-okay' sign to the driver. The expression on Ghanda Hari's face was one of mild irritation, like when you hit the enter key on your keyboard and it doesn't register or you find your stapler is empty. A slight inconvenience. He didn't look like he had just killed somebody.

I said to Johan and Sjaak, who were facing the other way, 'Shit, I think they've killed Martin.'

I could hear Tilly on the patio screaming and shouting.

I felt a blanket and then a cargo net being dropped over us and secured.

I lost the light.

The driver revved the engine and the vehicle started to move.

I didn't know it, but the longest journey of my life had just begun.

CHAPTER TWO

Steve McGown

'We've all been raised on television to believe that one day we'd all be millionaires, and movie gods, and rock stars. But we won't. And we're slowly learning that fact. And we're very, very pissed off' – Chuck Palahniuk, *Fight Club*

I often think about a DMC (deep and meaningful conversation) I had with my sister Leigh-Anne, sitting on top of a sandstone mountain on the cherry farm my family used to own in the Free State.

I loved that farm. It was about 16 kilometres from the Lesotho border, at the foothills of the Maloti Mountains. It was an amazing piece of land with rolling hills and *koppies* to climb and a big dam down the middle shaped like a bird in flight. It was a place of big skies, psychedelic sunsets and clean, cool air. In the spring the cherries would blossom *en masse* in a burst of colour. When I say it was heaven, it's literally how I imagined the afterlife would look.

Leigh and I had been running around there since we were just out of nappies, so even though Johannesburg was home, going to the farm was a huge part of our upbringing. As I got older it became even more important. Whenever I could, I'd escape Johannesburg and the strictures and rules of city life to bomb around on the farm on my grandfather's 125cc motorbike, go fishing or hang out with friends who came down with me from the city.

On this occasion, my sister and I had climbed the mountain to catch the sunset. She was talking about how sometimes in life you really have to mull things over; really think deeply and analyse stuff in order to find a way through the tough times. I was in my late teens at the time and I remember finding the concept so strange. What was there to think about? Life was straightforward and easy. It was about friends, good times, good conversations and laughter.

That was roughly 17 years ago and at least three lifetimes away. While we share the exact same DNA, the Steve McGown I was then was basically another guy. Up to that point, I'd had a very easy ride. Wherever I looked, doors opened. Everything seemed possible and within my reach.

When you live a charmed life, you don't realise it. I was popular at St John's College in Johannesburg. I can actually say that, because against the odds and despite a heavy stutter that runs through my family, I was narrowly elected to be head of one of the boarding houses, Nash. It wasn't the result the housemaster was expecting – there was another much more suitable candidate, a top sportsman, and obvious leader. Surprised at the outcome, the housemaster requested a second vote and again, the democratic process spat out the same result and I won. It was also a surprise to me, and not an altogether welcome one. For starters, I would have to board, which would be expensive. Then there was the issue of public speaking and my stutter. My dad stuttered, my cousins stuttered, there seemed to be something in the bloodline. Even my wife Cath stutters, and became a speech therapist. It's just something connected to the McGown clan.

So, when it came to the question of being head of house, the housemaster asked me if I wanted the role. I said, 'If I have to read in chapel, you can keep it. Thank you but no thank you.' Fortunately, he pointed out that as head of house you are technically in charge so you can actually delegate readings. I was voted in because I enjoyed people and vice versa, so I took the position.

Aside from the stutter, my life was carefree. While there was always financial strain on the family, I had amazing parents and the warmest family environment you could imagine. I've always been drawn to the outdoors, so whenever I could I went to the farm, to help my dad, Malcolm (aka Magoo), and my grandfather, Peter.

Peter was a World War II POW and mechanic who loved motorcycles. He was incredibly handy. He basically built the farm up, planting the cherry trees, getting the irrigation sorted. The farm balanced my life. There would be the craziness of Johannesburg, and then I'd have the farm environment, where I could run around and be knee-deep in mud.

By the time I got my driver's licence, I was organising regular trips down with my mates. On a Friday afternoon there would be five cars leaving Johannesburg in convoy, zigzagging down the highway. We'd lie on mattresses under the poplar trees by the dam drinking beers with a barbecue on the go, playing board games and talking about our plans for the future. Years later we all still reminisce about that golden period.

That's why I couldn't understand what Leigh was saying about complexity. I had not experienced that. Then, I got a job in banking and I started to become someone else.

It was never my dream to go into banking. I enjoyed the outdoors, so I thought of becoming a game ranger or getting into farming – not that I understood the nitty-gritty of what it takes to run a farm. I applied to the University of Pietermaritzburg to do a BSc in agri-management with a view to helping my dad in his business in some way. Then one morning my dad sat me down to say that farming was a tough game and that it would be difficult for us to sustain two households on what it earned. Bottom line: consider doing something else, son. I ended up getting a BCom Honours in risk, finance and marketing.

I'm not sure if anyone goes into banking for the right reasons, but I most definitely did not. I went into banking because I thought it would be lucrative, that I would look like somebody who is happening, someone who has the right credit cards stashed in his designer wallet, someone who has all the cash in the world, someone who people look up to.

In 1998 I got my first real job at a financial services company called Gensec.

Initially, there was a thrill to this new world. I was excited to become a big swinging dick banker, one of Tom Wolfe's Masters of the Universe. The starting salary was more than I'd ever earned before. I could buy rounds of drinks for my friends at bars in Sandton. It was just a matter of time till I made it to the top.

The gloss rapidly wore off. I found the job utterly demoralising – it was soul-destroying, menial work that would see me at the office till 9pm each night. In a matter of months, the 'glory' of becoming the big hotshot had completely vanished. I was selling my soul to the devil at a discount.

Everything that defined me as a youngster – that enjoyment of the outdoors, positive people, flexibility, freedom of movement – was evaporating in real time. I was stuck in a negative environment, behind a computer. I was always indoors, like a pale, blind fish at the bottom of a lake in a cave. This was not what I wanted.

My father always told me, 'If you want something in life, you have to push through. You can't quit.' I've spent a lot of time – too much you could argue – poring over the finer details of my life, and I think my reading of what my father was trying to say was the start of big

STEVE MCGOWN | **19**

problems for me. Instead of focusing on the part about wanting something in life, I hung on to 'you can't give up'. So every day I would grit my teeth and push on, sacrificing more and more of the person I was at the altar of pride and perseverance. After four years at Gensec and another two at Investec, I'd become a shell of who I used to be.

My mom had also been battling depression. I remember sitting at the kitchen table with her, both of us in tears. I said to her, 'I've completely lost myself. I don't know who I am, there's no colour in sunrises and sunsets now. If this is what I'm supposed to be, then I'm gone.'

I knew I needed to get out of banking, but my dad's words were on repeat in my mind. I could not shake that underlying message: if things get hard, you've just got to find that grit and push through.

I decided a change of scenery would make a difference.

CHAPTER THREE

North(ish)

Guided by the belt of Al Jabbar

I was sure Martin was dead. I could feel one of the mujahideen climb up onto the vehicle as it moved into second gear. They had just finished trussing us up under a brown blanket and a cargo net that was cinched tightly to the hooks on the outside of the Land Cruiser's carry bay. I still had my watch on, and even trussed up tight under the blanket I could just make out the time. It was 3:15pm.

I could not see much, so when the man spoke it seemed to be aimed at no one in particular, and everyone in earshot.

'Do you know Al Qaeda? *We* are Al Qaeda!'

As he said it, he must have lifted his AK-47, because a volley of shots went off centimetres from our heads. It was the flourish of a showman, an exclamation point not just for the final syllable that left his mouth, but for the entire operation this four-man crew had successfully pulled off. It was also a middle finger, as if to say to the authorities and to the people of the sleepy streets of Timbuktu: we came, we saw, we took these *kuffar* (non-believers) and we conquered.

We are Al Qaeda.

My body was already awash with shock and adrenaline; now my stomach fell even further, a whirlpool of acid panic bobbing with mines made of terror. Oh fuck. Not these guys.

As I lay there in the back of the vehicle, unable to see anything, I tried to let my body feel its way through the streets like a finger reading Braille. In my semi-delusional, panicked state I felt that my life depended on me keeping track of our direction. My starting point was all I knew for certain. I paid acute attention to every turn that the vehicle took.

We drove west down the road in front of the Alafia, turned right and began to head north, or at least that was the feeling I got. I was lying under the blanket, trying to get a peek as to what was going on.

There was no space for our faces and Sjaak, who it turned out had an on-going nasal problem, began to hyperventilate. He had to beg our guard for a small space to stick his head out so he could get air.

Squished half onto my back between the two wheel hubs, all I could see was the sky above our heads, so I tried to make sense of our direction from the way the vehicle moved. I could feel when we left the road and hit the desert, because the car started snaking around on the thick sand. It felt as though the driver was treating the Land Cruiser like an untamed horse, giving the vehicle its head a little, letting it navigate its own course through the sand to a destination that at least three of the seven passengers had never been to before.

The only ally I had was the sun. It was winter so even though the sun was sufficiently low that I could not quite see the edge of the Land Cruiser from where I was lying, I could at least get an idea as to which side was brighter. It wasn't much, but I knew the sun rises in the east and sets in the west; if I could tell which side of the sky the sun was on, I could identify where west was. Once I did that, I could tell we were heading north, fast. The driver was gunning the engine, trying to put distance between us and Timbuktu. After about 20 minutes, we turned sharply towards the east. By now we were bouncing around less, just sort of slithering our way through the sand.

About 40 minutes after we left Timbuktu, we stopped and I could hear another car nearby. There was a pattern to the way we stopped that I would come to learn; just before we came to a complete standstill, the driver would drive in a circle so when we stopped we would have created a corral in the sand and would be facing back the same way we came. This played havoc with my ability to keep track of direction.

I could hear voices as people from the two cars spoke to each other in what I assumed was Arabic. Their voices were calm and collected. There may have been a third car, it was hard to tell at this stage, because the engine of our vehicle was still running and, with my body wedged against the chassis, I was struggling to differentiate between sounds. There was a pause, they appeared to be waiting for something, but after a few minutes we were moving again, in what felt to me like the same direction we had just come from.

I hadn't really studied the map of northern Mali, because I'd had no intention of going north of Timbuktu and into the desert. Now I really regretted not having spent hours mulling over the Malian Sahara, because I had no idea about the area we were heading for. I had no idea about distances, where the towns were, or where the borders of Mauritania, Niger and Algeria were. For a long time to come, all I had as a point of reference was Timbuktu, a town that, for the rest of the world, is synonymous with the end of the road, the farthest place you could possibly go to. We were going much, much further than that.

Save for one rest break, we literally spent the next 15 hours and what I estimate was about 500 kilometres, going north-northeast. The reason I say 500 kilometres is because I actually tried to do the maths both in the car and later with Sjaak and Johan, who is a mathematician. Being able to quantify something is to create order, to understand the scope of problem. I was desperate for something to hang on to, and if I knew how far we were from Timbuktu, I would at the very least have an end point to this dark horizon, a light at the end of the proverbial tunnel. Without vision and desperate to keep a grip on what was happening to us, I kept trying to track every slight change in our movements, hoping that if I escaped I might be able to reverse-engineer our route.

North, then a push to the right for ten minutes, and then straight north. As the adrenaline wore off and the gravity of who these guys were sank in, all the energy just drained out of me.

Northeast, north, northeast, north, northeast.

Jammed against the two wheel wells, I attempted to put my cuffed hand under my head to protect it from constantly bashing and bumping against the steel bed of the Land Cruiser. As the hours went by, there were times when the desert felt incredibly flat and we went at great speed. At other times we went much slower, navigating mounds and humps, corrugations and divots I could not see. It always felt a little out of control, like it was a race that our driver had to win, but we were willing him to lose. I could hear the vehicle's engine fighting against the sand and the continual changing of gears. You could sense the urgency from the driver and feel the tension – our captors were trying to get us as far away from civilisation as quickly as possible. That meant they were expecting people to find us.

I had no idea what the protocol would be, whether there were surveillance planes and choppers on standby or if a platoon of Foreign Legionnaires would pop up around the next sand dune. Praying and hoping somewhat naively for the cavalry in the form of Western intervention, technology, planes, choppers, *Terminator*, ANYTHING to ride out and rescue us, I might as well have had a nap. As for local government forces, they were poorly equipped with inferior hardware, underpaid and less committed than our captors. At that stage, when it came to government authorities both in the region and around the world, either nobody knew where we were, had any reach, cared to give chase or gave two shits.

I found out years later that the Malian Army arrived at the scene of our abduction an hour after it happened. They got in their vehicles, drove to the edge of the road where the sand started and then, because they were not equipped for long-range desert pursuit, turned back. That was the extent of their efforts to try to find us. There's a French expression, '*tant pis*', that would encapsulate Francophone/Sahellian attitudes to our predicament for years to come. It means 'the situation is regrettable but now beyond retrieval.' Essentially, 'Oh well.'

North, northeast, north, northeast. I watched the sun go down and the sky get dark and I imagined us, a small boat tacking into a sea of sand, our pursuers so far behind on the map that they had effectively not even left port.

It was winter, so it soon got bloody freezing on the back of that vehicle, even under a blanket. We lay there shivering, trying to find a place for our feet. We bounced all over the hard, steel base of the Land Cruiser, expelling little 'oofs' of breath when we landed on our ribs and had the air squeezed out of us. I fought to stay conscious despite the nightmare of what being awake meant. Irrational thoughts did sloppy lengths in the pool of panic that was my brain. I was consumed with the timing of what had happened. I thought, 'Cath has given me six months to do this trip. I can't take longer than that.' I remember thinking that I'd cut my hair about four days prior and shaved the previous day, so at least I wouldn't have to worry about having to do those things. In retrospect, it is laughable that the grooming habits of the person I had been, a suit-and-tie-wearing city banker, were still something that mattered.

At the *auberge,* when Tilly screamed at us to take cover from Adam, I left everything that wasn't in my pockets on top of the table. At one stage I thought they might just steal my phone – that perhaps petty theft was what the gunmen had come for. For some reason they had not frisked us, so now my worldly possessions consisted of my wallet, my Suunto watch – bought for this trip because of all its nifty survival features, including a compass, which I couldn't access now – and the clothes I was wearing. These were a pair of black quick-dry shorts and a grey quick-dry T-shirt, both from a shop on the high street in Putney, and a pair of flip-flops from a Walmart in Arizona. The only other thing was my wedding ring. That was it. Or so I thought. Around 8pm, while squirming to find a comfortable position, I felt a small rectangular shape in the pocket of my shorts. It was my British passport.

It took a split second for me to understand my situation. I felt the blood drain from my face and the last vestiges of hope began to spin away. I knew very little about Al Qaeda, except the main atrocities of the last decade, but one story I did know was about a guy called Edwin Dyer who was kidnapped by Al Qaeda in January 2009. A British national, he was taken just north of Timbuktu on his way back from a Tuareg music festival in eastern Mali. At first Al Qaeda demanded a multi-million pound ransom. Then they demanded the release of Abu Qatada, a Jordanian cleric and associate of Osama Bin Laden. When the deadline expired for the British government to act, they beheaded Dyer. Although I was proud to be naturalised British and to have dual nationality, I was born in South Africa and was heading home. But I now realised that if Al Qaeda found the little book in my pocket it would say otherwise. Judging by what happened with Dyer, the British government does not negotiate. My British passport was going to be the death of me.

From the imprisonment of their leaders like Abu Qatada, to bombs flying through the air, to boots on the ground in Iraq and Afghanistan – they would not care who I really was. The place I called home, the colours of my flag, the nuances of my accent, the fact that the years I spent in the UK were just a detour for a young South African looking for adventure ... none of that mattered. To them I would simply represent the sins of the British Empire, both past and present. I had to get rid of the passport.

Watching over us, sitting on the spare wheel behind the cab, his face still hidden behind his *imamah*, was the mujahid who had announced that they were Al Qaeda. As we left Timbuktu, he had told us to stay quiet, and whenever we'd tried to talk under the roar of the motor he had threatened us again. With what happened to Martin fresh in our minds we obeyed, but I realised I had to do something.

I leant over to Johan and said, 'Fuck, my passport is in my pocket.'

He said, 'Give it to me, I'll throw it out the back of the vehicle.'

The problem was, it was now night-time. We were being followed closely by one other car, maybe even two, and because it was pitch-black, their dim lights lit up the back of our Land Cruiser like a faded yellow spotlight. I couldn't see much, but whenever we changed direction, they changed direction and their lights would pan across the back of the vehicle and light us up again. British passports at that time were burgundy-coloured. Unless there's a giant Saharan moth of that colour out there, seeing that drop from the car would look odd, even if I managed to free up my hands enough to get the passport out of my pocket, over to Johan and off the back of the vehicle without getting noticed by our guard. The odds were that the second car would stop to pick it up. They would know immediately that I was technically British. It would make me look guilty, and their hatred for me would only increase.

My next idea was to eat it. Seriously. I thought maybe I could tear the passport apart, chew it into a manageable cud and swallow it. Again, there was a problem. To combat counterfeiters and partygoers alike, modern passports are incredibly hardy, with stiff reinforced covers, electronic chips, holographic overlays and untearable, waterproof vinyl pages. So, if you fall in the sea after an all-night bender in Ibiza, the Foreign Office has you covered; your passport will still get you home to Essex with a hangover. Where they do not have you covered is if you are stuck in the back of a terrorist vehicle driving deep into the desert and you want to eat all evidence of your identity.

I decided that my next best shot would come when the vehicle stopped. I figured it had to stop at some stage, either to refuel or for a toilet break. Even Al Qaeda must need to pee. My plan was that if we were allowed to go to the toilet, I would try get a few metres off into the dark, drop the passport, force it into the sand, kick more sand on it and then pee on top of it.

As my brain spun out with plans and panic, I tried to focus on what I knew. The sun had been down for hours now and the stars were out. I watched Orion's Belt rise up in the east. It gave me a sense of comfort, because it was something I could relate to. One year, our family went to the Kruger Park, and I remember being given a stargazing book. It wasn't too technical on the astronomy front, but I enjoyed learning about all the different constellations. I hadn't thought about that book in years, but in a way having a rudimentary understanding of the night skies had become part of what I knew. It was a great technique for picking up women at varsity parties. I would dance with someone, ask them if they wanted to go chat outside and then say, 'When's your birthday, what's your star sign?' and identify their stars in the sky. I know … smooth operator.

Orion and his belt are very much a southern hemisphere constellation. It's a summer constellation, and at basically every barbecue I had ever been to in my life in summer, you would have a beer in your hand, a chop on the barbecue and Orion over your head, a constant companion.

As we drove further and further into the desert, bouncing around, getting battered, I used Orion to give me a sense of direction. I would come to learn that in Arabic, Orion is known as Al Jabbar, which means 'giant' or 'the almighty', and is also one of the 99 names of God. I already knew Orion as the hunter from Greek mythology, and that he stood in a north-south direction. His belt and his sword started to create the most vivid image in my mind, an arrow pointing towards his head, which points north. So as we swivelled and swerved, Orion moved towards the front of the vehicle, which meant we were now driving northeast. As Orion moved towards the back of the vehicle, we were driving northwest. When Orion was directly in front of my feet, we were driving directly north. North, northeast, northwest. Away from Timbuktu. Away from South Africa. Away from home. Away from Cath. Away from my comfort zone, away from my norm.

At 10pm, we did stop. Not because we had run out of fuel – I soon learned that Al Qaeda's vehicles had long-range fuel tanks for massive drives across the desert – but because Sjaak's phone began to beep. Just as I had a passport I did not want Al Qaeda to find, he had his old Nokia on him. The battery was getting tired, so the thing gave off a few plaintive beeps. The guard on the back heard it and banged on the roof to get the driver to stop.

We were in the middle of nowhere, it was pitch-black and amid much shouting everyone climbed out, unhooking the cargo net and pulling us from the vehicle. The second vehicle parked behind us, with only its orange parking lights on, rather than bright halogen lamps. They cast this yellow light for five, six metres and then the sand just disappeared into the darkness. Pulled from the vehicle, we were forced to stand while they did what they should have done in Timbuktu and frisked us. On Sjaak, they found his Land Cruiser car keys, his phone and his wallet, one of those old Velcro jobs with the neon colours we all had when we were kids.

They started interrogating us. 'Who are you? Where are you from?'

We mumbled back our answers in a blend of English and French until something registered. Holland, Hollandaise and Pays-Bas for Sjaak. Sweden and Suédois for Johan. South Africa, Afrika Zuid and Afrique du Sud for me. My answer was met with blank stares as if I had said something that did not make sense, like saying I am from 'Asia North' or 'the United States of Brazil'.

As they frisked me, they came across my body wallet. In it was €1,500 and $2,000, money that was meant to pay for accommodation, fuel and sundries on my way home. They took the wallet away and squatted down a few metres away in a little circle. I could hear them getting excited as they took the cash out and started counting it. While that group counted the cash, another guy was still patting me down. He came across the zip pocket on my shorts, found that small burgundy booklet, opened it up and walked over to the others, who were sitting in the light. As I watched them thumb through a booklet that would reveal an identity and destroy the last vestiges I had of safety and control, it felt like I stopped breathing. I became dizzy. My world was spinning out of control.

I could see that initially they could not figure out the lettering. One guy snatched it and looked at it, then somebody else snatched it from him. Everybody thought they could read better than the other person. It probably took them a minute to figure out what they had, and then I heard a word that was to plague me for years to come.

'Britannia!'

All hell broke loose. Everyone started shouting, *'Allah hu Akbar!'* and the mujahideen started dropping to the ground on their knees, one to my left, another to my right and more a few metres in front of me.

They were hitting the sand in prayer, to give thanks to Allah for a gift he had bestowed on them.

Me.

CHAPTER FOUR

London calling

'And I envy you. You have the one thing that matters. You have all your discoveries before you' – John Fowles, *The Magus*

Some kids wanted to open the batting for the Proteas or sail across the Atlantic or sleep with Charlize Theron. From the age of about 15, I had bored the living daylights out of my family and friends with my constant repetition of two big goals: I wanted to ride my motorcycle through Africa, and I wanted to travel and see as much of the world as possible.

On the latter I must have been getting a reputation for being all talk no action, because after studying and going into banking, I had gone nowhere and done nothing. I began to develop a fear of the consequences of finally going travelling. Would I be throwing my career away? Would I end up poor, destitute, unemployable? Would I be seen as a failure? I was only 25 years old and already consumed with stress and fear. It all sounds laughable now, but all of this kind of shit used to keep me up at night, and during the day it would weigh me down and cloud my thoughts.

Life, as my sister foretold on that mountain, was now complex.

Leigh-Anne was living in the UK working as a vet, and I thought I would go there too. It was common for young South Africans to move to the UK, get decent-paying jobs and maybe even dual citizenship; you could return to South Africa with some solid global experience, having made some money and travelled around Europe for a few years. Or, if you liked life in the UK, you could stay there and live relatively stress-free, with low crime and a strong currency.

South Africans had a pretty good reputation in the job market as being hard workers, so I was confident I could find a job. Still, it took me a while to get the courage to make the move, and to get permission from the British government. Finally I got a visa that would allow me to work in my industry, banking. I moved to the UK, and within two weeks I had a job in London working for JP Morgan.

For a while, things were exciting again. I had an incredible Canadian boss and I worked in a cosmopolitan team with a Nigerian, an Iraqi, an Australian, a Kiwi and an Indian. It really felt like the United Nations, and with more money involved I even started enjoying banking.

I went through a few ups and downs, as you do when you're trying to find your feet in a new country. I'd moved over with a girlfriend, who soon became an ex. I went through a stage when I would live off one single Tesco pie per day. Gradually, I started to grow up, get fit, save a little money and get in with my own crowd. That was when London became amazing. I stayed in various flat shares with Armenians, Poles, Israelis, Germans and Brits, the kinds of places that had moss growing in the shower. I was looking for a new place to live when I met Cath.

My sister attended a church in Southfields called St Michael's that had a large South African contingent. I wasn't particularly religious, but I started going there to anchor myself in the UK and develop my friend-ship group. At the same time I found this ad on Gumtree for a house share, one guy and two girls looking for a fourth. I phoned and asked if I could come for an interview. The person on the other end of the line, asking me if I was a weirdo or a murderer, was Cath, a fellow South African in London. I mentioned that I went to St Michael's, she said she also went there and I got the nod to come see the place. When I went there Cath wasn't around, but the other two housemates thought I was okay, so they said I could move in.

The funny thing is, a week before I even phoned about the house, Cath had been 'checking out some guy' at St Michael's; it turned out that guy was me. In due course, she spoke to her housemates and connected the dots that the guy she was eyeing out as he went up for communion was in fact that brother of Leigh-Anne, the tall blonde girl she knew from church, and also the guy who wanted to move into the house.

I moved in and in no time Cath and I hit it off. It was fantastic. We had a lot in common, and a lot of fun. We used to hang out together, sitting up till the early hours of the morning just talking – proper con-versations, which was something I really missed from those carefree days on the farm. After staying up half the night, I'd go to work com-pletely out of it from lack of sleep, and sit behind the computer with red eyes, wondering *why am I staying up all night talking to this girl?* She rapidly became my best friend in London.

About two months after I moved in, Cath made her move. 'Look,' she said, 'I've got feelings for you, so think about that. I'm just putting it out there.' The next day, she left for Switzerland on a skiing trip, so there was a bit of long-distance back-and-forth while she was gone. Then, as she got back, I was leaving on a skiing trip to France with some mates. When we were both back in residence she gave me what in retrospect seems like a slightly unreasonable ultimatum. She said, 'I've got feelings for you. If you don't feel the same way, you've got to get out, because this is my house, and I've been living here for a few years. You've created a very strange dynamic in the house and I can't live like this.'

In short: you can date me and stay, otherwise bugger off.

This ultimatum threw me, because in all honesty I wasn't quite ready for the next step. The breakup with my ex had been bad so I was in a bit of a weird space. I was still down about being in banking, and a little raw from having lived in scaffy places surviving off pies. Now, I had finally shaped a life that made a little sense – church, home, friends and a new best friend. I figured, *if I do date Cath, I could screw it up, but if I don't date her, then it is screwed up already and I'll lose my best friend. Either way, I've got problems.*

In the game show of my life, I chose to see what was behind the curtain. Decision made! Elation! Adrenaline! Love is in the air! And then Cath played her next move.

She said, 'Well now that we're dating, you've got to get out anyway, because this is a Christian house.'

Love is blind in more ways than one, because for a relatively strategic guy, I had been completely outmanoeuvred.

We met in December 2005, started dating in January 2006, and by April Cath dropped a prophetic bombshell on me. We were walking around London holding hands, and she said to me, 'I think we're going to be married within the year.'

I burst out laughing, because that wasn't even on my radar. I was running the numbers, overanalysing things and creating unnecessary pressure on myself, but Cath was more at peace with the world. She just has this way of saying how things are going to be and, more often than not, that's how they turn out.

We got engaged on Christmas Eve in Norway and on 31 March 2007, almost a year to the day that she first brought it up, we got married.

We settled into life together in the UK really well. I had a motorbike, a red and blue Honda CBR, and I got a second helmet for Cath. This was our mode of transport. We would travel all over the country on that motorbike, in summers and in freezing winters. I would strap down a small tent to the back of the bike, which had these little pannier bags, so we had to pack light. I had a saying at the time: 'If you can't fit it into a rucksack, you shouldn't have it.' It was an attitude both for the way we travelled and how I wanted us to be in the world: to live simply and without extraneous baggage.

At times it felt like the luck that had been part of my youth was back. As the years passed, I worked a number of banking jobs in the UK, from JP Morgan to Royal Bank of Scotland to Bank of America. Whenever I needed a new job, I always got one, even when other applicants had much better qualifications. My ability to talk to and connect with people was what made the difference.

Somehow I even came out fine when the 2008 credit crunch decimated the banking sector. As the crunch hit, the project I was working on for Royal Bank of Scotland ended, so without being laid off like so many others I was still out of a job at a very bad time. With time on my hands I would meet up with Lloyd Robinson, another South African mate of mine, in Richmond Park. We'd do a couple of laps of the park on our bicycles each morning to try to stay busy and to have a routine. It was hard to be positive in that climate of doom and gloom. We lamented our luck, saying that our lives were probably ruined and we would never get another job. My UK visa was based on work; without a job I would have to go back to South Africa long before I was ready to. As we rode round and round that first week our conversation was always the same. 'You know, we've got troubles, what are we gonna do? What are we gonna do?'

I went for an interview with Bank of America, and the next day I was back with Lloyd going around in circles. One day later, Bank of America came back to me to say I had the job. I remember thinking, 'You know what, you're a jackass. You wasted your time worrying while you could have been out enjoying the summer.'

It was a major lesson for me – not to waste time worrying about what may not happen. There's always good stuff you can take from tough times, and life can change in a second.

As we closed the front door each workday morning, Cath and I would part ways on the pavement. She would head off in one direction to her speech therapy job; my work was in the other direction. At night, we would come back to our place, have dinner, and at around 8pm we'd go for a walk around Putney. That was our daily quality time together. Those cool winter evenings were beautiful, quiet and dark. Walking around Putney at night, holding hands, talking about our day and discussing our future plans and dreams was incredibly special to us.

Going back to South Africa was something both of us were ready for. Cath had been in the UK for 11 years, I'd been there for seven. We'd made a bit of money, travelled and gained enough experience in our respective careers to make a living when we got home. I still disliked banking with every bone in my body, but I had picked up some incredible skills and experience that would help me in the future. The plan was to go back home and go into business with my dad, who had just passed retirement age. 'You created this thing but you're going to retire soon,' I told him. 'I want to come back and get involved.'

Magoo was on board with the idea. In fact, towards the end of my time in the UK, my father was actually giving me flak for taking so long. He was ready to take it easy.

As our homecoming crept closer, there was a definite countdown element and a lot of excitement among our loved ones. Cath and I were coming home, to be near family and friends, for me to have a career change, for us to have a fresh start in life and to have kids. Starting a family was a big part of the plan for our future.

The only thing stopping us from coming home sooner was that we were so close to securing our British passports. It's one of those things thousands of young South Africans who do a stint in the UK try to do. You move to the UK, spend years working your way up the food chain and finally, with sufficient years on the clock, you qualify for a British passport. When I first moved there it was not really my intention but, by the time we started to plan our trip back to South Africa, both Cath and I had been there so long we were now eligible.

I was blown away by the amount of time, effort and money it took me to get the passport. If only I had known what its real cost would be.

CHAPTER FIVE

Cath

As told by Steve's wife, Cath McGown

The last conversation I had with Steve before he was taken happened on Tuesday, 22 November. It was supposed to be my last week in the UK, just before I got on a one-way flight to South Africa. I was walking down the road in Putney on my way to the dentist when he called on my cellphone; by the time we said goodbye, I was in the waiting room. The reception was not great, but I could hear that he was happy. He was in his tent at the Sleeping Camel Backpackers in Bamako, enjoying life on the road and living his dream.

Just four days later he was kidnapped.

I was staying with Steve's sister Leigh-Anne and her husband Gregg when Steve's dad Malcolm called. We had been to Nando's in Putney for dinner. Using the 'free whole chicken' cards Steve handed over when he left on his trip, we'd ordered a whole chicken and spent much of the evening chatting about Steve's route and our plans for life back in South Africa. I stayed with Leigh and Gregg that evening on the couch of their eighth-floor flat in Roehampton overlooking Richmond Park. Just before I went to sleep, I got a voice message from a friend saying that there was a report that three people had been kidnapped in Timbuktu. Most people knew that Steve was on his way to Timbuktu – it was a bit of a joke, because you don't get to say something like that often in life. I told Leigh, but we didn't think too much of it, and I had a good night's sleep.

I woke up the next morning a little after 9am when Leigh's phone rang. It was Magoo. I could immediately hear the panic in her voice. She asked him to clarify something. I jumped off the couch and followed her into the kitchen, trying to make sense of the look on her face and the questions she was asking. She reached out as if to reassure me. She hung up and told me that Steve had been 'taken by some rebels', and they were waiting to hear more news. It was like the air had been sucked from the room, as we both tried to process what this meant. Then, all we had were questions and very little idea about how to get answers.

Magoo was already several steps ahead of us in terms of contacting the various authorities. He told Leigh that the British government was trying to get hold of me, so we called consular services by dialing 999. Eventually I was connected with Jim Collins from the British High Commission. His first words to me were: 'Catherine, you are a difficult person to get hold of.'

This was not a great start. I felt frustrated and irritated. I hadn't changed my phone number in years and I had filled in hundreds of documents during my stay in the UK. If the British government could not track me down in their own country, how were they going to find Steve in Mali?

Jim said, 'Your husband is in a very dangerous position. He is going to be away for a very long time.'

I wasn't expecting to hear that. In fact, I didn't believe Jim. At that stage, the reality of the situation had not yet hit home. As far as I was concerned, Steve would be home in South Africa in 12 weeks for our fifth wedding anniversary, because that is what he told me he would do.

Jim said he would be in touch to set up meetings at Scotland Yard to see the police, and at Whitehall where I would be briefed by the FCO (Foreign & Commonwealth Office).

Magoo had also given Leigh a number for me to call in Mali. I will never forget that call. The line was not good. I spoke to an official, who had a very strong accent. I kept on having to ask him to repeat himself because I didn't understand what he was saying. When I put the phone down, my first thought was that I would never be able to find Steve again as the communication was so poor. I felt a wave of panic flood through me, followed by heaviness in my gut.

My Steve was gone.

I didn't know it at the time, but I would be told by people with experience in these matters that the first 24 hours after a kidnapping are the most important. All I knew was, as long as I was doing something and not sitting around anguishing, I could keep it together.

I made a lot of phone calls. My pastor said that I was welcome to come over and pray with him and his wife, Judy. Leigh and Gregg dropped me off at their home. Steve and I started attending their church after we got married. Pastor Ray came to the UK from Zimbabwe. From the start he had a special place in his heart for us – Steve especially, because they had similar schooling and a lot in common. Both Ray and Judy embraced me when I arrived. I blurted out the information that I knew, then went off on a wild tangent of irrational thoughts. Ray quoted some verses from Psalm 91 and Isaiah 61 that never held relevance in my life before, but now seemed like they were written with us in mind.

'He will cover you with his feathers, and under his wings you will find refuge; his faithfulness will be your shield and rampart.' (Psalm 91:4)

'He has sent me to bind up the brokenhearted, to proclaim free-dom for the captives and release from darkness for the prisoners.' (Isaiah 61:1)

These verses would come up again and again for me like a mantra over the next few years, even when they fell on deaf ears. I knew that He was a loving and forgiving God, but I struggled with what had happened to us. I went to another prayer gathering that evening with Leigh and Gregg in Kingston. We prayed for strength, that Steve would not be harmed, for supernatural intervention, for the shackles to be broken, for hearts to soften, for Steve to feel His presence. A wave of guilt passed through me as I felt I had not been a good enough Christian. I resolved to change my ways and be more dedicated. I would read the Bible more. I felt like I had a purpose in life now: to bring back my husband.

After the church gathering we headed back home in silence. My tummy was rumbling – I had not eaten since breakfast. I was going to starve myself so that I could feel what Steve was feeling. When I felt a hunger pang, I would endure it. This kind of thing would always be present in the years to come – guilt at eating, guilt at relaxing, guilt at feeling any form of joy, like from a song on the radio. I could never bear the thought that while Steve was enduring hell, I was not.

I didn't sleep well that night. I was used to sleeping in strange places – I'd been backpacking for the last five months – but despite being cosy on the couch, my mind would not stop whirling. Leigh also couldn't sleep. She was five months pregnant, so she woke up a lot at night. She came through to check on me. She prayed for me, and after that I was able to sleep.

Waking up was awful. The closest thing I could compare it to was a breakup; from one day to the next my life was different, only my heart was not broken from rejection, but by terrorists. Steve still loved me; he was just gone.

I set off in the cold for Scotland Yard. These were the same streets I'd walked so often to get to and from work, but never before had I carried such a load on my shoulders. At the front desk I announced my arrival and a detective came to fetch me. He sat me down in his office, brought out some official-looking documents and kicked things off with, 'Sorry to be meeting under such circumstances.'

He said that he was going to ask me a lot of questions. Most of them had to do with Steve's character profile, the reason for his journey, how he looked and where his dentist was. This last comment made my blood run cold; I knew where that question was leading. Steve had not seen a dentist since I met him, so I presumed the records would be with his dentist in South Africa. I would need to ask his mother, Bev. He asked if Steve had any distinguishing features. The only things that came to mind were a scar on his chest from a possible melanoma being cut out, and a bald patch on the right side of his head from where the forceps were placed when he was delivered as a baby.

I enjoyed talking about Steve. I gathered that they wanted to know what type of hostage he would be. I felt more assured that Steve would be fine, because he was not hot-headed or quick to anger. He was a hap-py-go-lucky type who was smart enough and streetwise enough to know what was best for him at the time. The detective asked me some possible Proof of Life questions: What was Steve's cat called? Where did he go to school? What were our nicknames? The last one had me blushing – Steve has a tendency to hand out strange nicknames. The detective said, 'We've heard it all before. Trust me.' One of the names was 'Knucks'. The detective asked me to spell it; I said that it was short for Knucklehead.

The detective ran me through what I should do if I got a phone call from the kidnappers, like asking who is speaking and using the person's name when responding. He gave an example, 'Okay Mohammed, thank you.' He said that I needed to ask if Steve is alive, make a note of the time of the call, and to listen out for background sounds to give them any clues as to where he was being held. Prisoner rescue by echolocation.

The detective gave me some information on Hostage UK, a group that supports the families of kidnap victims. Lastly, he gave me an earpiece and a recorder to insert into my phone when the kidnappers called.

How did I land up here?

I called my friend Bridget on the way to the tube station to tell her the meeting went well. Now I didn't want to talk for too long; I had to keep the line free for the kidnappers to call me. Steve knew my phone number by heart. While I walked I turned my phone on to its loudest setting and clutched it, the recorder and the earpiece ready to be inserted. I had taken off my gloves – special gloves that Steve bought me because I have difficulty with circulation – and my hands were getting cold. They would just need to be cold.

The night before I went to Whitehall, I stayed over with Karen and Guy, some friends in Putney near to where Steve and I used to live. When they went to bed, I borrowed their laptop to log in to my and Steve's emails. Word had started to spread about Steve's kidnapping but it was still being kept out of the press. I compiled an email to a group of friends and family, giving them as much information as I knew at the time.

I woke up to an inbox full of replies. One of my friends in Australia thought his account had been hacked and asked if this email was genuine or not. I tried to reply to all the different questions. I realised that I couldn't keep up with this. I received two phone calls – my heart pumping each time – but both were friends phoning from South Africa. Lee had a few choice swearwords for Al Qaeda. Rich gave me a taste of what was to come: he was angry.

So many people phoned to say that they knew someone who knew someone who could get Steve back. They had 'trained in the military'. They 'worked for the Foreign Legion'. They 'knew a guy in Mali'. My head was spinning. Everybody wanted answers and I didn't have many. I was still at the information-gathering stage. My phone's ringtone would soon become a sound that sent me into a panic. I ended up changing the ringtone as soon as I arrived in South Africa and had to get a new phone number. I kept my UK phone going for another month just in case I got a call.

I set off for my meeting at Whitehall at about 9am. I went to get my post from my old flat first. The caretaker, Stuart, was totally shocked to hear what I had to tell him. I was getting tired of retelling the news already, and it was only day five. This would become a new thing too: telling people about Steve.

I arrived at Whitehall feeling very underdressed – I was still travelling, so I was wearing jeans and trainers, and carrying a backpack. At the security gate I had to put all my belongings into a scanner. They wanted to take my phone away, but I said I was expecting a call from the kidnappers. They didn't argue with me as Jim Collins arrived to fetch me and just nodded his head. Jim was very chatty, which was a relief as I was processing everything around me. He took me past the Foreign Secretary William Hague's office. I knew his name from the papers and TV, but I had to read up on who he was exactly afterwards. I had a lot to learn.

We continued up the beautifully polished wooden staircase. The carpet underneath me was soft. Many an important person had walked up these stairs. *What was I doing here?* I was just a regular dual-nationality citizen with a normal upbringing, schooling and job. Here I was in my jeans and trainers. At least they were Salomon. Steve got them for me: fast-drying and lightweight, for our travels. Right then it was me who felt lightweight, walking the corridors of Whitehall.

I was taken to a conference room with a few officials already sitting in a semicircle in front of a large screen. Only afterwards did I realise that they were from the Secret Services, MI5 or MI6. I sat down and took out my A5 spiral-bound notebook that had travelled with me around the world. It was the only thing I had in my bag. I was introduced to the people around me and made notes of their names. The British consul in South Africa, Joanne Olivier, joined us via video call. I liked the look of her. Jim explained that I would meet her when I was back in South Africa.

An attractive young woman with dark hair started talking. I tried to keep up with what she was saying as everything, from the acronyms to the place names and people she was describing, was new to me. She spoke about AQIM, the Tuareg, nomadic traders, the Algerian civil war and Gaddafi. She could see I was struggling to keep up, so she just said, 'You don't need to write anything down. It will all become clear to you in time.'

She spoke about the last kidnapping in 2009 of a British citizen, Edwin Dyer. They didn't tell me he'd been beheaded. I would find that out later. She asked if I had any questions. I felt really embarrassed that after this high-level conversation all I was worried about was malaria, since Steve no longer had his medication. I was also concerned about things he would need, like sunblock and toothpaste. I asked for help in talking to NatWest. The bank staff I had spoken to were unhelpful; even though I was his wife, I had no authority over his accounts. All

I wanted to do was block them. I was worried that Al Qaeda would withdraw all of Steve's cash from the ATM in Timbuktu. I could see Jim suppressing a smile.

'We can arrange to have Steve's accounts frozen,' he said, 'but you don't need to worry about that. These guys don't want Steve's money, they want the government's money.' Jim said he would arrange an official letter that I could give to people to explain the situation.

Before I left, I asked if I could stay on in London; I was nervous about how the South African government would handle Steve's abduction. At that stage I felt that Steve stood a better chance if I worked with the Brits, because he would not be a huge priority for the South African government, which had plenty of other things to put time and money into. Jim and his colleagues reiterated the importance of playing the South African card. Al Qaeda had more leverage against Britain.

When I look back at those days, I have memory flashes of phone calls and meetings, instructions and rules.

Jim instructed me to close down all social networking sites like LinkedIn and Facebook; our aim was for the kidnappers to know as little about Steve as possible. They emphasised that it wasn't that Steve was not important, but the idea was to paint him as grey as possible. There should be no colour or feeling linked to Steve in any way, because it could give his captors something to work with.

Jim also said that there must be no reference made to money anywhere. This meant closing the BackaBuddy charity page for Steve's ride that my stepdad Alan had set up a few weeks prior.

No matter how counterintuitive it seemed, publicity was not a good thing. Jim said it was extremely important not to talk to the media. No comments and interviews in the tabloids with the 'wife of British prisoner Steve McGown'. I asked him why – when Paul and Rachel Chandler had been kidnapped by Somali pirates a few years back, it was all over the news. Jim's response, once again, was that we didn't want to make Steve look important to the kidnappers. The less they knew the better. He said that the FCO would be in charge of 'crafting' the lines for the press.

All of this was new to me. I didn't know many people who had been kidnapped. I knew of the Chandlers, and little Maddie McCann, of course, but that was a child kidnapping. This was Al Qaeda, a force to be reckoned with. I had been in London at the time of the bus and tube station blasts in July 2005, but other than that Al Qaeda and the associated Iraq and Afghanistan wars were far removed from my thoughts. I felt safe in London. I loved London. It was where I met Steve.

The rest of my time in London was rushed. I had had to finish packing, among all of the emails and phone calls that I was receiving. I slept on a few more couches, prayed more, cried more. I was blessed to have so many friends who were happy to help me out. By the time I left the UK, the British government officials I was dealing with said that the chances of Al Qaeda calling were slim now that a week had passed.

I remembered the first fight Steve and I had had after we got engaged. It was something I thought about a few times when Steve was away. It was New Year's Eve, our first one together. For me, celebrations are important and should be shared. They were not as important to Steve. I would continue to celebrate his birthday when he was away as well as our wedding anniversaries. That is just the way my family is. I realised that I was going to go back to South Africa and would spend a lot of time with Steve's parents, who I did not know well at that stage. I had only met them on a few occasions.

A wave of anxiety washed over me as I thought of all the things I needed to do when I got back to South Africa: new accommodation, new ID, new car, new driver's licence, renew my Speech and Language registration ... the list went on. Everything was already set up for me here in London. Steve was gone and there was no knowing when he would be back. I had to start again, but on my own.

CHAPTER SIX

McGown, the Mechanic

'I finally felt myself lifted definitively away on the winds of adventure toward worlds I envisaged would be stranger than they were, into situations I imagined would be much more normal than they turned out to be' – Ernesto Che Guevara, *The Motorcycle Diaries: Notes on a Latin-American Journey*

Call it a midlife crisis, but somewhere between 30 and 50, a lot of nine-to-five working people break with the established routine of their lives to take on a big challenge. Marathons, Ironman, cycling up Kilimanjaro backwards on a unicycle – for some it's about physical endurance or claiming a first, while for others it's about undertaking a journey that shakes the dust off their lives and returns them to their true selves. I fell into the latter group.

Riding a bike through Africa wasn't new. It wasn't a first in the slightest. That was never the point. It was something for me. To see a truly different part of the world, to rid myself of at least a part of who I had become, to reprogramme myself and return to South Africa more like the old Steve (I liked that guy), with a fresh outlook on life, ready to settle down and have a family.

This trip had been a long time in the making, at least eight months in terms of practical planning, but in terms of daydreaming it felt like it had always been there. Cath knew about it from the moment we met. I had been banging on about 'riding a motorbike through Africa' for as long as I could remember, but life got busy and the opportunity had just never presented itself. When we decided to move back to South Africa I had the perfect gap.

When I was 11, my grandfather taught me how to ride the little Yamaha 125cc motorbike we had on the farm. My mate, Gregg Lister, used to come down with me from Johannesburg, and he'd jump on the back. We were kids so we weighed nothing, and once I got the knack of cornering, braking and accelerating at the right times, we'd zoom past the cherry orchards, over the mountain and around, over and over again. We'd fall off all the time and burn our legs on the exhaust pipe, but the battle scars were part of the appeal.

I loved the freedom that a motorbike gave you to explore the outdoors, but my folks would never let me have one in town. Even when I hit 18, they said there's not a chance in hell I was getting a motorbike. Still, I always wanted one, so when I moved to the UK I got a Honda CBR superbike. I rode it in the UK for years, but as the trip home started to take shape, I realised I needed an overland bike that could handle tough roads, was easy to fix and could go huge distances without having to refuel. After doing extensive research, I bought a Yamaha XT, a bike I classified as a 'farmer's bike', easy to fix with no fancy electronics. It was an older model from 2000, but with about 200 miles on the clock it was an absolute baby. My baby.

To say that I doted on that bike would be an understatement. In order to save my XT from unnecessary extra mileage, and to keep fit, I rode my bicycle to work. The summer evenings were long as I cycled through the parks en route home; the winters were cold and I'd get drenched, but I loved it. As I rode along the Embankment, I'd watch the reflection of decorative lights draped in the trees dancing off the Thames. It was beautiful. Later, I would come to realise what a privilege it was to move around at your own speed so safely.

In a way, my commute felt like I was in training for the trip, learning to keep things simple by packing exactly what I needed to shower and change at work. *If you can't fit in in your backpack, you don't need it.* That's the thing; if you're prepared, life's actually pretty easy. It was as if I was feeling the transformative effects of the journey home long before we said farewell to the UK.

Motorbike sorted, the next thing I needed to decide on was the route. I considered taking the well-trodden East African route down to South Africa, made famous by Ewan McGregor and Charley Boorman in *Long Way Down*, but their journey did not inspire me at all. With a camera crew every step of the way, and fixers sorting out their visas, McGregor and Boorman's escapades actually put me off the East Coast, because they made it look vanilla. More than anything I wanted to experience something different. If everyone did the East Coast, which was mostly tar road, I was going to go down the West Coast. It had more mud, jungles, bigger fish, colourful birds – and it would give me a unique story to tell.

Turning my attention to a West Coast/Central Africa route, I began to get serious with my planning. Cath was incredibly supportive. I was going to begin my trip in October, and I had six months to complete it, because I had to be home before our fifth wedding anniversary on 31 March 2012.

One of the old, established overland routes went through Algeria via a tarred road to a town called Tamanrasset, which is slap-bang in the middle of nowhere in the heart of the Sahara desert. From there you have to either wind your way into Mali or work your way into Niger. From what I could establish, the Tamanrasset to Mali road looked like a no-no route. No one spoke about it, because no one really went there. The road from Tamanrasset into Niger, down to a place called Arlit, was a much better known route, but it was known as bandit country and had recently got a reputation as a place where terrorists were active. As much as the idea of driving through the area appealed in a geographic sense, I had zero interest in getting kidnapped so that was out. In fact, there was a lot of talk about how the area that consisted of the eastern side of Mali near the town of Gao, the western side of Niger and the lower side of Algeria had become a real terrorism hotspot. With the rise of Al Qaeda in the region, it was an area you most definitely did not want to go to. That settled it for me. I was going to avoid any chance of terrorists in the Central Zone and do the West Coast route instead.

I needed to take in as much as I could in as few countries as possible. Going through Mali was ideal because Mali has a lot of borders. If I went from Morocco, through Mauritania, Mali and then into Burkina Faso, rather than riding through all the coastal countries of the bulge of West Africa, I would skip a lot of small countries like Senegal, Guinea-Bissau, The Gambia, Sierra Leone, Liberia and Côte d'Ivoire. It would have been amazing to visit them, but I didn't have time for it. I wanted to spend as much time as possible around the equatorial countries further south, ticking cool birds off my lifer list, fishing in crazy rivers way off the beaten path, seeing giant trees and riding through muddy jungle tracks. That's why, when I got kidnapped on the edge of the Sahara, it felt doubly cruel: in my mind, my 'real' trip going through Central Africa – Nigeria, Congo, Cameroon, Angola – had not even started.

Next I needed to establish who was going to come with me. I was happy to do it alone, but for safety reasons, and because it's nice to share experiences, I was looking for someone to join me. So I began marketing the trip.

First prize would have been Cath, as we would get this shared six-month homecoming journey. Trying to pre-empt this idea I bought Cath her own bike, a Honda XR 125. We used to go to a quiet road behind our house in Putney where I could teach her how to use the accelerator and get a feel for the clutch. Riding a motorbike can be tricky at first, a little like playing a piano with your feet and your hands, and she kept falling off into the street. I felt really bad and would run up the street after her in case she came off again. Cath is tough as nails, though, and persistent, so eventually she got it and we started riding around together. She even started biking to work and back, but she was never really sold on the whole motorbike thing. One day she went to visit a friend and her bike broke down. She tried calling me a few times to help her, but I was in the pub with a friend and missed her calls. She had to half-push, half-drive her bike all the way home to Putney from Worcester Park – a hell of a long way. I think that was the day her interest in biking back to Johannesburg died.

Initially, when you float the idea of a big adventure around a crowded barbecue or dinner party with like-minded friends, there will be a lot of interest. Most people, South Africans, Ozzies and Kiwis especially, love the idea of The Big Trip, whether it's sailing across the Atlantic, traversing the USA in a camper van, backpacking around South America or India, or overlanding through Africa. Plenty of friends expressed interest in joining me, but as time went by they all dropped out as they weighed up the ask (time, money, risk) against the reality of what was possible in their lives. Unless it's part of a bigger life change, very few people can just chuck it all in for six months.

I'd been spending a lot of time on a website called Horizons Unlimited, an unofficial forum for the world of motorbiking and 4X4 overland trips through Africa and elsewhere. On a forum like that you're speaking to a like-minded tribe, so inevitably there was interest in my trip, but there was a lot of uncertainty too because of the seismic geo-political shocks reverberating through the region. In 2010 the Arab Spring uprisings kicked off across North Africa and the Middle East, and while I was prepping for the trip throughout 2011, they were still underway across North Africa in various shapes and forms. Some countries, like Morocco and Mauritania, only experienced minor protests and underwent constitutional reforms, while others, like Libya and Egypt, saw massive upheaval. In Egypt, two successive governments were overthrown. Libya saw the biggest impact when, after a vicious multi-faction civil war, long-ruling dictator Colonel Muammar Gaddafi was overthrown and killed.

What this meant was that most of North Africa was regarded as a bit of a tinderbox, although it seemed the conflict was restricted to the eastern side of North Africa. While I was concerned that my dream trip might have to be called off if sparks flew in the wrong direction, I was confident that, if the relative calm in Morocco and Mauritania held, there would be a window period for me to get across from Spain into Morocco and then shoot south through Mauritania. If my timing was right I'd soon be in Nigeria sipping *ogógóró* (distilled palm wine) from my hammock, with my gas cooker next to me boiling up some couscous to eat with my tinned sardines and olives.

Many of the bikers who had initially expressed interest on Horizons Unlimited fell out of contention, but one guy called Fokke was on board. A Dutch motorcycle policeman, he was a bit younger than me and judging from his Facebook page, which had pictures of him jumping out of planes in a Batman suit, he was quite a wild guy. We spoke on the phone, he seemed like a decent dude, so we agreed to do it together.

By this stage I had fallen deep into the rabbit hole of overlanding through Africa. Cath was tolerant as I systematically dismantled all that was warm and nice and beautiful about our home and turned it into a biker's cave of gear and grease. I pasted maps of West Africa on the bedroom wall. Guidebooks were strewn across my bedroom table and the lounge. The couch was constantly loaded with gear, and I'd use the armrests to build and rebuild my pannier bags, because they resembled the back end of my bike. From spork to tarp, every item I took had to have two or three functions. I'd cruise eBay at all hours buying 'essential' bits of gear for the bike and the ride. Long-range full tank that would give me 500 kilometres to the tank? Yes please! Bike rack, centre stand, bash plate, hand guards, luggage rack and hammock? Take my money! Every Wednesday evening for three months I attended a motorcycle mechanics course in Croydon and with my newly acquired skills I would break down and rebuild engine parts in the kitchen. I even managed to bring Cath's Honda XR 125 back to life. The trade-off was a Tupperware full of bike parts and a kitchen that stank of petrol. I had a very tolerant wife. Having been chained to a computer keyboard for so many years, I relished getting my hands dirty and grappling with the practical nature of fixing the bike and getting it going again.

I was finally ready.

All that remained before I got on my bike was an epic round-the-world blitzkrieg backpacking tour with Cath. It was a brief thing by Phileas Fogg's standards, around three months, but just as I had obsessed over my African motorbike thing, this was something Cath had dreamed of. We'd worked, we'd saved and this was our last hurrah before we settled down back in South Africa. We had an absolute ball and it was an awesome way to get travel-fit before getting on the bike. One week we were packing up the house, selling off our belongings and preparing to leave our life in London, and the next we were winging it to New York. From there we went down to Washington, then over to Cancún in Mexico, then Belize, Guatemala, Nicaragua, Costa Rica, back to the US to visit some of my family in Arizona – where my uncle, a former US military officer, warned me about travelling through North Africa – and then off again. Route 62 to California and San Francisco, then on a plane over to Thailand, checking out Bangkok and the islands down south. In Hong Kong we parted ways. Cath flew to Australia to see some of her friends and I flew back to London where my bike, my gear and a few last bits of admin awaited me.

We thought it would be six months until we saw each other again.

With Fokke locked and loaded to leave the Netherlands at the same time, I jumped on my bike on 13 October, settled onto my new black ram's skin saddle cover and set off on to the A20 down to Dover. France, Spain, Portugal, Gibraltar and a ferry crossing to Morocco lay ahead before I would finally be back on African soil.

CHAPTER SEVEN

Steve of the Sahel

'It's not about the bike' – ~~Lance Armstrong~~ Steve McGown

Say what you like about Coldplay's Chris Martin and conscious uncoupling, but the man knew how to put a hit together. Take 'Viva la Vida' and its instantly recognisable intro sequence, used the world over in adverts, political rallies or any other moment that demands an uplifting entrance. It's got everything from a soaring, orchestral string section, to a marching drumbeat, triumphant timpani, bonged gongs and clashing cymbals, all accompanied by Martin's uplifting (yet somewhat Old Testament-hymnal) lyrics about ruling the world, being a king, castles that stand on pillars of salt and sand, missionaries, Roman cavalry, Jerusalem bells a-ringing, and even revolutionaries waiting for heads to be served on platters.

As I gunned my bike south out of Morocco, shooting deeper into the vastness of the Sahara desert, that song was blasting through my headphones and hitting me right in the feels. I was undergoing a conscious uncoupling of my own. While I had loved many elements of my years in the UK, I was leaving London, Excel spreadsheets, derivatives and dividends, Liverpool Street Station, the City Line and echoes of 'Mind the gap' behind in my dust.

I was already high on life, and the sun baking down on my back made it even better. From London all the way down the west coast of France and on to Spain, it had rained nonstop in what felt like Europe's worst autumn in years. I felt like I was permanently soggy. It probably didn't help that from the get-go I wasn't staying in hostels. I would just ride until I was absolutely buggered, pull over on what I thought were quiet back roads and set my hammock up in the rain in a bus shelter. I had intentionally given myself a limited budget for the trip, so I would not be tempted to take it easy. As part of my preparation, I bought cooking gear; a pot and a small multi-fuel Coleman, which allowed me to cook with anything from petrol to vodka.

Now, in Morocco, we had clear skies and surprisingly modern motor-ways near the coast. As the bike bucked up a gear and cruised forward, the Dutchman, Fokke, was just a high-speed speck on the horizon. This, I'd come to realise, was normal.

Fokke-the-police-motorcyclist seemed to have a death wish. Hitting the corners knee to the ground, his waterproof bags and other gear piled high behind him, he pushed the limits all the time. I felt that in Fokke's mind he was Evel Knievel, jumping through fiery hoops. It was as if he was the polar opposite to me. This ride down Africa was not about the journey for him: it was all about the bike.

The ferry from Gibraltar to Tangier was the calm between two high-speed storms as Fokke and I put our feet up on the railings and had a beer. I was bubbling over to soon be back on African soil. But watching him push his bike to its limits on those Moroccan highways, and again as we hit the off-road stuff, it was clear that we had vastly different approaches both to how we rode our bikes and to what we wanted from this trip. I wanted to cruise like an old granny biker at 80 km/h so I could take in the birds, the bush and the animals, and let Africa get under my skin again.

The other stark difference was in the way we had prepared for the trip. I'd spent months researching and prepping my bike, my gear and my route, from my mechanics course to researching the best cellphone, best point-and-shoot camera, best tyres, best route and all other eventualities, whereas Fokke appeared to be flying by the seat of his pants. It felt like he had just climbed out of bed in Holland and hit the road – he was that disorganised. We seemed to stop at every Carrefour in Morocco to buy something that Fokke had forgotten. My trip to Africa was not meant to be about malls and car parks. I just wanted to get away from human clutter.

Take driving in sand. You're meant to deflate your tyres when driv-ing in sand to get a bigger surface area, but because he didn't buy a pressure gauge, he let too much pressure out of his tyres. He then hopped on the bike – which was already in the sand – and let rip with the accelerator. The result was he ripped the valves out of his inner tubes, so we had to replace them – but he only had one spare.

He had also not modified his petrol tank, so because he was going as fast as he could, we had to stop more frequently to get fuel. I had long-range tanks because I heard that there was a very long stretch between Western Sahara and Mauritania where there were no fuel stations. It turned out there were plenty of fuel stations, so Fokke was in luck, but I was confident that those long-range tanks of mine would come in handy later down in the Congo.

The pressure was growing between the two of us and our different expectations.

The longer we spent on the road, the more often we met and re-met travellers following a route similar to ours. Inland from the Moroccan coast in the city of Rabat, we met Dutch couple Sjaak and Tilly in the overlanders' campsite the guidebooks recommended. They were there in their Land Cruiser with its rooftop tent, and they were down-to-earth and friendly. While Fokke and I were setting up camp, two Swedish bikers, Tommy and Johan, arrived on super-kitted-out KTM motorbikes. Money and machinery personified, theirs was an entrance akin to pulling up outside a restaurant in a Ferrari in a one-horse town. Everyone looked up and many judged them, myself included. I stood there watching them, in their RoboCop riding gear, thinking, *UFOs have arrived and are landing in our dirty, dusty campsite*. They seemed so out of place. To put it into perspective, my entire set-up cost me about £4,000, intentionally, while one of these bikes went for about £15,000. I figured they must be professional bikers, but it turned out one of them knew what he was doing while the other just had loads of money. The Swedes and the Dutch couple were heading the same way we were, down the West Coast, so we hung out a bit comparing notes, then we all went to get our visas in the slow-motion queue of the Malian and Mauritanian embassies.

Customs officials the world over are not known for their people skills, but the Mauritanian authorities in particular were an obnoxious bunch, tripping on power and rude to all and sundry. No one was actually allowed into that embassy, and there was a big queue in the street up to a closed door in the perimeter wall. The door would open slightly, a face would appear, grab some documents from the person at the front of the queue, close the door and disappear. Later the door would open again, same face would appear, documents would be handed out and the door would close again. It was like a Disney film, a magical door in a forest of enchanted Moroccan streets, hiding all kinds of secrets behind it.

Fokke and I made our way from Morocco down into Mauritania, skirting the coastline of Western Sahara – a disputed area that claims to be a sovereign state, but which is also claimed by Morocco. Here we felt we had to tread lightly and watch our conversation with the locals, as there was a tangible heaviness in the air. As we rode, there was no sign of life in the rolling sand dunes to our left, while to our right the Atlantic Ocean was marked by the occasional sardine factory, strange blocks jutting up out of the desert with hundreds of kilometres of nothingness between them. I remember looking inland to the endless desolate reaches of the desert and thinking, *God has forsaken that land*. It was hot, and a continual wind was blowing slithering, snake-like formations of sand across the road. There was no sign of water, no flicker of fauna or flora, and it went on for what seemed like interminable distances.

I could not relate to the Sahara region. It was very different from the Africa I knew. In my mind, North Africa may not have even been Africa at all. It was undeniably beautiful in its own way, but I was looking forward to getting into the arid savannah of Mali and further south into the equatorial rainforests of central Africa. I was salivating to get into baobab country with large rivers, hippopotamuses, sausage trees, colourful birds and open plains.

After the two major coastal cities of Mauritania, Nouadhibou and the capital Nouakchott, we cut inland above Senegal. Fokke and I agreed early on that we would use tar roads in the more Westernised countries so we could make up time to be able to relax and go slow in the less-developed countries, where there were more things to be seen and adventures to be had. We were now arriving in those lands. We rode from the Maghreb states of North Africa into the semi-arid Sahel region.

The Sahel is not a cultural alliance of states like Scandinavia, or a politico-economic union like Benelux, but rather a much more informal eco-climatic belt that sits between the Sahara to the north and savannah to the south. It runs from northern Senegal and the Atlantic, right across Mauritania where we were, into Mali, Burkina Faso, Algeria, Niger, Nigeria, Cameroon, the Central African Republic, Chad, Sudan, South Sudan, Eritrea, Ethiopia and Somalia before it hits the Red Sea. It is still a dry zone, but compared to the Sahara it is much more fertile. The further south we went, the greener it got. I defined that transition by the first baobab and cow that I saw. Cows need water to drink. They cannot survive in the desert proper. Along with cows come water and human settlements: the real world.

We were riding through places that for months had just been names pegged to the bedroom wall – Aleg, Kiffa, Ayoun el Atrous – and then crossing over the border into Mali. We could have pushed on to Bamako, but instead we went to the town of Kayes up in the far western corner of Mali, right on the Senegal river. By now, Fokke and I were not seeing eye to eye and there were undercurrents of frustration building. We were trying to communicate what we each wanted to achieve, but the end result just never played out. We would stop just before sunset and ride a kilometre off the road to make camp. On paper this was still fantastic, sleeping rough among the birds and the bugs, but it still defeated my objective. I wanted to stop at 4pm to allow myself two hours to walk around with my binoculars, do some fishing and take it easy, off the bike. I wanted to take things in, nice and slowly. I wanted to live my African experience, get myself filthy. I could feel that, soon enough, we would go our separate ways.

Our next stop, Bamako, was an important point on my African trip. It was a key spot for embassies, so in one fell administrative swoop I could get visas for Burkina Faso, Nigeria, Togo, Benin and a bunch of other countries that lay ahead. Fokke and I were staying at a well-known overland haunt, The Sleeping Camel, along with Sjaak and Tilly, and the Swedes. One night over a pork spit barbecue, we connected with an overland tour group who were heading up to Segou, Mopti and on to the fabled desert city of Timbuktu.

It was originally part of my plan to go to Timbuktu, but by the time I got to Bamako it wasn't, because I was sick and tired of riding through desert sand where I continually fell off. I thought I would skip Timbuktu and push on south into what, in my head, I called 'real Africa'. But now, hanging out with the overland truck crowd, enjoying the spit barbecue and lots of conversation and laughter, Timbuktu reappeared as an attractive option. To be honest, I wasn't that interested in the city itself, though I was certainly up for spending a night or two there and taking a couple of pictures. What I really wanted to do in the area was spend time birdwatching along the Niger River, and to check out the famous cliff dwellings of Bandiagara, from where the Dogon people managed to repel invaders for centuries. Caught up in the crowd's excitement, I decided to join them on their way to Timbuktu.

The Dutch Land Cruiser, the Swedish UFOs and the South African on the farmer's bike started the journey with the overland truck. Identifying each other as kindred spirits, Tommy and Fokke raced ahead together – but we ended up passing them between Douentza and Timbuktu, when Evel Knievel's bike broke down. Again.

All along the inland route through Mauritania, there had been road-blocks, armed by *gendarmes* who demanded our *affiches* (visas and travel papers). We would sometimes wait for a couple of hours until there were sufficient vehicles to ride in convoy, with military vehicles front and back. The questions and warnings of the soldiers – 'Where are you going? Don't stop for anyone! Al Qaeda!' – were sobering; there was definitely terrorist activity in the greater area. Throughout the ride, I quizzed people whenever I could about safety and security, routes and precautions, from the senior official at the Malian consulate in Rabat, to the Zimbabwean overland guide we met in Bamako, and the Australian who ran The Sleeping Camel. Everyone assured me that on the main routes in the main areas of Mali, like Timbuktu, it was very safe. In terms of history, they weren't wrong. Our abduction was the first terror incident to happen in Timbuktu.

It felt kind of weird arriving in Timbuktu, akin to actually finding Atlantis or El Dorado, if those places were bustling, dusty desert towns. Timbuktu was always that fabled place name, thrown into conversation metaphorically to imply something that was bloody far away. Even the Oxford Dictionary describes it as, 'used in reference to a remote or extremely distant place'. If you think about anyone travelling from Europe or from the Mediterranean Sea, Timbuktu was one of the first major trading cities you would get to once you crossed the western portion of the Sahara – if you made it at all. The heat, bandits, sand-storms and other dangers must have destroyed the majority of those early long-distance travellers. The way we got there, approaching from the forests and savannah of Bamako and Douentza in the south by 4X4s and motorbikes, was considerably easier.

We arrived in Timbuktu on the evening of 24 November 2011. It was dark and so dusty that we couldn't see anything through our headlights. The trip took longer than expected, and we were led off down Timbuktu's dirty streets to our *auberge* by some young children running in front of Sjaak and Tilly's Land Cruiser.

The following morning, we left our hotel at about 10am. There were four or five kids, ranging from around eight to 11 years old, sitting on a pile of rubble about 20 metres or so down the dirty road. The overland group had gone out earlier on an organised tour; we never saw them again.

As we walked past the kids, one of them came up to us and shouted, 'Hey, you want a tour around Timbuktu? We will give you tour!'

It's the kind of interaction that happens every day between poor kids and tourists in thousands of developing cities, where the offer (or the request) ranges from tours to sweets and pens, private dances, drugs and carpets. You learn to navigate them with a smile. Tilly, being the tour organiser of our informal group, had already plotted out a few things for us to see, so we gave a friendly, 'Thank you, but no thank you,' and kept walking.

The kid who asked the question looked to be the eldest of the group. He also looked incensed, and barked out a threat that as captives we would mull over for years to come:

'I'm going to get Al Qaeda to take you into the desert.'

The threat was so specific it shocked me. I remember turning to Sjaak and saying, 'That's pretty aggressive! Seems a bit of an overreaction. Do you know what brought that on?'

We carried on our way to the tourist centre where we had our passports stamped with a 'Welcome to Timbuktu' stamp. It seemed an inconsequential and somewhat gimmicky thing to do at the time, but I had my British passport with all my travel visas in my pocket, so I figured, why not get some lightweight memorabilia.

I'd decided to travel the northern countries of Africa on my British passport because I thought it would be easier and possibly cheaper for visa applications. Once I crossed the equator and moved on to SADC countries, I would change to my South African passport.

Later, when Sjaak, Johan and I pored over every detail of what happened that day, one of our theories was that it may have been one of the *gendarmerie* at a checkpoint that we drove through en route from Douetnza to Timbuktu who informed Al Qaeda where we were. We may have been seen while walking around town and they followed us back to our *auberge*. Al Qaeda didn't just randomly pitch at the Alafia hostel. Somebody told them. While they did not know our nationalities, they knew we were Westerners.

Another theory rested around what happened at lunch. We had zigzagged our way around Timbuktu, taking in both the mosques and the gravesites with their famous mausoleums (later destroyed by Al Qaeda when they took over the region in 2012). We stopped at the market where we saw a young French couple just walking around on their own, which seemed quite adventurous. From the market's rooftop there was a beautiful view out into the Sahara. Looking out there, I remember thinking about whether I should take myself for a ride that afternoon. I had seen what I wanted to in Timbuktu, and I wanted to go out, zoom around the desert off-road, have a bit of fun and work on my riding skills in the soft desert sand.

On our way home we got a bit lost in the bustling streets and chaotic whirlpool traffic circles of downtown Timbuktu, which is similar in layout to many European cities, just dustier. We came to one of the big turning circles, and as Tilly was turning her map this way and that trying to figure out where we were, we decided to get some lunch. With my pink skin I also wanted to get out of the midday sun. Right on the edge of the traffic circle was a grubby cafe of sorts. Plastic chairs, plastic tablecloths, in a four-by-five-metre room, five budget meals on offer on a single-page plastic menu – the kind of place frequented by locals, not tourists. On the right, down a single step, was a tiny kitchen, and this little Arab guy kept running in and out, taking orders and disappearing down the two stairs into his kitchen. We sat there, having soft drinks and eating a budget local rice dish that cost about a euro per plate.

After about half an hour, as we got up to leave, the place suddenly got crowded because a bunch of guys came in at the same time as we were trying to get through the door. They stood back for us; I think there were three of them. There was some awkward manoeuvring around each other, lots of polite, friendly, '*Merci, merci*' from us as we walked outside into the wall of midday heat. I wasn't paying particularly close attention to these guys – I had no reason to – but I remember they were wrapped up in desert gear and one of them was strikingly tall. Perhaps it's revisionist history, trying to find clues in what seemed like an uneventful morning, but I remember the whole interaction seemed a little charged, from the way they carried themselves to the way they looked at us, but they were polite enough not to leave me questioning anything until later.

To this day I still don't have a clue if they were following us or not, or if the tall guy was Ghanda Hari, but from the *gendarmerie* checkpoints on the tarred roads into town to the tourist office stamps and the kids and everyone in the area around the Alafia hostel, plenty of people knew there were foreigners in town.

An hour and a half later, Adam walked into our lives.

CHAPTER EIGHT

Magoo

As told by Malcolm 'Magoo' McGown, Stephen's father

It was about 8am on Saturday morning when the phone rang. I was sitting at my desk in my office at home, getting some admin done. It was Fokke's mother. Before they left on their trip I said to Steve, 'You better just leave a contact number in Holland, just in case. If something goes wrong, they will have a number for us on that side.'

When she introduced herself, I knew that something had gone wrong, because you do not get calls from the relative of your son's biking buddy for any reason other than catastrophe.

Fokke was not with Steve when it happened, because he and the other Swedish biker had broken down on their way to Timbuktu, but as soon as he found out what happened at Steve's hostel he made some phone calls. Fokke actually phoned the police in Holland first, then he phoned his mom, who phoned me. She only had the bare bones of the story at that stage, but as she gave me the what, how and who of what had happened, I got the message: Steve had been taken by Al Qaeda.

I walked from my office 20 metres down the passage to where Bev, my wife, was in the bedroom. It's a house we've been in for 45 years; both Stephen and my daughter spent a large part of their childhood here.

I told my wife Steve and some others have been taken, 'they think by Al Qaeda'.

As you might expect, the news left us utterly shattered. What do you do when you get a call like that? What can you do? The only thing that made sense was to take action, and start looking for help and information. So, I started making phone calls.

I started with Steve's cellphone, just in case there was a mistake and he might answer, or I could get through and find a way to get him help. I wanted to tell him to do just as they asked, and not to fight or oppose them. It's the same kind of advice we have received from experts in hijacking situations in South Africa. The phone just rang and then went to messages. I figured it had either been confiscated or they were out of a range somewhere deep in the desert.

A whole night had already passed since they were taken.

My next step was to find government contacts. I began looking through the pages at the back of the telephone directory. I was in panic mode. I started looking up all the relevant government departments to my mind – Department of International Relations and Cooperation (DIRCO), police, secret service, Home Affairs – trying to find someone to call who might be able to help. Every number just rang and rang. There was not a single manned emergency 24/7 number to be had in the entire superstructure of the South African government.

My next avenue was Radio 702, because they frequently have government ministers on their shows. I spoke to someone off-air, and told him about what had happened to my son. I said, 'Please can you get me someone to talk to? I need a number in Pretoria for any of our government ministers who can help.'

About half an hour later, I called the station again for an update. They may have tried phoning a few people, but they certainly were not giving me the action I required. They had not managed to get any direct ministerial contact. It was now around 11am. Then the phone rang. It was a Lieutenant Colonel Ernst Strydom who said he was in charge of dealing with abductions and ransoms in South Africa. It did not necessarily sound like a fit with an incident of an international nature, which Steve's saga was, but it felt miraculous to have someone to talk to. Within half an hour he was at our house – all the way from Pretoria.

Ernst would become our go-to man for most government interactions. He was one of the good guys, as was Mbulelo Bungane from DIRCO, who we were soon introduced to. They had our best interests at heart and assisted us wherever they could, but there were definite limits to what they could do, what they could tell us, and how far their influence stretched. Over the next five years and eight months, I learned that helpful officials like Ernst and Mbulelo were the exception rather than the rule. Government wheels turn very slowly.

With something like this, you soon learn to throw the net wide, because you have no experience of what to do and little feedback from those in the know. There are very few people in this world who can claim experience and understand strategy when it comes to terrorists taking hostages. I certainly had no idea, but I knew that the key to securing Steve's release could only be found by chipping away at this giant multi-layered puzzle that starts and ends with information. It started with something as basic as me – a businessman and farmer – googling Mali and trying to learn about Al Qaeda, Ansar Dine, and the various factions, rebels and other players in the region where Steve was taken. It started with Cath's mom, Sue Peiser, who is well connected and adept at networking, getting contacts at both the South African and British governments and their secret services. It started with me going to the Horizons Unlimited website forum where Steve had spent a lot of time in the build up to his trip, to dig around and try to learn as much as I could from other bikers and overlanders who had on-the-ground knowledge about what was going on there.

I had to create an account to access Horizons, and chose the username Magoo, my schooldays nickname from the 1950s cartoon character Mr Magoo. When I tried registering my username, it turned out it was already taken – by Steve. That really hit home.

I had to go with the username Magoo2 instead.

Once you start to get info, you have to evaluate each and every piece. Over time, you get told – and you learn – which bits of info are valid and which should be rejected. You start to get an understanding of who can actually help you and who cannot or will not. Many of these decisions are incredibly hard to make, because the game you are playing involves your son's life. On top of that, nothing is straightforward. There's no 0800-AL QAEDA-IN-THE-ISLAMIC-MAGHREB number to get in touch directly and find out what they want and how you can try to deliver it in exchange for Steve.

Money was one of the immediate issues. How much did we have and would it be enough to buy Steve back from Al Qaeda? I brought up whether it was viable to sell the farm to free up capital, but Ernst ruled that out. Even if I got R5-million to R10-million for it, that would be a drop in the ocean in terms of the money that Al Qaeda would want for Steve, Johan and Sjaak. To put it into perspective, one of their earliest ransom demands for Steve was for €15-million.

It was not even clear if it was money that Al Qaeda wanted; publicity and leverage hold immense power too. I subsequently learned that money is one thing Al Qaeda are not short of. The kidnapping business in which Steve was now an inventory item is a lucrative revenue stream for funding jihad.

Sometimes, as in Steve, Johan and Sjaak's case, Al Qaeda tried a few different approaches to see what would stick. Occasionally, it felt like they were just playing a game of their own, making overtures that they knew would be denied, but which would give them a pulpit to criticise Western governments for not coming to the table.

One of their demands in May 2012, about six months after Steve was taken, was the release of the Jordanian cleric Abu Qatada in exchange for their 'British' captive. A Spanish counter-terror judge once described Qatada as 'Al Qaeda's spiritual ambassador to Europe', and he had been tied to numerous terror cells and attacks. Imprisoned on and off in the UK for his ties with Al Qaeda, he was a real thorn in the UK government's side and an important talismanic leader to Al Qaeda. The UK wanted to send Qatada back to Jordan, where he faced a stiff prison sentence of 30 years for earlier terror activities.

The demand from Al Qaeda to exchange Steve for Abu Qatada got Steve's name wrong. They called him Steve Malcolm, which is his middle name and my first name. It read:

'The initiative to the British government is to release its citizen Stephen Malcolm, who also has South African nationality, if it deports Abu Qatada to one of the "Arab Spring" countries. If Britain ignores this offer it will bear the consequences of handing Abu Qatada to the Jordanian government.'

The last time Al Qaeda tried to trade a British prisoner for Abu Qatada was in the case of Edwin Dyer. When the British government responded with some variation of 'we don't negotiate with terrorists,' they beheaded him.

It's almost impossible to describe the double helix of anxiety and hope we felt as a family when Al Qaeda put this on the table. We were visiting our daughter in the UK at the time, and we sent frantic messages to Ernst Strydom to send Steve's South African birth certificate, his South African wedding certificate, his South African university degree and anything else to prove Steve was 100% South African.

It became crystal-clear right from the beginning that we had to get one message straight: Steve was a South African. That's it. He may have been caught with a British passport, but after discussing it with both the British and South African authorities, everyone agreed that Steve stood the best chance of surviving if we focused on his South African nationality. That meant, even though we tried to keep the press to a minimum, that whenever Steve was mentioned there was a sense of ownership, that he was, is and always will be South African. We wanted him brought home to his wife and family in South

Africa. We provided Oupa Mokau, then South African ambassador to Mali, with every document we could think of that confirmed his South African identity. Everything we did, repeated the message – South Africa, South Africa, South Africa.

It suited the British side too. If Steve was considered a British prisoner, not only was he more valuable if a ransom was paid (and the UK, like all governments, claims not to do that), but Steve would also give Al Qaeda more leverage when demanding the release of Islamist prisoners like Abu Qatada. Still, every trip that we did to the UK to see my daughter, we would end up at the Foreign Office for meetings with British intelligence in the hope that they had some good news for us, anything that might inch us closer to getting Steve back.

The Abu Qatada exchange never happened. He managed to game the system and avoid deportation for many years by appealing to the European Court of Human Rights on the grounds that if he returned to Jordan he would be tortured. The irony of a guy who had been a professor of Sharia sciences in Pakistan, and who did not believe in non-Sharia law, using Western democratic laws to his advantage made the whole saga even more bizarre. In the end, after he and his family had led a very comfortable taxpayer-funded life in the UK for many years, it took Jordan and the UK ratifying a torture treaty to eventually send him home in 2013. In 2014, he was acquitted of charges and released.

I can now speak with authority that negotiating the release of a hostage is a maze of diplomacy and sovereignty that each family has to navigate as best they can. There is no blueprint. From power to influence, to money, to integrity, to figuring out if anyone actually cares – the path you take is dotted with people both good and bad, those who are out to scam you and others who genuinely want to help.

When dealing with governments and government departments (who often do not communicate with each other), you have to follow protocol, something we did for the most part, until it became apparent that if we only followed protocol nothing would ever happen. Then you have to pursue the back channels, the whispers of connection and insider knowledge. Someone who knows someone who knows something that might be able to help. Sometimes they can, sometimes they can't. Often it will cost you. We got scammed, a lot. We knew this going in, but you have to try, because you will never forgive yourself if you do not.

Every step takes time. Every blind alley drains you physically, mentally and emotionally.

About the only thing I was certain of was Steve's character. He's one of those guys who just gets on with everyone. While I didn't think he was going to do anything stupid to endanger himself, I figured if anyone could make friends with Al Qaeda to secure his release, Steve could. He's also a chip off the old block; we see the world the same way in terms of strategy and leverage, like a chess game, so I knew that if I was working the game from my end, and Steve was working it from his end, there was a chance that we could navigate our way out of this mess. We had to.

CHAPTER NINE

Britannia

'And the world it didn't give a hoot / If his blood was British or Timbuc-toot' – D H Lawrence

The ride to our first Al Qaeda camp was tortuous, with multiple stops and, for us prisoners, so many unknowns. While I couldn't see much, I could feel, hear and smell everything around me; the engine revving, the constant gear changing, and the diesel fumes. It was like being on an interminable road trip where the only sense you want – sight – is offline, but by now I knew we were as far from civilisation as it was humanly possible to be. Just how remote we were started to sink in as we pushed further north on our journey into the desert.

After the frisking where my British passport was discovered, we drove on, sometimes at great speed over smooth ground and at other times slowly over rough terrain. Whatever we were driving over really challenged the Land Cruiser; I could hear from the way the engine strained and how often the driver changed gears, working hard to try to get through the sand, constantly revving. It felt like we were weaving through giant traffic cones and constantly hitting the lip. It turned out they were these huge mounds of sand that were probably three to five metres apart from each other. I know this only because I would return there a number of times in the years to come. It was an area I used to call The Mounds; in daylight it looked like thousands of anthills stretching off in every direction as far as the eye could see. The effect was created by sand continually blowing through the desert, building up around any hardy pieces of grass. These chest-high, metre-wide mounds would form, with grass tufts sticking out the top like trolls buried with only the tops of their heads showing.

On the edge of consciousness, I nodded in and out of sleep, fighting to stay awake to protect myself against the next unforeseeable jolt. After what seemed like an eternity, we eventually came to a stop. The other vehicle pulled up behind us, they undid the cargo net, pulled us off the vehicle, walked us 10 metres away and told us to lie down behind one of the mounds.

There was a freezing wind coming from the northeast so we lay on the southwestern side of the mound for shelter. It was the end of November, not yet mid-winter, but this desert was Baltic. In the years to come, I would unenthusiastically wait for winter and this wind. In my mind I would imagine it blowing from the snow-capped mountains of Europe, across thousands of kilometres of desert sand before finally finding its way to me through my cheap, single-ply Chinese blanket.

I was still in my shorts and T-shirt, with one flip-flop. My Suunto had already been taken – as we were being frisked, Sjaak kept asking me what the time was, which alerted Al Qaeda to the fact that I had a watch. Now, the three of us lay there behind a mound, huddled together for warmth from the wind. Our captors were also resting. Having driven hard for 11 hours to get as far away from any pursuing posses as they could, they too were exhausted. We couldn't see them, because there were mounds spaced out between us like an egg box, but I have no doubt somebody was above us on guard duty.

After a two-hour sleep they woke us, placed us back in the vehicle, secured us under the blanket and the cargo net, and started driving again. We zigzagged slowly through the mounds, but once we got on to a flat, hard surface, the Land Cruiser got up to speed. The darkness of the heavens above my head slowly began to lift, and the stars I was using to tell direction began to fade as the sun came up. We were still lying down and couldn't see much, but you could feel the change in the air. The freezing wind of the night ceased and the day warmed up. The vehicle stopped again, and this time when Al Qaeda pulled us from the vehicle we could actually see what was going on.

We were literally in the middle of nowhere. It looked like giants' country. There were huge, black, flat-topped massifs almost like carbon copies of Table Mountain dotted here and there, with vast sand plains between them. The sand ran all the way up the side of each mountain as if trying to consume the rock. The sky was so far above my head. Everything was enormous and overwhelming; I was tiny, insignificant and out of my depth. I was numb, and my head swirled with insecurity and confusion.

The feeling of agoraphobia was very peculiar since I love the outdoors and open spaces, but I felt vulnerable. I was handcuffed and surrounded by a large group of people with Kalashnikovs over their shoulders, talking excitedly among themselves in a language I did not understand. All I knew was that I, 'Britannia', was the focus of the conversation.

One of the vehicles had peeled off a little earlier, so there were about a dozen mujahideen watching us now. While two Al Qaeda guys climbed a nearby hill to get a vantage point to look for pursuers, the others brought us green scarves and turbans. The only thing in the desert made from proper cotton was the turban; everything else was cheap, plastic clothing from China. They could see that we had no idea how to dress ourselves so one guy came and helped me with my scarf. He literally wrapped me up. We stood around for a little while in the sun, defrosting and unfolding our limbs after hours in the back of the Land Cruiser. Then the *herassa* (Arabic for 'security detail') were called down from the mountain, and we were loaded back into the vehicle. For the first time we could sit with our backs to the cab, against two spare wheels, facing out the back of the Land Cruiser. I was on the left, Sjaak was in the middle and Johan on the right, with the blanket and the cargo net pulled up over our chests. Now that we were allowed to look out of the vehicle, we could take in our surroundings. There was a car in front of us and a third car behind us, and as the sun rose higher we could start to see the Sahara properly for the first time. It sounds ridiculous to be sightseeing when you've just been kidnapped by Al Qaeda, but the view inspired jaw-dropping awe – at least it did for me.

The Sahara is absolutely enormous, a huge expanse of space divided into just three colours. There's blue for the sky, there's black for the mountains, there's orangey-yellow for the sand. The colours are extremely vivid, except when you hit a sandstorm.

As we drove, gunshots rang out, sending immediate bolts of panic coursing through my body. We pulled up next to the lead vehicle – it turned out they had shot a gazelle. It lay there in the sand next to the vehicle, still twitching. Just the fact that it was there seemed incredible to me. When I looked around all I saw was sand and black mountains; there was absolutely nothing for these animals to eat. One of the guys climbed out, took a knife and cut its throat so it bled out right there next to the vehicle. Then they cut open its stomach to gut it, and chucked all the organs out onto the sand next to the vehicle. There was a little baby gazelle foetus, obviously dead now that its mother had been shot. The mujahid picked up the carcass of the gazelle, chucked it in the back of the other vehicle and we sped off again, leaving behind in our tracks a bright, shining red mess of intestines, stomach and an embryonic sac with the foetus still in it. I later learned that within Islam you can eat absolutely everything in the body of the animal, and you *should* eat everything. So technically we should have taken the foetus to eat.

Around 8am we found ourselves driving over small, black, shiny fist-sized stones that made up part of the mountains. This was a new area that ran alongside the sand of the Sahara. We drove along the black stones, watching the desert off to the right, until we literally fell off into a watercourse with a scattering of acacias inside it. What on earth would a drainage line be doing here, charting a course through this flat, black, stony landscape? It was incredibly beautiful, and with the addition of trees we now had a new colour in the palette: green.

We pulled over under the trees in this *wadi* (dry riverbed), which was deserted save for the carcass of a long-dead camel. Al Qaeda placed us against a cliff face while they reclined under an acacia in the middle of the *wadi*. It was getting a bit warmer now, and they were chatting among themselves, like you would if you were hanging out having a chilled picnic in the park. It almost felt as though Al Qaeda were just sort of wasting time, trying to fill a gap before we moved on again. While they were still alert, they did not look harried any more. It was as if they had re-entered their comfort zone. We were in their territory now.

With a four-metre high vertical sandbank to our backs, our options for escape were limited. We were exhausted and had not had a drop of water or anything else from the moment we were taken. If we were going to try to storm the mujahideen, we would have to run 10 metres and clamber over some rocks to get to them. Their guns were by their sides so they would have ample time to do to us what they did to Martin. And where were we going to go? We were 15 hours' drive into the middle of nowhere. As we sat back against that *wadi* wall, Sjaak, Johan and I started to have very quiet conversations, like three wannabe ventriloquists, because we had been told to keep quiet. We had a million questions and zero answers. Everything was still completely out of control in our heads, but the burning questions were, 'Where the hell are we?' and 'What are they going to do with us?'

While Sjaak had been in the Dutch army and Johan was a mathematical genius, when it came to navigation I had a better grip on things. Maybe it was my upbringing in South Africa, going to the farm and the bush, but from my stargazing I had a pretty good idea which way we had gone and for how long so I filled them in with my guess that we'd probably been driving northeast for about 15 hours. We started to do the maths and worked out, based on us driving fast in sections and slow in others that we must have driven approximately 500 kilometres in 15 hours. Years later when I left the desert, I actually had the GPS coordinates for that camp, and it turned out we were almost exactly on the money.

After a while we pushed on again and worked our way further into this endless undulation of black stones. Everything was just so big here. Around midday on the Saturday, approximately 22 hours after we were taken in Timbuktu, our little caravan rolled boldly into Camp 1, which was set in a copse of trees down in a *wadi*. Mujahideen appeared from all over the place; there were kids there too. There was a lot of excitement, chatter and embracing as they welcomed back their brothers in arms. These guys were conquering heroes returning home with the spoils of war. Everybody stared at us with mixed expressions of satisfaction and disgust.

We were lead to a small tree, about 30 metres away from the Al Qaeda gathering. We were told to stay there and to stay quiet, but as the mujahideen went off out of earshot to celebrate with their friends, we began try to make sense of the last 24 hours. Why did they not take Tilly? Was she dead? Was Martin definitely dead or just injured? Would we be rescued soon? What did they want with us? Would we be killed? How did this happen? What had we missed? Where the hell were we? And, there was that pesky little thought I was still having, that I really had to be home in six months to keep my promise to Cath.

Later, we would get confirmation on both Tilly and Martin. Al Qaeda have two versions for why Tilly was not taken, so you can choose which to believe. One is a somewhat funny anecdotal story and the other one is likely the real story. The funny story is that Al Qaeda say that they do not like to kidnap women because they are complicated. Women menstruate, and the mujahideen will have to buy tampons and other sanitary stuff for them in the desert, which just makes what is a boring job – watching prisoners – even more trying. The real reason that they didn't kidnap Tilly was because, within the Quraan, it says that old men, women and prepubescent children must be left alone, except if the person in question is combating Islam. So you can probably still kill a 12-year-old boy who has hit puberty but a 10-year-old boy, a woman or a proper geriatric is out. So Tilly's get-out-of-jail card was her gender, writings from the Quraan, and that she was not trying to promote Christianity or any other religion.

Al Qaeda did end up kidnapping women at a later stage. One of them was a Swiss missionary who they caught and released, warning her not to come back to the area, but she returned and was taken again. Sadly, just as this book went to print, we heard that she had been killed. There are currently two women being held in the desert for advocating Christianity.

As for Martin, he was definitely dead, but that feedback only came a year later from some of the younger mujahideen who were recruited when Al Qaeda took over Timbuktu in 2012. They were in Timbuktu when our abduction took place in 2011; when they heard the first gunshots going off, they hid in the mosque, along with every other civilian in Timbuktu. Eventually, after an hour or so, they started coming out of the mosque, and they saw Martin's body with brain matter and blood all over the street.

We learned that our abduction was just one successful part of a multi-pronged operation across the region. Not only had they managed to scoop the pot in Timbuktu with a Swede, a Dutchman and a 'Britannia', but the day before we were taken Al Qaeda abducted two French geologists, Philippe Verdon and Serge Lazarevic, from the village of Hombori. The news had not yet made it to us in Timbuktu, or I would have left immediately. Both our abduction and the abduction of the French were incredibly brazen firsts; the first-ever terror attack on Timbuktu and, with the Hombori abduction, the first attack south of the Niger River.

Verdon was executed in 2013, ostensibly as retaliation for France's intervention in the Malian conflict, but Lazarevic would be released in 2014 in exchange for four militants held by the Malian government. That was the official line. Al Qaeda later told me that it was in fact an exchange for seven of their fighters and €500,000. The only operation that had failed during Al Qaeda's multi-day shopping spree was the Mauritanian part. The same day we were taken, Al Qaeda had sent a long-haired guy called Isaac, who fancied himself a bit of a karate black belt, to Nouakchott. He was scouting one of the city's beaches for foreigners when some policemen recognised him and he had to make a run for it. Still, two out of three and five prisoners in total was a fantastic return for their efforts. Especially the fact that two were French and one was 'Britannia'.

I was really struggling with my new name or label. I wanted to explain that it was all a misunderstanding, that I was South African to my core. One thing I knew, judging by the reaction Al Qaeda had to my passport, was that I was both the jewel in the crown as far as prisoners went and the lowest piece of scum they had ever seen. The last 'Britannia' they had, Edwin Dyer, had been killed two years prior to my kidnapping.

Sitting on the ground with people walking about the camp, I felt like a scolded dog, desperately trying to get eye contact, to see a face that might at least want to engage with me, to tell me something about what had happened and what was going to happen. Were we to be ransomed? Executed? Beheaded in front of a video camera? Did they want to torture us? Mujahideen and kids kept coming past to look at us, like an all-day breakfast buffet, laugh among themselves and spit their disgust into the sand. Every expression was one of hate, and this scared me. Later I was told that at least an animal had value in their world, because you could eat it. Non-believers were lower than that, the lowest form of creation. Our wellbeing did not matter, our emotional or mental state was of no concern. Yahia, the leader of AQIM, was the only one to look at us slightly differently: he looked straight through me as though I did not exist. I may have been a prize, but it's difficult to put into words just how inconsequential or worthless I truly was to him as a life form. It was as though I was a ghost. We were merely a tool in the war against the West.

On that first day in camp, to celebrate their victory, the mujahideen slaughtered a goat in front of us. A deep fear took hold inside of me, branded deep into my psyche. I was never able to separate the ease with which they did that from the way I was seen or not seen. It was not done for effect, to scare us. That goat's death was just a job. Two guys, laughing and joking, dragged the goat out into the open and rolled it onto its side. One man knelt on it while holding its front and back legs, the other held its head back, took out a blade and cut its throat. Experienced, they both jumped away as the blood squirted out. Job done, they literally walked away and left it there next to us kicking in the sand, a big pool of blood growing underneath it. This had a huge impact on me, because it was so casual for them. Taking the life of an animal was not an emotional thing. It was just like turning on a tap in the kitchen or opening a can of Coke. Business as usual. In the Western world we believe every life matters. In the Sahara, people die all the time. Death is not a big issue. Life has very little value in the Sahara. As 'Britannia', a despised sub-human captive, I was going to have to do whatever it took to hang on to mine.

CHAPTER TEN

Hey Mate

As told by Cath McGown

I was heading to Heathrow on a one-way ticket back to SA. We had been waiting for this for years, but now I didn't want to go back. This was not how it was supposed to be. I was excited to see family and friends of course, but there would be so much change.

I was given a great seat on the plane. I sat upstairs and had three seats to myself. I didn't want to talk to anyone. I was restless. I couldn't sleep. I tried to watch TV, but it was too frivolous. Everyone seemed too happy. If I was going to watch anything it had to be a drama with trauma or sadness. That is what I could relate to.

I ended up watching the flight path over Africa instead. I knew where Mali was on the map now. I looked outside the plane window trying to see if I could spot Steve down below. A stupid thought. I tried to form an image of him in my mind. Where was he? What was he doing? What was he thinking? Is he hurt? Is he in pain? I looked up from the window into the sky where God was supposed to be and prayed. Maybe He would hear me more clearly now as I was closer to heaven. I tend to run out of words when I pray, so I just prayed the same thing: 'Please look after Steve. Bring him home safely.'

We landed in Johannesburg. I was told that someone would come and fetch me, and take me through a different entrance just in case the press was waiting in the arrival lounge. I spotted someone who I thought could be our guy, but he looked too casual in a bright South African flag shirt. He had a nice friendly face with white hair. *Spierwit* as one would say in South Africa. Turned out he was our guy, but I would only find that out afterwards.

His name was Ernst – Colonel Ernst Strydom. He would become a key player over the next few years, a friend and confidant. I just wish they'd said that someone in a bright South Africa shirt would be waiting for me at the exit. Was this the start of bad communication? I couldn't be negative. I gathered my luggage – I'd paid for an extra bag, so I loaded up a trolley instead of just putting on my backpack and heading for the exit. I was used to backpacking and travelling light after our round-the-world trip. Steve always said, 'What you can't fit into a bag should be left behind.' I used to get irritated with this. I ended up having to carry the heaviest bag as I had more stuff. I always had to remind him that I was carrying all the medication and toiletries, like sunblock, which he hadn't thought of.

I came through into the big arrivals hall and saw my mom smiling and waving at me. My mother-in-law Bev and my father-in-law Magoo were next to her. This was strange. Steve was supposed to be here with me. I hugged my mom and the floodgates opened. I was home. I was safe with my mother. I didn't need to hold it together completely.

They introduced me to some people who I presumed were part of the DIRCO team, Caty May, one of the SAPS negotiators, and Mbulelo Bungane. Ernst arrived to join us. I didn't say that I had seen him. I didn't want to start off on a negative note.

We decided to go to Mugg & Bean, the nearest coffee shop. We didn't waste time with small talk, which was good. We needed to get down to business and get Steve back. I took out my notebook, which was to become a standard of mine over the next few months. Caty spoke about her role; she was a hostage negotiator and had been working on the Somali kidnapping case of Debbie Calitz and Bruno Pelizzari, two names I was not familiar with, but which would come up a lot over the next few years. Caty said that I must write a journal. I thought that it would be a good idea for everyone to have tasks. Bev was good at organising things so her job was to collate info in a file. My mom had good contacts so she would be in charge of that. I would keep everyone updated, as I liked writing. During my time in the UK and on our travels, I wrote long emails to my friends and family updating them on life in general. We said our farewells, agreed to connect again at DIRCO to meet the task team. We were told, once again, to steer clear of the media.

The next few weeks were busy. I had to arrange a new phone number as soon as possible. I was still clutching my phone in case the kidnappers called. I had to get a new driver's licence and SA ID document. This required standing in long queues. I tried to achieve so many things in one day, but I had to lower the bar. I set a goal for each day.

It was December and I was back in South Africa, but it was difficult to get into the festive cheer. Everything just seemed far removed from my mind-set. I was living a different life. I got to see friends I hadn't seen in years and they were all deeply compassionate, but I was exhausted after seeing them. The questions were numerous and I had to relay the information. I felt so much envy for them and their perfect lives. They were well-meaning, of course. I felt safe at home with my mom, my stepdad Al, our old Labrador Rosie and the two male, twin Burmese cats.

Our first meeting with DIRCO was on 7 December, a week after I arrived. I was impressed with the government buildings; they were well secured, if a little prison-like. We were led into a small meeting room and there was a photo of Steve projected on the wall. I had to divert my gaze. It was a photo I had not seen. Steve's parents must have sent it. Everything was familiar to me; the checked shirt he was wearing, his smile, his facial expression – jovial, easy-going, happy – and his confident stance. I told them to take the photo away. Caty said, 'We did it to humanise him.' I guess they needed a visual. For me, Steve was in my heart. He was so part of me.

We sat around a table, and listened to presentations about the structure and the role of DIRCO. One guy, Anthony Moeni, really impressed us. He delivered a good PowerPoint. Magoo asked lots of questions. None of them could really be answered, which was another scenario we would relive.

Mbulelo would head up the South African team. They were in contact with their counterparts in the Netherlands and Sweden. They explained that it was a waiting game; still early stages, still gathering info from other countries. They spoke about other hostage cases – Monique and Callie Strydom, who were held by Abu Sayyaf in the Philippines, and the Baghdad Four who were taken in 2004. No ransom demanded. In 2010 Nick Greyling, a SuperSport sound engineer, was taken in Nigeria for a few days. I ended up meeting his wife years later. She gave me a complimentary back massage at her beauty salon in Melville, and I went to their book launch. The only other case that was currently active was that of Bruno Pelizarri and Debbie Calitz, who were taken by pirates in Somalia. A very different case to ours, with different dynamics. The DIRCO team warned us about scam artists and the many different people who would come out of the woodwork offering to help.

They explained how important it was to foster co-operation and not offend the sovereignty of Mali. We had to tread carefully. Mali hadn't offered much information yet, but DIRCO said they were sure that Mali was committed to the case, and that South Africa would intervene if they thought this was not the case. DIRCO also said that it was up to the host government to take responsibility, as the crime was committed in their country.

The first option was to negotiate a settlement. A capture or tactical resolution would be more risky; but if there was enough intel then that would be a possibility. However, South Africa would need to wait for an invitation from Mali. It would be an act of war if South African troops went to rescue Steve. Talk of hiring a private negotiator came up. The government said that they could not stop us, but that it would make things more complicated if a third party was involved.

We learned about the history of Mali and the local tribes. They explained how the people in the north were victimised by the government and how the desert is their sanctuary. We were told that the people in the north are lawless, have no IDs, come and go through porous borders as they please. We had to trust the Malian government to engage with them, because they know their people, customs, language and history. They said that South Africa has good relations with Mali and that their president had already made an impassioned plea to Al Qaeda for Steve's release. They explained that Steve would be covered during the day with a turban of sorts, and that they would rest during the day as they were in hiding.

DIRCO reiterated that negotiation is preferred over military intervention, but that it is difficult with three nationalities involved. They reassured us that even if things seemed quiet, behind the scenes they were working the case. They could not divulge info that would compromise the efforts they made, and that it was okay, even expected, that we would get agitated. We just had to be patient.

We left feeling deflated but a little more optimistic. There were so many unanswered questions. But we had met the team so at least we knew that Steve's case was not in the hands of idiots.

The first real news came after two weeks on 9 December. There were some rumblings that something might happen on the Friday night. When we woke up Saturday morning, I was told to look at my email. It took forever to download. It was a photo: the first Proof of Life. As the PC buffered, we slowly started to make out bodies in the picture. I couldn't sit on the chair, I was too anxious. I vaguely recognised the other two hostages from the photos I had seen on Facebook. The last image to come clear was Steve. He had that concerned look on his face, a look you wouldn't normally see in any photo of him. He was wearing a pale-pink shirt and he was kneeling, with his hands on his knees. When I saw his image, I fell to my knees and put my hands on my head. The tears started for the first time in ages. My mother let out a cry too and wept with me. The only words I had were, 'It is real, it isn't a dream'. I studied the photo in detail. There were four men behind the hostages, with guns.

We had an emergency meeting at the McGowns' home with Ernst. He explained that AQIM had used AFP to communicate their message. He said that things had become more political; they may be trying to get the government involved as leverage to get the French out the country. The French army already had a presence in Mali in 2011. He suggested that we get a phone number for the kidnappers to call and keep the phone charged at all times.

We arranged to meet with the French embassy as well as the Dutch. Both meetings appeared futile to us – they probably gained more than we did. They did seem genuinely concerned and interested, but once again their hands were tied. They said that too many people were involved, and it would disrupt progress to tell us what they knew. The best bit of news from the meeting was that I learned that Sjaak was a train driver and that his partner Tilly worked in a bank. This was so special to me. I just wanted some information about the people involved. No more political talk.

Christmas, New Year and my birthday on 3 January came and went. For each date I kept believing that Steve may come home. Steve's birthday, 28 January, was the next significant date. I had to do something. Steve's friend Lee offered to have a barbecue at her home with some of Steve's friends. Magoo and Bev were invited too.

Before we left London, Steve had bought me a video recorder to use for my work. On his birthday, I used it to record some of his friends making a message for him. It was an awkward kind of celebration, part birthday, part wake, part memorial. Many put on a brave face, as one does in front of a camera, but some couldn't even talk, they were too emotional. Steve's guy friends tried to hit the balance between stoic and upbeat: 'Hey, mate...'

What do you say on video to a guy, a friend, a husband who is not dead, but could be very soon, while his wife stands and records it?

CHAPTER ELEVEN

Proof of Life

'Things don't happen for a reason. They just happen' – Alice Bowman,
Proof of Life

In 2009, we took a trip to the bush in Mpumalanga with my family.
My dad and I were playing chess, sitting around this little swimming
pool with birds singing in the trees above us. I had my binoculars and
my bird book. I'd make my move, pick up the binos, check out a bird,
and once my dad had had his turn, I'd make a move again and repeat.

To my surprise, I beat him. It was not the first time, but it was the first
time it was easy. There was always a lot of banter around our games so,
as was custom, I chirped, 'Must be losing your touch old man!'

We had been playing together since I was about five years old. It was
one of those father-son things, and with my dad there were no gimme-
games. I had to beat him fair and square.

Getting out of the desert wasn't chess, but it was a high-stakes
game with kings, queens and emirs, knights and mujahideen, bish-
ops and mullahs. The board was massive, with many moving parts,
ancient genesis stories, long-held vendettas and alliances that shifted
with the sand. For once, my father and I were playing on the same
side – we were just thousands of kilometres apart and unable to
share our moves.

Even though my life was at stake, there were times where I could
not believe how ridiculous the situation was. Here I was, engaged in
marathon labyrinthine games of avowed and disavowed provenance
with Al Qaeda, and I wanted to laugh hysterically at the stupidity of it
all. I wanted to point out where we found ourselves, sitting in the sand
in the middle of nowhere, arguing about where we came from, who
we belonged to, and what we believed in. Wars and proxy wars over
religion and trade, from spices to oil and power, had been fought for
millennia. Nothing had changed, other than that in this millisecond

on the continuum of space and time, fate or Allah had decided that I was the pawn in play.

Here I was, a South African, relaying in great detail how un-British I was to a mixed bag of Sahelian jihadis, most of who had a very rudimentary grip of world geography. I did everything I could to distance myself from that flipping passport. From the fact that my family are McGowns of Irish descent ('the Irish hate the British'), to the Boer War ('South Africans hate the British'), to my disavowal of every British government move of the last 500 years; I even compared Al Qaeda calling me British to me calling them Yemeni because their Arab ancestors moved from Arabia across into North Africa. Far from being anti-British, this was all part of my game to stay alive.

I took comfort in knowing how dogged and strategic my father is. I take after him, so I was gambling on the hope that back home in South Africa, my dad would be playing a similar game to me, working with the authorities and whoever else could help to get across the message that I am South African.

The first time I knew that my dad and I had the same game plan was when we saw Yahia, the regional Al Qaeda leader, just before we shot a new Proof of Life video in early 2012. In his hands were a bunch of identity documents from South Africa. It was a massive moment – the first solid evidence proving to Al Qaeda that I was what I said I was. Even though Yahia never shared these documents with the rank and file – having a British prisoner was better for their morale – it was a start. I sent the old man a mental high-five.

'Proof of Life' videos were a big part of the whole saga. For hostage takers, a Proof of Life is an essential tool for communicating with the other side. Whether it's a photo of the kidnap victim holding up that day's newspaper or a video, the message is simple: 'Your boy is alive, now give us what we want.'

For Al Qaeda it was a vital means of communication, because while they have their own websites and propaganda channels on the dark web, sending a Proof of Life video got them out of the dark and into the limelight of mainstream news channels. From suburban lounges in South Africa to the boardrooms of French corporates invested in the Sahel and the halls of government across the Western world, each video was a chance not only to make demands around their prisoners, but also to promote their goals, from Sharia law to the plight of Islamic nations under the oppression of Western forces.

From time to time we got feedback about negotiations – Holland or Sweden is going well but 'Britannia' is not, or vice versa. It was hard to know what to believe and what to ignore, especially because we never had the full picture and we could never know if Al Qaeda were simply engaging in prisoner psychology with us. My hope was that we would be seen as a package deal. You could tie your brain in knots thinking of possible ways this could play out, but *if* I assumed that my dad and Cath had successfully owned me as a South African and *if* the British government had played along in the interests of keeping me alive and *if* none of my friends in London had posted photos of me on social media standing in front of Big Ben (a real concern if any Al Qaeda members wanted to snoop around), then I could make a bunch of new assumptions.

Fear compounded upon anxiety because I had so little information about what was happening on the other side of this chess game. South Africa, especially in the Jacob Zuma years, did not have a great track record. From corruption to nationwide electricity-grid failures, they had myriad other issues to take care of before anyone dedicated time and resources to a white South African male stuck with some jihadis in Mali. Even if the Swedish and Dutch governments managed to negotiate a package deal, would the South African government come through for me? Would my family have to sell everything to pay to get me out?

It was bad enough feeling terrified and sub-human every day, but I knew that my kidnapping was so much greater than what was happening to me. I had massive guilt about what I had done to my family. My dad was about to retire; my getting kidnapped must be ruining what was left of my parents' lives. What about Cath? My beautiful wife, who I was meant to meet that March for our fifth wedding anniversary, was waiting for a man who might never come home. We were planning to start a family. What if I was held here forever? I could not expect her to put her life on hold indefinitely for me.

As the years passed, the idea of being hopeful about home seemed more futile than ever. I was kidnapped at 36 and Cath was 34. I wanted her to move on with her life. A few years in, I started making Proof of Life videos saying, 'Cath, I will love you and I will support whatever decisions you make. If you need to move on, I know it's not because we don't love each other, it's because the situation is so ridiculous. When I come home we will still be friends. It's not that our marriage didn't work because we fought. It didn't work because of this situation that we've been thrust into.'

The lack of direct communication was a huge frustration. All I wanted was five minutes to phone my family. Despite Al Qaeda coming to me once or twice telling me I was going to get a chance to make a call, I never got the opportunity. That didn't stop me from agonising over phone numbers. I knew my dad's phone number and the landline. I had forgotten my mom's phone number. My dad often wouldn't answer his cellphone – he was just very relaxed about it and wouldn't realise it was ringing. If Al Qaeda were going to drive 400 kilometres away from camp for me to make the phone call (and then leave the area immediately because we would be using a traceable satellite phone), I could not risk going to voice mail. There would not be a second shot. Calling the landline was also a concern – what if my folks were out and the phone just rang? The stress of these things ate away at me.

In total we did about 20 videos, of which only eight made it home to my family. Over time I discovered that a lot of thought, strategy and pageantry goes into each one. To keep their enemies guessing, Al Qaeda shot the videos in various geographies and styles. Most often we would have a tarpaulin thrown over two vehicles as a backdrop to completely hide our location. On one occasion in April 2015, we travelled a long distance to the southern parts of the desert to shoot a Proof of Life with the sound of birds and trees in the background, and then travelled back into the desert. This could only have been misdirection to confuse our would-be rescuers as to where we really were.

I used to get excited when a Proof of Life was in the offing. Not only did it mean that negotiations were underway, but the journey would often give me small pleasures, like the time I saw an African Golden Wolf. Of course, in no time, Al Qaeda were hanging out of the Land Cruiser windows trying to shoot it (they shot everything). Fortunately, it escaped.

There are levels of communication in Proof of Life videos, over and above what we said (usually according to a script). Some of it is the way we looked. For certain videos we wore bright orange jumpsuits, carbon copies of what Al Qaeda prisoners wear in Guantanamo. That was not by chance. In others we wore local clothing, to show that, even if the French or Malian Army forces spotted us, it was unlikely they would be able to differentiate us from the mujahideen or other locals, and we were likely to be killed in a rescue operation. In some videos we had our heads shaven, in all we were bearded. Sometimes we were separated; one of us videoed in a bunker, the others above ground.

Whether the negotiations were for us as a group or as individuals, misdirection and subterfuge were the name of the game. If Al Qaeda made one slip-up, attack helicopters would descend on our camp. We knew that, they knew that.

Our first Proof of Life video happened on Sunday, 27 November, just two days after our abduction. For that they used the classic approach: prisoners kneeling in front of a group of masked mujahideen – except for Abu Osama, the Algerian veteran of the Afghanistan war, who was confident to show his magnificent bearded face. Each of them was armed with an AK-47 or the heavier PK machine gun and ammunition vests.

For the first few years, Al Qaeda kept us largely in the dark about what was going on with our negotiations. *When does the negotiation start? How does the information get back home? Is it uploaded via YouTube? Could that be traced? Would they send it back to Timbuktu, Kidal or Bamako on a USB via camel or Land Cruiser, and then upload it from an internet cafe? Maybe they just get a street kid to drop it off at an embassy? Do our families know we are alive? Are they going to torture me, cut off an ear or a hand before the next video to show they are serious?* With no one willing or able to answer us, Johan, Sjaak and I threw these questions around non-stop.

The longer I stayed in the desert, the more the video strategy changed. Al Qaeda clearly felt they had to get a little more creative to get a response. Towards the end they even started asking us for advice.

In 2015, we shot a Proof of Life down in the south that was definitely inspired by both ISIS (in terms of music and outfits) and perhaps a FIFA Xbox game (in terms of nifty graphics). It opens with Al Qaeda walking towards a line-up of vehicles on a sand dune. They are wearing their black outfits, which were reserved for special occasions. The voiceover, by Abu Farida, his British accent unmistakeable, says, 'Welcome to the world's largest prison. A prison that has no walls, no cells, no bars. A prison where the fear of a prison break is non-existent. This is the mujahideen's prison of the Sahara.' With that, they get into mud-spattered vehicles and drive off as the opening title appears: *A Trip to Interview Two Prisoners – Johan Gustoffson and Stephen McGowan.* Both our names were misspelled.

The next scene opens on a heavily wooded area, with the sound of a dove cooing. The camera pans across the cab of a Land Cruiser, where Abu Farida in the passenger seat says, 'So we've reached the place where the prisoners are being held. As you've noticed, there's no desert, no blazing sun, no extreme temperatures. In fact, this is the new territory under the control of the mujahideen.' *Subtext: you kuffar nations have no idea where these guys are.*

The next scene features solo shots of Johan and then myself, zooming in on our faces in slow motion as our bios are narrated and the details of our governments' failings listed. As per Abu Farida's stage direction, I turn my shackled hands to look at a watch I was given, as if impatient to be rescued (I was). Then, the vehicles pull up next to us, covered in branches and other foliage that we had helped decorate them with not five minutes earlier. Throughout, there's a suspenseful, action-film background beat; when the mujahideen jump from the vehicle onto the ground, there are soaring jet-like sounds. Our handcuffs are unlocked and we gather together under a tree with Abu Farida, for the interview.

Johan and I rattle off some scripted questions: 'Do you have any information for us? Have you heard anything from our families? Have you heard anything from our governments? Is there any update on the negotiation?'

Abu Farida says, 'Unfortunately we haven't received anything official from your governments. The French and Malian secret service are trying to gain as much time as possible in the hope that your freedom will be gained without having to submit to the mujahideen's demands. It's come to our attention that the French are impeding your negotiations. They are making it very difficult for your governments and for the mujahideen to come to an agreement.'

Waving flies away from my face, my wedding ring visible on my hand, I say, 'We were kidnapped at the same time as the final French hostage. We were hoping that the negotiation for the last French hostage would include us...'

Johan rubs his face and says, 'I don't know what to say.'

Abu Farida pulls out a Dell laptop, and the three of us sit under the tree on a blanket and watch a clip of French hostage Serge Lazarevich as he arrived back in France. There's a bit of back-and-forth as Johan and I discuss how baffled we are that we cannot get the same sort of attention. We ask what Lazarevich was ransomed for, and Abu Farida says it was in exchange for seven mujahideen in Bamako and Niger. Suddenly the seven in question drop down, superimposed onto the screen, resplendent in purple-blue robes and AK-47s, like the player selection panel of an Xbox soccer game.

My involvement ends with a message to the South African government and my family. I thank them for all they have been doing, and wish my mother happy birthday for two weeks ago. I told them I had not heard anything from them for over three years. 'To my beautiful wife, happy wedding anniversary for last week. I have now been in the Sahara for almost half as long as we've been married. I know we had some big family plans for our life. I pray we still get to do all these things, and I pray that my release comes soon and I come home to you.'

On two occasions, we received parcels and letters from home, I imagine via the same system that took messages from Al Qaeda to the outside world. Sometimes the letters would be used as props in our videos, making it look like we had received them, but they were often taken away before we could actually do so. That happened on my birthday, 28 January 2012. I was given a letter, but as soon as they'd filmed it they snatched it from my hands before I had a chance to read it. The second one was when we did the Guantanamo orange jumpsuit video. I still have that letter – I ended up almost laminating it with Scotch Tape to hold it together. I didn't know then that it would be my last message from my mom.

Cath had sent two Tupperwares with useful things like a French dictionary (by far the most prized possession among us prisoners and the source of many fights), a razor, a chessboard, some suntan lotion, Jelly Tots and dried fruit. I ate the Jelly Tots one a day, until they ran out, turning each into a five-minute experience, savouring every little sugar granule with my tongue.

In December 2016 I got to keep a letter from the South African government. They spelled my name wrong. I could not believe it – after five years as a hostage. If they wanted to devise a soul-destroying move, that was it.

Initially, a Proof of Life video was something that brought a lot of hope to us. Before one of the first Proof of Life videos, a mujahideen told us, 'You do this, you go home.' Unfortunately, we took him at his word (despite his rudimentary English) and thought our release was imminent; what he meant was that if we engaged in Proof of Life videos, we would one day be released.

Sometimes, we could tell when a video was going to be shot, because Al Qaeda started treating us a bit better. The first time it happened we were given some instant coffee and biscuits. Because we thought we were about to go home, we celebrated like idiots and drank most of the coffee instead of rationing it out for weeks.

As the years passed, I never grew tired of recording Proof of Life videos, even though they seemed to make no difference. It meant getting my hopes up again and again, only to have them dashed by sand and time. Even so, I would play a game of bluff with myself. I realised I wasn't going home, but I allowed myself to believe I was, because a two-week mental holiday was a break from reality.

If nothing else, the videos were proof that something was happening out there and that I wasn't forgotten, stuck in a game of endless moves with no checkmate in sight.

CHAPTER TWELVE

Azawad

'To him who puts a cord around his neck, God will supply someone to pull it' – Tuareg proverb

If you've ever flown to South Africa from Europe on an overnight flight, there's a point at which you lose the glow of urban civilisation. You cross over the Mediterranean, and the lights of the coastal cities of North Africa dissipate into blackness as the plane flies deeper south over the continent. There might be a last few specks of light if you pass interior cities like Fez in Morocco, and a few small desert towns in Algeria, but as you cross the Sahara there's nothing save for the vast inky abyss below you. I was in that abyss, my life force pulsing ever so slightly; muted, minuscule and as insignificant as a speck of glitter on the floor of the deepest ocean.

This vast land is what the local Tuareg tribesmen call Azawad. In their language, Tamasheq, it means 'land of transhumance' or, in layman's terms, 'land where you move livestock from one grazing ground to another as per the seasons'. It's a land without borders, at least borders that anyone cares to acknowledge. It's a land of pastoralists and traders, rebels and smugglers. It's a land I would come to know intimately and, ultimately, in a deep, respectful way, a place I would come to love for the beauty of its incredibly tenacious flora and fauna, which had to fight as hard as I did to survive in such harsh conditions.

But from that frantic escape from Timbuktu to Al Qaeda's desert lairs, for years all I could feel was fear. Fear of death by bullet or by blade, and fear of the unknown. Not only was everything around me alien and unwelcoming, but everything about the future was uncertain. I was a prisoner in one of the hottest places on Earth, but I was always kept in the dark. For most of my years in Azawad I felt submerged, fighting for air, and I had no idea if I would ever break the surface and breathe again.

To understand the what, the where and the 'how the hell?' of my situation, you need to understand a bit about Azawad's history, its geography and its traditional inhabitants, the proud people of the Tuareg desert tribes.

The Tuaregs are found across the central Sahara from southwestern Libya to northern Niger, Mali, Algeria and Burkina Faso. Descended from the Berbers of North Africa who gave the Barbary Coast its name, the Tuaregs are Islamic, semi-nomadic pastoralists who belong to a confederation of tribes and clans, rather than feeling any affiliation or allegiance to countries as we know them. These are of course broad strokes, because some Tuaregs play by the rules of nation states and engage in formal politics.

Save for the introduction of guns and cars among the wealthier Tuaregs, the modern world we inhabit is very different from the ancient world they know, where life is dictated by the seasons, livestock, grazing and water. Many of them see the land they have always inhabited as their own, and the lines drawn when European powers divided up Africa at the Berlin Conference in 1884 as illegitimate and arbitrary. They are old colonial hand-me-down doodles, dictated in centuries past and adhered to by politicians sitting in air-conditioned palaces in capital cities far away from the baking interior of the Sahara and semi-arid Sahel.

It's not hard to conjure up a parallel version of this for Westerners. Imagine your clan has lived in the UK or France for centuries, and all of a sudden the Malians or Mauritanians arrive with an agreement made with a bunch of other African powers that bestowed upon them your ancestral land. They took what was yours, spread their religion and treated you as sub-human. You and your people would fight them for centuries if needs be. In a place as harsh as the Sahara, where everything about daily life – from feeding your family to access to water – is about survival, people are quick to take up guns to settle disputes.

That is why the last couple of hundred years of first colonial oppression, and now government suppression, has been especially cruel to the Tuareg. Whether it is France, 'Britannia' or the Great Satan America, the Western world is not looked upon kindly in these parts, and for good reason. Some of the hatred is linked to global Islamic oppression and the wars in the Middle East, while some of it is more directly aimed at a colonial legacy like that of the French or a government like Mali's, which the Tuareg see as having illegitimate control over them.

The Tuaregs have fought for their independence for centuries. They fought against the French colonisation of the Sahel states time and again (there have been seven Tuareg uprisings in total). After the French left and African states gained independence in the 1960s, the Tuaregs watched the extraction of mineral wealth from their lands and experienced neglect from their new governments.

Even if Mali's government, which sits hundreds of kilometres away in the verdant south, wanted to contribute meaningfully to the administration of the north, the sheer size of the area does not help. Of Mali's eight regions, the three north of the Niger River – Timbuktu, Kidal and Gao – cover 827,000 km², around 66% of Mali's total landmass. That's an area the size of Texas or twice the size of Germany, populated by just over a million people, most of whom live close to the Niger River.

Save for the two main towns of Timbuktu and Gao, which are just above the Niger River, there are only a handful of towns in the northeast, the Tuareg stronghold of Kidal being one of them. There are even fewer villages dotted north of Timbuktu in the great expanse of the desert. The rest of the sparse population of the north is rural and nomadic, moving goats, camels and sheep from well to well and between grazing areas. Even this nomadic way of life is changing as climate change means the desert expands year by year. As herders' animals die of thirst and starvation, more poor people – whose carbon footprint is almost non-existent – are pushed into the cities by habitat change generated largely by industrialised nations.

The people may be dirt-poor in Western terms, but there is vast wealth in that dirt if you participate in an extractive economy, something that both France and the governments of Mali, Niger and other Sahel countries have taken advantage of. French companies are very active across the Sahara and Sahel, drilling for oil and mining uranium and other minerals in Tuareg ancestral lands. Uranium from Tuareg lands, mined under rights in northern Niger, keeps France running as a nuclear superpower. Three-quarters of France's energy comes from nuclear power and the country exports this cheap power to the tune of €3-billion per year. While France gets the power and the fat cats in the Niger government get rich from the deal, the Tuaregs and other regional tribes in the northwest get sick from the toxic dust.

French nuclear interest in Azawad goes back even further. In 1960, six years before the French started blowing up Polynesian atolls, they tested their first atomic bomb in southern Algeria. This was in the Tanezrouft region near Reggane, just over the border from where we were being held. Named the *Gerboise Bleue* or Blue Jerboa, after the cartoonish kangaroo-like mice found in the desert, at 70 kilotons it was four times more powerful than Hiroshima, and the largest first nuclear test bomb to date, superseding anything the Americans or Russians had tested at that time. To this day, the residents of the area and nomadic people who pass through there suffer from a litany of cancers, deformities and blindness as a result of the radioactive fallout. Whether from this testing or not, I saw many of these kinds of deformities within the ranks of Al Qaeda. That bomb and the four that followed in the same area were crimes against humanity, yet virtually no action has been taken by way of reparations.

With such a long history of oppression and exploitation, it makes perfect sense that Azawad proved such a fertile place for Al Qaeda to infiltrate and grow strong. While Al Qaeda was made up of mujahideen of all sorts, from Arabs to Bambara, Fulani and other southern tribes, there was a strong Tuareg presence in their ranks.

Shortly after Johan, Sjaak and I were taken, the main Tuareg rebel group, the MNLA (National Movement for the Liberation of Azawad), began another rebellion. After the Arab Spring uprising swept through North Africa, Libya fell into a civil war as its citizens overthrew long-ruling dictator Colonel Muammar Gaddafi. Gaddafi had long-standing ties with the Tuareg, and often espoused the idea of a 'Great Islamic State of the Sahel'. He had supplied arms and funding for numerous uprisings in Niger and Mali, and also recruited thousands of them into his army, a mercenary force loyal to him. They were encouraged to reject their hereditary chiefs and fight against governments in home countries that excluded Tuaregs from power.

Gaddafi was killed in October 2011, a month before I was taken, and the Tuareg forces loyal to him began the long journey back into the desert to their homes in Niger, Mali and elsewhere. What also came back from Libya was a huge amount of Gaddafi's weaponry and money, which armed and funded both the MNLA and Al Qaeda's operations.

When an army-led coup overthrew Malian President Amadou Tomani Touré in March 2012, the MNLA took advantage of the situation. One of the army's main motivations for the coup was having to fight up in the north where they routinely lost skirmishes and battles. Now, with their government in disarray, the poor, underfed, underarmed Malian military, made up predominantly of Bambara tribesmen from the south of Mali, were absolutely annihilated in the north by the exceptionally well-armed, battle-hardened Tuareg forces. These included the MNLA and an acronym word-salad alliance that included AQIM (Al Qaeda in the Islamic Maghreb), Ansar Dine (an Islamist group led by Tuaregs with ties to AQIM) and MOJWA (Movement for Oneness and Jihad in West Africa, another AQIM ally heavily involved in fighting and abductions).

This temporary alliance took the towns of Kidal, Gao and Timbuktu from the government forces, and the MNLA announced the formation of their new state: Azawad. The problem for the MNLA was that many of the citizens of these towns were not Tuareg and had no interest in seceding from Mali or being ruled by Tuaregs in Azawad. It also did not help that, as a guerrilla force, the MNLA were not particularly adept at maintaining the rule of law. They were adept at fighting the Malian government or Ganda Iso (an anti-Tuareg paramilitary group made up of Songhai, Bambara and Fulani tribesmen), but policing a town, running hospitals and schools, and providing basic services requires administrative skills.

On the other hand, AQIM, assisted by Ansar Dine, and MOJWA believed it was their holy duty to fill the void and implement Sharia law. By June 2012, the alliance between the MNLA and the Islamist groups was broken. AQIM and their allies attacked and defeated the MNLA in the Battle of Gao and pushed them out of the cities. They imposed Sharia law and enforced it with an Islamic police force, banning alcohol and cigarettes, and insisting that women cover themselves fully. As they settled into governing, Al Qaeda even had T-shirts printed and pass cards made for their soldiers.

Initially, Al Qaeda was welcomed into the cities by applauding crowds who had been let down by the Malian government and disliked the MNLA, but with time these crowds turned to dislike Al Qaeda too, as they were not allowed to drink, play music or have parties. Men and women could not mix, and people could not dress as they pleased.

The more military success Al Qaeda had, the more Al Qaeda brigades joined from elsewhere in the Sahara, along with tribal militias who did not want to be ruled by the Tuareg. By the end of 2012, the MNLA was totally defeated. Al Qaeda even hunted down MNLA leaders in their homes in Kidal and other small desert villages in the middle of the night, executing them in their beds. Seemingly invincible, Al Qaeda was in full control of Azawad and was beginning to push further south into Mali, below the Niger River.

In January 2013 France finally stepped in and, 100 years after they conquered the Sahara, returned to the region to fight AQIM and all affiliated groups.

When the French arrived, they were met by applauding crowds and Al Qaeda were booed out of the towns and into the desert. A year later those same crowds would turn on the French too.

All of this – the fall of Gaddafi's Libya and the spread of Libyan money and weapons; the coup that toppled the Malian government; the Tuareg uprising that turned northern Mali into Azawad; the hegemony of Al Qaeda, plus centuries of oppression and domination across racial, national, economic and religious lines – was coming to a head towards the end of 2011.

And here I was, a banker on a motorbike with a bird book and a fishing rod, who took the wrong detour on his way home.

CHAPTER THIRTEEN

Al Qaeda (Pty) Ltd

'We are the children of a nation and we are an inseparable part of it'
– Osama Bin Laden, October 2001

No matter how many times I closed my eyes at night in the Sahara, hoping that I would wake the next morning from the most God-awful, never-ending nightmare, every morning I woke up and I had to face the terror once again. It was not just a bad dream. I was a captive of Al Qaeda.

When they think of Al Qaeda, most people imagine masked men, Kalashnikovs, terrified prisoners and vicious-looking hunting knives. These are the guys who blow things up, fly planes into buildings and go on shooting sprees in Western cities screaming, *'Allah hu Akbar!'* It makes sense, because that's the part we are exposed to on TV.

The idea of Al Qaeda was a little more grounded in reality for me. Like most people I had watched 9/11 unfold in real time. I was 26, at work at Gensec, my first job in Johannesburg. We all sat there staring at the TV screen in absolute amazement, transfixed by what was happening, wondering if it was real. It turned out that a high-school friend of mine called Nick Rowe, my inside-centre on the rugby second team, was on the 106th floor of the North Tower when American Airlines Flight 11, hijacked by Mohamed Atta, flew into floors 93–99. Realising that the fire was unstoppable and escape impossible, Nick managed to make a phone call to his family to say goodbye.

On the day of the London tube bombings, I was working at Royal Bank of Scotland. Just up the road from our office, a suicide bomber hit a train leaving Liverpool Street Station. The effect on the city was exceptionally eerie. Everybody left work early, still nervous about commuting in case there were more attacks. I had my bicycle so I cycled home along the Thames, but I remember how the streets had a strange feel to them.

That was the sum total of my experience of Al Qaeda before Timbuktu, just a few degrees of separation. They were more an idea or a concept.

Contact with Al Qaeda or one of their attacks was something that happened to other people, unfortunates like Nick, who worked in the wrong building, got onto the wrong plane or train, signed up for the wrong war, bought a ticket to the wrong concert or walked down the wrong street.

I suppose I could apply that kind of filter to hundreds of decisions minor and major in my life that led me to this point. I had done my due diligence for my trip; I just got incredibly unlucky as seismic, geopolitical shockwaves spread through the region and Al Qaeda embarked on an ambitious shopping spree outside of their usual range. Still, I could play the shoulda-woulda-coulda loop of hypotheticals for days:

> – *I should have just gone southeast from Bamako down to the Central African countries instead of joining the overlanders on their way to Timbuktu.*
> – *I should not have believed the embassy officials and others who said Mali was safe.*
> – *I could have taken the 'boring' East Coast route in the first place.*
> – *I could have just jumped on a bloody plane in London and been home in Johannesburg the next day.*

In Islam, the stories of the Prophet Muhammad (Peace Be Upon Him) are called *hadiths*. One of them warns about the errors of asking 'if'. After missing something, he forbade a person from saying, 'If only I had done such and such, then such and such would have happened.' The message was that obsessing over 'if only' scenarios opens the door to Satan and makes you vulnerable to grief and fear, which are ultimately of no benefit to you. Instead, Muhammad (PBUH) guided people to God's plan, which is to say '*Qaddarallahu wa maa sha'a fa'ala*' (Allah has ordained and as He willed, He has done).

In the early days, long before I learned anything from Islam, I realised playing 'what if' was a pointless game. I could not change where I was.

As the days turned into weeks and the weeks into months and the months into years, I grew to know Al Qaeda, or at least this branch of the organisation, as well as anyone who spends every day and every night in their company can. The fear of being killed, beheaded, never left me in that time, even after I converted to Islam and came to understand some of the laws that govern them, and their treatment of prisoners and fellow Muslims. While my fear of death as Al Qaeda's captive was constant, my understanding of who they are, what motivates them and how they see the world evolved.

There's a scene in Monty Python's *Life of Brian,* where the anti-Roman rebels argue over which splinter group they are: the Judean People's Front, the People's Front of Judea or the Judean Popular People's Front. Similarly, the Islamist groups and sub-groups of the Sahel can seem like a swirling alphabet soup of ever-changing acronyms. As power and influence wax and wane, regional alliances form, break and re-form. The mujahideen who held me were from Al Qaeda in the Islamic Maghreb (AQIM, or the French acronym AQMI). Before AQIM existed, it was called GSPC (Salafist Group for Preaching and Combat), but it became AQIM in 2007 when they pledged allegiance to Al Qaeda's top brass, Osama Bin Laden and Ayman al-Zawahiri, who AQIM told me was the old Egyptian puppetmaster hiding in the mountains of Afghanistan, sending out the occasional video to his global crew.

In 2017, AQIM created a union with Ansar Dine, the Macina Liberation Front and Al Mourabitoun, and they changed their name again to what it is today, *Jama'a Nusrat ul-Islam wa al-Muslimin* ('Group to Support Islam and Muslims'). To keep things simple, I am going to refer to my captors as Al Qaeda, or AQIM when I need to differentiate them from Al Qaeda as a global organisation.

Make no mistake, Al Qaeda is a global organisation and a remarkable one at that. AQIM is just one franchise of that organisation. From Al Qaeda in the Arabian Peninsula (AQAP) to Al Qaeda in the Indian Subcontinent (AQIS) and myriad other off-shoots and affiliates from the Philippines to Malaysia, Caucasia, Spain and beyond, their franchises can fight, break economies (and make money while doing it), move food, soldiers and prisoners, and most of all strike fear into the imaginations of billions of people. What I saw of Al Qaeda's skill at logistics and distribution, communication, talent acquisition, staff training, workforce management, revenue streams and branding was truly impressive. Years later, when I was being interviewed by the British secret services, I referred in passing to 'Al Qaeda middle management' and they laughed, but it was accurate. They are most definitely highly organised and well structured. You do not get to be as widespread, effective and long-lasting as Al Qaeda have been, with so many opponents, without brilliant management skills. Incorporating the strategic money-making capacity of a Goldman Sachs, the logistical genius of a Fedex, the hearts-and-minds branding of a Coca-Cola, and the experience and precision of a Blackwater, Al Qaeda would be one of the world's greatest companies if they were motivated by the world of stocks and bonds, dividends and IPOs. But the trappings of life in *Dunya* (the temporal world) are just flash and glitter to them. They are motivated by something else entirely: the word of Allah.

Al Qaeda loves chaos, which is why northern Mali and the greater Sahel region was the ideal place for them to franchise their brand. If a country is in turmoil with rebellions, coups, disenfranchised people or neglected communities, all of which engulfed Mali circa 2011/2012, it creates the perfect opportunity for Al Qaeda to come in and create an Islamic emirate ruled by Sharia law.

When Al Qaeda decide to take on a new country, the procedure is to send the government a letter stating that they have three months to implement Sharia law, or enter into war with Al Qaeda. They can keep their government, salaries and ministers. All they must do is implement Islamic Sharia, and Al Qaeda will leave them alone and move on to the next country. Even a country like Mali, which is 98% Muslim, is not exempt. It is not enough to be the majority; Al Qaeda Muslim countries must reject all man-made laws and live by Islamic laws. After all, we were made by Allah, and therefore He knows what is best for us. Democracy and democracies are *haram* (illegal or forbidden). If someone steals, you chop off their hand. The five prayers are obligatory. Adultery, idolatry, apostasy and all the other sins must be punished. If the government comes back and says, 'Yes, we will do this,' Al Qaeda will literally leave the country. Of course, this never happens.

When a government inevitably rejects Al Qaeda's ultimatum, the mujahideen go to war. Al Qaeda does not fight direct wars; they are not stupid. Blending into local communities, they engage in guerrilla warfare, which traditional armed forces struggle to contain. Conventional wars against the might of the Americans, the British, the French or the Russians would result in them getting massacred, so because they have God on their side, they are *sabr*. This means 'patient', and it was a word I heard many times in the desert when I asked Al Qaeda when I was going home. '*Sabr*, be patient,' they would say. By being *sabr*, they will outlast their enemies and ultimately win.

Al Qaeda's argument to me was that, beside the fact that the entire world should be run by Allah's Sharia, Mali was 98% Muslim. The people wanted to live by Allah's law and it was the *murtadeen* (heretic) government, the 'puppets of the West' who kept the people from this. These *murtadeen* will be going to a very hot place in Hell, (*Jahannam*), and they were high up on Al Qaeda's hit list.

By entering a region, making alliances with the downtrodden, aiding insurrection and destabilising the government, bit by bit Al Qaeda will take over a country. If you are a Westerner looking at this, you might be tempted to ask, 'Well, would that be so bad? Mali is 98% Muslim as it is, so why not let Al Qaeda call the shots there and leave the rest of us out of it?' You would be wrong, because while Al Qaeda would gladly take Mali, they would not stop at one country. After Mali would be Burkina Faso, Niger, Chad, Nigeria and so on. They believe it is their holy duty. The word of Allah as written in the Quraan is law, and it is beholden upon them to implement that. Anyone who does not comply, who stands in their way or who fights them is *kuffar*, a non-believer, and must be destroyed. They are the lowest form of creation. While Christians and Jews and the nations most associated with these religions are the old enemy, Al Qaeda also criticises any Muslims who do not believe what they believe. Liberal Muslims, Shias, Sufis and anyone else who interprets Islam in any way that does not align with Al Qaeda's are legitimate enemies and targets and are going to Hell. With their Sunni Salafist jihadi approach, what Al Qaeda wants is a return to the roots of Islam and a literal, strict and puritan interpretation of the Quraan.

In my nearly six-year experience of living with them in the Sahara, I got to know Al Qaeda on several levels. I got a slight understanding of them as a global force, and a decent grasp of them as a regional power, and came to know a few quite well as individuals. I learned that Al Qaeda see themselves as both soldiers of God and the policemen of the Sahara. Live by Sharia and they will treat you well. Everything will be fine, because that is God or Allah's will. Even if it is not fine from a human perspective, well, that is also Allah's will. We may not understand it. Only He knows how everything will play out, because God's plan always has *hikma* (wisdom). This pre-determination is a major thing in Islam, and for Al Qaeda it provides both purpose and finality. They are put on this earth to execute the word of God. If they die in this service, that is part of God's plan.

Apply that to conventional battle, firefight or certain death (think suicide bombers), and you have a formidable enemy.

Contrast that promise with the desperate and dire reality of life on Earth for many of the young mujahideen who volunteered to die. I was told many stories of how they had been suppressed by the French or had their families murdered by the Malian army over disputed allegations of theft. Many of them were ill, with no medication or any prospects of a better life besides living hand to mouth in the heat and dust of the Sahara. If, however, they made it to *Jannah* (heaven), there was so much water that the rivers flowed underground and 72 virgins awaited each of them. It was little wonder that, when volunteers were needed for suicide missions, there was a long waiting list of names.

The other thing to get your head around is the fact that these guys not only believe they have God on their side and that they are doing his work, they also see themselves as being the good guys in a battle against evil. It's hard to comprehend from a Western viewpoint. In *Star Wars*, did the Resistance see themselves as the bad guys in the face of the Empire? No. Neither did the Viet Cong, the Boers or the Aztecs, and nor do Al Qaeda. They see themselves as a plucky band of brothers simply doing what God tells them to and taking on the Evil Empire (aka the West). All they see of the West are colonial forces that stick their noses into everyone's business under the guise of human rights, but are most likely to fly their own flag for world domination, Christianity and economic gain. One need only think about French vested interests in the Sahel region or the USA's relationship with Middle East oil to concede that they have a few very valid points.

The ranks of the mujahideen I met were drawn from across the Islamic world. At first, the majority were Arabs from Algeria, Mauritania and Mali, then Libya, Morocco, Tunisia, Egypt and elsewhere in North and West Africa, with the balance made up of Tuaregs and a few black Africans from the more southern tribes in Mali and the region. As time wore on, this began to change. Buoyed by their success, more foreigners from France and Britain joined Al Qaeda after they took over the northern towns in 2012. People would literally drive up to Timbuktu, wanting to pledge allegiance to Al Qaeda. As more of the middle-management types from Algeria were killed by the French, Al Qaeda actively looked to recruit mujahideen from the south, because ultimately they wanted to take over the whole country.

In 2017, when a southern imam called Amadou Kouffa (aka Mohammed Kofa) joined AQIM, bringing with him his predominantly Fulani forces from the Macina Liberation Front, it was a major signal to the rest of Mali that Al Qaeda was an inclusive, cosmopolitan organisation, a band of Muslim brothers passionate for Allah. On paper, irrespective of colour, language, wealth, age and country of origin, everyone was equal, accepted and loved in Allah's eyes.

In practice, things were a little different. While a team photo would show a diverse bunch, there was definitely a class structure and some inherent racism and tribal tension at play. Historically, the Tuaregs hate the Arabs and the Arabs hate the Tuaregs. The Tuaregs hate the Bambara and vice versa and so on *ad nauseam*. In the past, the Arabs would raid the south, pushing to below the Niger River, where they would plunder and wreak havoc, grab a young Black child and return to the desert where no Black African would dare to enter. The Sahara is huge and would eat anyone alive who did not know how to survive it. The child would become a slave, and the Black family would lose a member forever. These were ancient tensions, but also fresh. Slavery is still present in the Sahara (I saw an enslaved person at a later stage), and a country like Mauritania is notorious for taking a relaxed approach towards slavery. The way Al Qaeda frame it, Islam is the solution. Everybody hates everybody until you become a Muslim. When you become a Muslim, you are all brothers and you are tolerant. That's where Al Qaeda fits in.

Al Qaeda says we are here to unite the people, everybody together under one banner. That might be the official line, but it did not always work like that in day-to-day camp life. The Arabs, and to a lesser extent the Tuaregs, were at the top. When we made camp, they would take the tent. The prisoners would get put under a tree, where we would build our own hut. The black mujahideen would get put under a tree, even though they were mujahideen as well.

Even when it came to food, which was meant to be shared equally, that did not always happen. Whenever they slaughtered an animal, the liver was a sought-after delicacy. Whoever was cooking would share the liver equally among the men. On one occasion, when a Bambara and a Fulani mujahid weren't there, the young Arab guys just ate it. That would never happen the other way around. I could feel the tension in the camp following that.

The way Al Qaeda saw their enemies differed on race and nationality. They saw the Malian and regional ECOWAS (Economic Community of West African States) forces as mere cannon fodder. When they told their battle stories, they would not even count the lives of these poor, Black soldiers, instead only giving points for French, or if they did really well, American lives.

Race and tribe aside, among Al Qaeda you had all the archetypes of any army. They had their officers (emirs and deputies) and their grunts (normal mujahideen), GI Joe juggernauts and their Beetle Baileys, their musclemen and their madmen, stone-cold killers and even the odd sympathetic soul. Some were locals, peasants and pastoralists, while those from wealthy families were more worldly and better educated. Some were relatively open with me about who they were, while I only gleaned snippets of information about others over the years from listening to their fellow mujahideen.

There was Abu Osama, an Algerian, who frequently appeared in our Proof of Life videos in the row of mujahideen standing behind us; while everyone else kept their faces covered, he stood proudly unmasked, staring at the camera. He had quite high status in the group; he was a veteran who had fought in Afghanistan. To him, an AK-47 was a multi-tool, nothing more. Sure, it could kill people, but he would also use it for DIY, to hammer things or shoot a hole through something when there was rigging required. He would even detach the thin cleaning rod that ran along the underside of the barrel to use it as a kebab stick over a fire.

There was Abu Ali, who had been a chauffeur in France before fighting in the desert. We used to call him 'chef de cuisine' because he was good in the kitchen. After one too many battles he was on serious meds; he landed up marooned in camps far out of harm's way, slurring and incomprehensible.

There was a guy called Noah, as in the Ark, who was probably my biggest opponent among Al Qaeda. While some of the mujahideen engaged with me, got to know me and even had sympathy for my situation, no matter how many years passed and how hard I worked to counter my status as 'Britannia', Noah never trusted me and he never believed me. He was a cruel person, who had serious clout with the decision-makers, which was always a huge concern for me. I felt if anyone was going to chop my head off, it would be him. Even his eight-year-old son took joy in telling me I was going to get my head chopped off.

There was Talha, the young bespectacled guy originally from Timbuktu, raised in exile in Mauritania, and groomed to be a leader. When Al Qaeda took Timbuktu in 2012, he ran the city. In an interview with Al Jazeera, he looks personable, engaging and calm, like he would not be out of place sitting on the lawns of a European university, debating

Marxist theory. I cautiously respected him. Often aloof, when he inter-
acted with me he genuinely seemed to want the best for me and hoped
that I'd go home soon, '*Insha Allah*'.

A few of the mujahideen, like Adam, the baby-faced mujahid who led
our abduction, and brothers Abu Bakr and Anas, had been fishermen
in Mauritania. At about 6'5" Abu Bakr was an absolute beast of a man.
The leader of Al Qaeda's attacking unit, he would go into villages and
camps and destroy everything and everyone he saw. He could shoot a
PK (a larger calibre weapon than the AK-47) while standing Rambo-
style, which got everyone's respect. You would hear his name being
whispered in reverential tones by young mujahedeen in small secret
gatherings. It felt like he could literally tear your limbs off your body
with a glance, but when he smiled, he became the gentlest giant.

Anas was also massive. He used to come to us to learn English. He
had the same smile as his brother and exuded peace and gentleness –
as far as a gun-toting member of Al Qaeda can. Anas was a one-man
workforce. He would build the hut, slaughter the goat, prepare the
meat, make the fire, cook lunch and dinner all at the same time, with
a deep warm laugh and no help from anyone. He had endless energy
and a passion for Allah. That was the funny thing about many of these
guys: they were 'tough on non-believers, but gentle to Muslims'.

There was Abu Farida, a short guy prone to chubbiness, who ran
Al Qaeda's communication division. From what I could put together
his father worked for a British airline and his grandmother was from
Kenya or Ethiopia. He had attended a fancy public school in the UK.
He enjoyed swimming and his favourite stroke was breaststroke. We
used to do 'gym' together in the desert and got on quite well, even
though I thought he may be trying to connect with me to establish
whether I was actually British or not. Similarly, I was never quite sure
if he was British or Kenyan or maybe even part South African, because
he had a very neutral accent and was familiar with South African
establishments like Wild Waters in Boksburg, Spur and The Meat Co.
He told me he knew plenty of South Africans from the mosque he
attended in London. They weren't mujahideen, just normal Muslims
who were his friends before he entered jihad. This made me realise
how few degrees of separation there are if a guy like Abu Farida, with
his Western upbringing and exposure, could land up here, making
jihad videos for the cause. Abu Farida was almost as much of an out-
sider as me in the desert because the Arabic he spoke was Classical

Arabic (al-Arabiyah al-Fus'ha) and not the Hassaniya Arabic dialect of the western side of the Sahara.

Abu Darda was the son of one of Mauritania's richest men. He was passionate about Islam and gave up a lot of comfort to join Al Qaeda. I liked Abu Darda and respected him. He brought me a box of Weet-Bix on one occasion; because it was South African, he thought it may remind me of home. Small gestures or gifts like that were priceless to me, as I had nothing as a prisoner. They helped me feel human and accepted. I relearned how to be grateful for the small things in life, a quality that slips away as your payslip grows. Abu Darda also gave me his old Quraan, an item that not even every mujahid had.

Before joining Al Qaeda, Abu Darda used to drive around Nouakchott in either a BMW X5 or a Mercedes ML, while his brother drove a Range Rover. He studied in France and Tunisia, and would go on holidays all over the place, from France and Spain to the Canary Islands. He told me about his father charging him with the responsibility of chaperoning his sisters and his grandmother on a month-long beach holiday to the south of France. There was no shortage of cash or comfort, but he battled with looking after his sisters because they wanted to run around and behave more secularly than he could accept.

In Islam, *fitna* is temptation, something that draws you away from the religion. All the nude beaches, clubs and bars (half the reason the Western world visits the south of France) left him incensed. He eventually told his father he couldn't stay in France one more day with the barrage of *fitna*. Not long after that, he was in the desert, dividing his time between waging holy war and babysitting us hostages.

Arabs, Tuaregs, Fulani, Bambara, a British public-school boy, an Algerian Afghan war vet, Mauritanian fishermen and a trust-fund kid from Nouakchott: all watching over a South African, a Dutchman and a Swede in the blazing sun of the Sahara. Religion, the great equaliser.

CHAPTER FOURTEEN

Another World

'Sahara, aghir kokib' (The Sahara is another world.) – Al Qaeda

When we think of prison, we think of cells, bars and cramped, dimly-lit spaces: Nelson Mandela's tiny cell on Robben Island, Al Qaeda operatives in solitary confinement in Guantanamo, or the clanking of automated doors at Rikers Island shutting the inmates in at night. Our prison was far from that, but it was no less oppressive. A vast open-air cell, with no bars, just endless horizons of nothingness where the shimmering heat guaranteed death for those who did not have knowledge of the area, ample water and a means to get around. It was a prison in the way that a cartoon desert island is a prison – except that we had guards.

If, to the Tuareg, Azawad meant finding grazing pastures for their animals, for Al Qaeda the whole point of using this massive, sparsely-populated area was that they could move us, their human chattel, around relatively easily without being seen. We stayed away from people, wells, trucking routes, desert markets. Even if an area held the odd nomadic family, we'd be kept out of sight as our white skins were very obvious. Nomadic Arabs live so remotely, they are always inquisitive as to who is in their area, even if they are only looking for a free bag of tea or a leather pouch of sugar. Because of this we moved at least every two weeks, from one remote area to another.

The distance we moved could be anywhere between five and 500 kilometres, but we never stayed too long in one spot. Al Qaeda referred to areas with lots of fighting and military activity as being 'hot' (*sakhen*), so their goal was to keep us far from the frontline and any hot areas as much as possible. In total, we moved camp (*makan*) over 150 times in the five years and eight months I was in the desert. As the raiding party escaped with us from Timbuktu, I remember worrying if I'd be held in a prison or an underground bunker, but in the end we spent six years in the sand. It was a long camping trip – just replace the campfire camaraderie and hipflasks of whiskey with constant terror, the sound of surveillance aeroplanes, the odd big bang from a long way off, cuffs, blindfolds, and the incessant yearning for family and home.

I went to Mali as a traveller, curious to see that part of the world, so despite having fear as a constant companion, with time, as I got control of my mind and began to understand my situation a bit better, I was able to look out over endless sand dunes or across the black stone plateau, or watch a massive sandstorm engulf the world, and appreciate the beauty of our prison. In a way I was privileged. As Al Qaeda would say to me, *Sahara, aghir kokib*. 'The Sahara is another world.'

We camped in five distinct regions. There was The Mounds, the area we drove through on our way to Camp 1, which looked like thousands and thousands of little termite mounds randomly placed to the horizon in every direction. Without a bird's-eye perspective, my life was mounds.

Camp 1 was in the rocky foothills of the Adrar des Ifoghas mountains, which lay perhaps 80 kilometres west in an area we called the Edge of the Mountains. It was an undulating, yellow-orange sand landscape with a scattering of black Liquorice-allsorts mountains, bordered by well-placed acacia trees that hid us and our vehicles from the searching eyes of surveillance planes. Just as Timbuktu was a beacon against which we compared everything, Camp 1 was our Saharan equivalent. As we changed camps, I would relate all positions back to Camp 1; *now we are 50 kilometres northeast of Camp 1, now we are 30 kilometres west, now we are 500 kilometres northwest.*

We could not actually see the mountains from Camp 1, but in early 2012, we made a trip east. We drove a full day, hard and fast. I was blindfolded, but I managed to peek and I saw these mountains approaching. This area I called The Black Mountains. We spent the next five months camping among them. Years later, with the luxury of a map of Mali to hand, I could see that, extensive as they were, these mountains too were an island surrounded by the Saharan sea. Just as with life, everything comes to an end, even the mounds and the mountains.

When the rain fell in the mountains, the *wadis* would begin to trickle. A few minutes later you would hear the rush of water approaching, and then a wall of water would come charging past like a freight train, killing camels and anything else in its path, before running out into the sands of the Sahara. Where the floodwaters sank into the sand there were shallow three-metre wells among a relatively dense acacia trees. These formed a perimeter around The Black Mountains. You would get this row of green acacia trees on the edge of the *wadis*, these undulating hills of shiny, black, fist-sized rocks and this yellow-orange sand. Where the mountains didn't obstruct the wind you would often see a string of acacia trees literally buried in sand up to their upper branches. All you saw were a few green leaves poking out the top.

I experienced a couple of floods in the mountains. On one occasion we were parked next to a *wadi* when the rain started to come down hard. I thought, *Why do Al Qaeda always get the dry spot? This time I'll beat them to it.* I took shelter in one of the vehicles. Then the *wadi* started to flow. This was an almighty storm with crashes of lightning and thunder. In no time, the dry riverbed had transformed into a rushing metre-high torrent. With rain tearing down, the roar of the water and the thunder, it was hard to see or hear a thing, but it was clear the car was in danger of getting washed away. One of the mujahideen came out of nowhere, jumped in, threw me out into the storm and just managed to reverse the vehicle away from the flash flood before it was too late. On another occasion, they were too late, and had to spend two days digging a half-buried Land Cruiser out from where it got buried in the *wadi*.

After the rains, pools of leftover water, called *gelters*, would form in the *wadis*. One pond would be for drinking water while another would be for washing clothing, kitchen stuff and entertainment. As organised as Al Qaeda was, it was bizarre how they sometimes lacked logic: we would wash in the pond, which flowed into the drinking pond, so we were in essence drinking our bath water. On other occasions, if management weren't watching, the big sooty kitchen pot or a pair of feet would be washed in the drinking pond.

As the chaos of captivity began to settle and we became more integrated, we were allowed to join Al Qaeda and swim in these ponds. In April 2012, after finding a *gelter* with a decent length for swimming, I knocked out some lengths, climbed out the water and lay on a big black boulder with the sun on my face. I was at peace; this felt euphoric. I was a million miles away from being a prisoner held by Al Qaeda. Then the realisation hit me: while I was lying on this rock feeling as though I was on holiday, my family back home was going through absolute hell. How could I feel joy when I was causing so much pain to my family? I was overwhelmed by guilt.

Further up north into the desert, a world away from the rain and occasional mountain flood, was an area I used to call The Breakers or The Waves. It was as flat as the proverbial pancake; I could literally see the curvature of the Earth as the land sloped away to the horizon. However, every five kilometres to the north and south there were strings of giant sand dunes, 50–70 metres wide, that ran from the eastern horizon to the western horizon as far as the eye could see. We would camp in the nooks and crannies of one of these giant dunes. If you climbed a dune and looked to the other side, they looked like sets of slow-motion sand tsunamis.

This area was close to the salt mines of Taoudenni. There used to be a military base there that housed political prisoners who had to work in the salt mines until they died. Think Siberian gulag (with an average summer temperature of 46°C) meets Anakin Skywalker's hometown of Mos Espa on Tatooine, and you start to get close to understanding how harsh life in a settlement like that is.

The last distinct area was The Holes in the northwest, adjacent to the Mauritanian border. When we camped out in The Holes, it felt like we were far from everywhere. The northeast of Mali, towards the mountains, had life; there were trucking routes, markets, rain and good grazing. The northwest of Mali had nothing. It was an extremely difficult terrain to navigate so nobody went there. We would frequently get stuck and spend hours digging out the vehicle. It was tough, hot and frustrating. There were no *gelters*.

The Sahara is enormous and has so many faces, the beauty and contrast was mind-blowing. I got to see places that I wager few, if any, Westerners have ever seen, landscapes and geological formations that in any other part of the world would be overrun with tourists and branded UNESCO heritage sites.

I just wished I had someone to share it with. On cold nights, I'd pull my blanket up under my chin, wrap my head in my scarf and look up at the moon. I'd think about my family and wonder if they were looking at the same moon at the same time. People talk about seeing a rabbit in the moon, but I used to see a bear, a bit like a honey badger. Every time I looked at a full moon, its brightness almost blanking out all the stars, I saw this bear in a bubble.

Music is *haram* for Al Qaeda, but I would sit there humming and singing gently to myself. The song on loop in my mind was Paul Simon's 'Boy in the Bubble' from the album *Graceland*. Deeply entrenched in my psyche as a South African, it reminded me of going to Southbroom on the KwaZulu-Natal coast with my family as a kid, long days on the beach and never-ending avocados. As I sang along under my breath about dry winds, dead sand and distant constellations, I'd swap out 'boy' for 'bear'.

The bear had his back to me and he was looking over his right shoulder, looking back at Earth, looking back at me. The despair on his face made me so sad. Completely alone, he was floating further and further away from Earth. Further away from his hopes and dreams and family and everything that was dear to him.

CHAPTER FIFTEEN

Camp Life

'Remember, you have no companions but your shadow' – Genghis Khan

If you go to Google Maps and zoom in on the area we called The Holes, it looks like thousands of tiny dimples, like those on a golf ball or ostrich skin. The potholes would vary in size, from a tennis court to a rugby stadium. The larger ones could house 21 people, plus vehicles, and we could all still have a bit of space. Plus, the larger ones had one or two trees for shelter from the sun and from surveillance planes.

We gave the camps names, like 'Camp 1', 'Oasis Camp', 'Comfy Chair Tree Camp' or 'International Camp', where the beaten and injured multi-national force of mujahideen regrouped after the French pushed them back into the desert in March 2013. Al Qaeda had their own nomenclature. If Jaffar, as emir, found a strategic spot that worked for Al Qaeda in terms of access to wood and water or concealment, he would tell all the other groups of his find and hand out the GPS coordinates. It then became known as 'Camp Jaffar'.

The way Al Qaeda structured their prisoner babysitting brigades of mujahideen was not dissimilar to workers on an oil rig. They worked in groups in two-month shifts. A group would consist of 21 people at a time, with one emir or leader and one deputy. Each car would have seven guys; three up front and four on the back. In the early days, when the three of us were together, we had three vehicles and there were seven guys on each vehicle – except they would lose a person for each vehicle because of the three prisoners. So, it was then six muja-hideen per vehicle plus one prisoner, for the total of seven.

Within each group, we would have a minimum number of four camps, changing camp every two weeks. (After the French arrived in January 2013, we would have many more camp changes because we kept having to flee from them.) At the end of a two-month group cycle, three cars would arrive with a fresh batch of 21 to relieve the guys who had just babysat us. They would do a handover and the old guys would head back into the greater pool of Al Qaeda operatives across the southern Sahara and further south, where they conducted other *amaliyas* or operations.

The exciting operations, for them, were military operations, like attacks on Malian army bases or suicide bombings, which they loved speaking about around the campfire, raising their fellow soldiers up as heroes. These stories filled me with terror. I felt that the stronger Al Qaeda got and the more chaos they could inflict on West Africa and the west in general, the less chance there would be of a successful negotiation and of me ever going home.

Besides these operations, Al Qaeda was an organisation with people and vehicles that needed to be fed and watered. Task groups were responsible for getting fuel or food from markets and burying it at specific GPS coordinates in the desert, gathering intel on various towns and military camps and roadblocks, or babysitting other prisoners. Some of our guards, like Abu Laith, we never saw again. With his eyes set on what awaited him in *Jannah*, the afterlife, he volunteered to drive a Land Cruiser laden with explosives into a Malian army depot just northeast of Timbuktu, killing multiple West African soldiers and damaging some French helicopters.

Periods of change were tricky. Whether a change of group, camp, area or protocol, I could feel Al Qaeda's stress levels altering. The lack of information always left me feeling anxious and vulnerable.

The process of changing camp was terrifying. We never knew what was happening or what the plan was. We would be blindfolded for the drive, which could end at a scenic spot for a choreographed on-camera execution. The only time I got excited was when we went further south; it felt like we were inching closer to Timbuktu, to the real world, to tarred roads, to me potentially going home, back to my family and Cath.

Change brought about opportunity; a new area, scenery, people and potential information. But new groups brought a new wave of old problems. With little else to do except pray and recite the Quraan, the mujahideen discussed us, their charges, and my passport always resulted in a fresh set of lectures about Islam and about the evils of the Britannia. A new group also meant that I had to start, all over again, with arguing the case that I was South African, not British.

While we were bored out of our minds, our captors were too. For soldiers of God, guarding POWs is not exciting work. Most of them would have preferred to be in the actual fighting rather than be stuck in the desert for two months, looking after a wallflower South African, a lunatic Dutchman and a calculating Swede. The guys recruited from further south in particular hated the Sahara. They would rather be back home, where at least they could get some shade from proper trees and have easy access to water. One mujahid, a Bambara from Niger, told the group, 'Sahara is not good. There's no water and no rabbits here.' Like us, he just wanted to go home and appreciate the simple pleasures in life.

Usually, the changeover happened 60 days to the day. If a vehicle arrived early at 58 days, there would be celebrations and everybody would get very excited. If it ended up dragging on to 62 or 63 days before relief arrived, there would be a lot of grumpiness in camp. If there was a delay, it could be because guys were battling to find food in the markets due to a heavy military presence, or they were more urgently needed for an operation elsewhere. I think our longest group changeover delay extended by almost three weeks. Our group became incredibly cantankerous. When the sounds of the cars started coming in from the south, there was an immediate frisson of excitement running through the camp.

As boring as it was for the mujahideen, for the organisation this was a vital role. They literally had one job: do not let the prisoners escape. That was pretty much the only thing that they had to do. If we escaped or were found by the French, Malian or ECOWAS troops, it would result in incredibly bad publicity, and huge embarrassment, for Al Qaeda. If we died on their watch, well, it was not ideal, but it also wasn't the end of the world. Al Qaeda had multiple hostages in camps all over the Sahel, so their inventory was well stocked. No matter if we died by snakebite, the bullets of French guns in a rescue attempt, or heat exhaustion from trying to escape, Al Qaeda could at least use our deaths to their advantage. They could get mileage out of the PR war by proclaiming, 'We kidnapped a British guy, and we were trying to negotiate, but in the end due to the inefficiencies of Western governments, one of their children died.' Subtext: 'To the people of Britain, Sweden or Holland – your governments do not care about you. Had your government actually negotiated, this guy would not be dead and he could go home to his family.'

Within a group, each Al Qaeda emir ran their camp in much the same way. Some, like Noah, kept us on an extremely short leash, but most felt comfortable that escape was impossible, so in time they allowed us a few minor freedoms. Days involved prayer before sunrise, breakfast, prayer at midday, lunch, prayer in the late afternoon, prayer at sunset, dinner, and then often we'd sit in a *halaqa* (a circle for a meeting) and one last prayer between sunset and midnight. As prisoners, we spent a lot of time doodling, sleeping or exercising.

As far as the structure of the camp went, there was a place for Al Qaeda's hut, a place for the prisoners, a place for the kitchen, the larder, the fuel drums, the vehicles, the water drums, an area to eat, to relieve ourselves, a place for the prayer line and places to sleep. Some mujahideen were on *herassa* (security detail), others were on firewood detail, preparing food or working on the vehicles, while the rest took it easy in their tent or lounged under a tree. Some of them would be sent off to fetch water from the closest well. They would use the vehicles if pressure from our pursuers was not too intense or, if Al Qaeda felt the area was being watched, they might get hold of some camels and fetch water the old-school way, with 100 metres of rope, a well pulley (*karkarrah*), a bucket and water drums.

In the early days we had a really small area in each camp, about four by four metres, to move in. After we had been held captive for a month and understood the dynamics and the rules, that area was increased to about 10 by 20 metres. At that point we were allowed to exercise, something that was incredibly important to us and about which I will go into detail in due course. We would arrive in a camp and be allocated an area, 'from that rock to this tree to that patch of camel dung, that is your spot'. If you wanted to go to the toilet, they would point in a direction and say something along the lines of, 'You go over that hill for the big toilet, for the small toilet, you cannot go far.' Other than that, we could not leave our area. If anybody came near the camp, we were under strict instructions to sit down, get in our hut and hide our things. No matter what, we could not be seen.

When it came to sleeping arrangements, initially the three of us started off sharing a single hut. It was about two by three metres and we would all sleep in there, packed tight like sardines. Because the hut had a single door on one side, inevitably you would have to crawl in over somebody's blanket or mat to get to your little portion of the sardine can. You can imagine, when somebody comes crawling in and their flip-flops throw sand in your face while you're sleeping, tempers run high – especially when you've been doing it for three years! Plus, if you consider who we were – two bikers and an overlander – the very nature of what we chose to do with the leisure portion of our lives was to explore, independently, away from crowds. Being held captive by Al Qaeda was bad enough, but being confined in a tiny space in the sand made it worse. There were fistfights, kicking and beard pulling, and the most common line thrown around inside our hut was 'we are *not* friends'. I think Al Qaeda realised that, before they would get to kill us, we may kill each other. So they allowed each of us to build our own hut.

I still don't know why, but Al Qaeda called this a 'boogie' – which is the way the word sounds in *Arabya Hassaniya*, but whenever I built my hut, I would imagine myself on a Caribbean beach under palm fronds, with music and colourful lights, cocktail in hand, having a bit of a boogie.

Making a quality hut in the Sahara is a science, because the engineering and architecture have to factor into everything from the limitations of your natural building materials to light, wind and sandstorms, as well as Al Qaeda's paranoia over surveillance from the sky. As with any building, foundations come first. The best sand on which to place your hut is hard sand, as your poles will stay true for longer. You want your hut to run from east to west for best protection from the sun; this also allows direct access of wind from the northeast.

The best poles for creating the hut frame were acacia tree branches, which were strong yet flexible. For the roof structure I would use acacia roots. These roots were quite amazing; they were dead straight, some thin like dowel sticks and others quite thick, like a broomstick. The combination of these roots would create a frame and cross slats on which you could lay grass. They were strong enough to handle a sandstorm or thunderstorm, and also the weight of my blanket if I needed to hang it from the roof to create extra shade.

The grass for the roof and sides of the boogie grew in tufts in randomly scattered patches in the sand. Depending on the direction of the prevalent wind, these holes tended to have a steep edge and a long edge like a golf bunker. You would take the camp axe or spade and start chopping and digging out the grass. You had to be careful, because in a land that is 98% sand and stone, living things like horned vipers and scorpions like to shelter and hunt from the base of the few bits of grass they can find.

Using grass for thatching, acacia roots for scaffolding and the odd ropey (the name we had for bits of elastic and cloth we used as tie-downs), I got better and better at building my huts. The most important thing was not to make it too high – chest height at most – because any-thing taller would cast a dark shadow that surveillance planes might see. While trees and bushes obviously cast shadows too, they are a bit vague, whereas a tall solid structure like a hut can cast an unnaturally dark shadow. That said, it was important to get the roof as high as possible to keep the temperature inside as cool as possible. It was a fine balance between what Al Qaeda wanted for security and what we wanted for comfort.

We also could not have too big an entrance, because a dark entrance-way would show up as an unusually black cave-like mark from above. This fear of shadows was the same reason we were under strict instructions to sit down whenever a surveillance plane flew overhead. It wasn't so much the colours of what we wore that Al Qaeda was afraid of, but the shadows we cast.

Over time, I learned more and more tricks to get as comfortable as possible in the desert. An obstacle to sleep behind, like a mound or a hut, would help break the desert wind. A scarf (*amama*) covering my ears would keep insects out and keep my head warm.

The winters were freezing. I was probably the only person who pre-ferred sleeping outside my boogie in winter. Sleeping outside under the stars and a full moon allowed me to dream of being back home. Some Al Qaeda members would build a small screen at night to keep the light of the full moon off their faces. They would say that, just as the sun gives you a headache, so does the full moon. I found this peculiar, but after five years in the desert, I too was creating a screen.

Sleeping with my head into the wind helped with preventing lower back pain, which was a constant problem for me. This was an Al Qaeda trick. In summer, some Al Qaeda members would make a grass mat and sprinkle it with water before lying down; this would keep the ground cool, which would also help with back pain. In winter, it was important to have some kind of roofing over your head, even if it was not a full boogie with walls. It still trapped some heat and kept the cold from entering your bones, as Al Qaeda would say. In summer it was okay to sleep directly on the sand to keep cool, but this always concerned me because, while snakes would not climb on your mat or blanket, they would have no problems on the sand. I did not want to wake up with an unfriendly viper under my blanket.

I grew to love desert sand. Sand gets everywhere. You learn that letting it stress you out is a waste of time because, whether you stress or don't, you will have sand everywhere anyway, so it is best to accept it rather than fight it. Sand in your water is not a problem, because it sinks to the bottom. Sand in your blanket is not a problem – just shake it all out when you stand up. I would sit in the desert and imagine how amazing it would be if I could just click my fingers and swop the sand from all the beaches in the world with Saharan sand, because there is no comparison. Beach sand has a humid clamminess to it, whereas desert sand is amazingly granular, made of tiny one-millimetre stones. It's not dusty – most of the finer powder is sitting over the Atlantic somewhere courtesy of the strong winds blowing it off the Sahara and out to sea – and it's clean. We used it to clean our hands, our pots and pans. You could get caught in a sandstorm and be absolutely covered in sand and then dust yourself off and be spotless again.

Besides the sand, the Sahara is hot and sterile, and almost nothing is filthy. Sometimes I didn't shower for a month and still wouldn't notice any body odour. Either we all stank, or no one stank. I think no one stank. It was quite bizarre. In the Quraan, the Prophet (PBUH) used to speak about how the desert sun made things clean again. Even urine and faeces, once they've been in the sun long enough, get completely neutralised and are no longer classified as dirt.

Sometimes, if there was pressure from the French or Malian forces, we would have to leave a camp at extremely short notice. The mujahideen would run up to us, rolling their hand over each other and shouting, 'Baggage!' The literal translation of the French is 'bags', but it essentially meant, 'get your stuff together ASAP!' Then we would be blindfolded, bundled into the Land Cruisers, and hit the road again. If there was less panic and we were just moving camp, we were sometimes allowed to pack up our hut with all the grass we had harvested, so the Land Cruiser landed up looking like we were farmers heading off to feed cattle hay. But for the most part, we pretty much only took our poles and left the grass behind.

In a land so vast and sparsely populated, you would think that hiding away would be the easiest thing, but the desert is a funny place. Al Qaeda knew all too well what gives you away if you are not careful. While it was unlikely that the Malian army and later the French could find us of their own accord, the fear of *jasoos* (spies) informing Al Qaeda's enemies of our location was real. All it took was one guy with a camel seeing us at a distance; if that guy visited a town and either let slip our location or intentionally shared it with the authorities for a reward, death would soon arrive in the shape of a French helicopter gunship and commandos.

As we abandoned a camp, we had to take precautions about what we left behind. When we cut somebody's hair or shot a bird – as we did with every sizeable bird, even the beautiful Nubian bustards and white storks – we had to bury the evidence. If we did not, and the hair and the feathers blew across the sand, it would announce our presence in the area. When we were preparing to leave a camp, the mujahideen would dig a hole into the sand, half a metre down, and bury everything. Weeks of sardine cans, milk cartons and other rubbish all got chucked in there. The desert was essentially a giant tip to these guys.

One thing Al Qaeda were incredibly sensitive about was smoke. It was funny how they would play with guns, shoot and kill people, drive like maniacs and fall off moving cars, literally everything extreme and dangerous, yet at the slightest whiff of smoke they would complain. If you made a small fire and the wind was blowing in their direction, they would go absolutely crazy, saying *dukhan lesa jayed! Dukhan* is the word for smoke, *lesa jayed* means not good.

Their complaint was partly due to the fact that smoke is bad for their health – and many of these guys were asthmatic – but also because there are almost no odours in the desert. The desert targets very few senses besides sight. So if we had a fire and the smoke travelled on the wind, it would effectively broadcast that people are here. Because there are so few people in the desert and most people know who should be in the area, if an Arab on a camel, five kilometres away, picked up the smell of smoke, it was more than likely he would come to the camp to investigate. If he was a *jasoos*, we were in trouble.

The only other smell would be petrichor, that earthy warm smell that comes off the ground in late summer as the first rains hit; or the rare smell of an acacia blossom.

The latter had a real effect on me in February 2012. We were on the edge of the mountains, and being held prisoner was still new for me. I was walking in circles around a small bush for exercise. It was a still day and a gentle breeze blew in from the northeast. I got a face full of this incredible scent. I remember walking straight through it and actually turning around and trying, almost like Pepé Le Pew, to follow it to its source. It was the acacia bush I was walking around. It had these small yellow flowers with bits of pink. For months, everything in the desert had seemed so bland, so one-dimensional, and this sensory overload from the scent and the flowers combined was so powerful.

As I stood there, eyes closed, breathing that scent in through my nose. It took me back to a specific moment in time and another flower – the May bush we had next to the swimming pool at my folks' place in Johannesburg. It was a sunny Sunday afternoon, I was 13 or 14 years old, and my sister was by my side. We were wet from the pool, our skin rippled with gooseflesh, getting dry in the sun. My parents were laughing on the patio, my mom always stylish even in her casual Capri pants and a T-shirt. The music played softly in the background, and as I lay chest-down on the sun-baked bricks to dry, I could feel the vibrations of the pool's Kreepy Krauly chugging through the ground. Out of half-closed eyes I could see the May bush and hear the bees buzzing around its small white flowers, leaving a beautiful scent on a beautiful afternoon.

The wind changed slightly, I lost the scent and the spell was broken. I stood there with tears running down my face, a wrecked 36-year-old desert prisoner torn apart on the inside with nothing but memories and hope to hang on to.

Group email from Cath, 25 May 2012

Today marks six months of captivity for Steve, Sjaak and Johan. Time has flown by, but it has also dragged on, often appearing as though this nightmare were endless. Time has been a major factor for us as we wait patiently and pray fervently to see some light. Although much has happened since 25 November, it also feels as though nothing has happened as our Steve is still in captivity.

The past few weeks, since we heard the news of Steve's release being linked to Abu Qatada, have undoubtedly been the hardest, especially with the knowledge that Steve's fate is at stake. The uncertainty has been difficult to deal with. We have had meetings with British and South African authorities, and the stance is still for the South Africans to lead. Steve's parents were in the UK and were debriefed in Whitehall at the Foreign Office where I first received my debriefing all those months ago. Things are still very confidential at the moment so we can't say much, but there is some movement.

In our desperation to do something to secure Steve's release, we as a family have attempted to open a few doors – one of which was Thabo Mbeki's. I was amazed when I walked into his offices that there was a picture of Timbuktu in the entrance hall, and a picture of the famous manuscripts too. Although he did not offer much advice, he did inform us about some of the history of Timbuktu. He was instrumental in arranging for a library to be built in Timbuktu to house the precious manuscripts – some of which I heard were destroyed in the riots recently. As I am sure you may have read, Mali is still in turmoil and things do not look like they will be improving any time soon. Their interim president was attacked in his presidential suite and had to be hospitalised.

Because we felt so helpless, we took it upon ourselves to send numerous emails and letters to various people around the world (including David Cameron and Theresa May) to appeal for Steve's release or to just lift him and the others up in prayer. One special email was sent to Beatrice Stockley, the Swiss missionary who was kidnapped in Timbuktu and released shortly afterwards last month. My stepmom in the UK was instrumental in arranging this for me. Amen!

We were very close to making Steve's story public – we even went as far as having an interview, but this was halted with immediate effect when the government officials found out. They felt that the British media would get hold of the story and it would run wild, which is not want we want. Al

Qaeda love the press. I must say it was very cathartic to talk to the press, as we have felt all along that we have had no voice. Our silence has been frustrating, as we feel that Steve's story has not been heard by the nation. I hope that one day it will be.

Steve's motorbike has finally arrived. It came on the ship with one of the South African mining companies in Mali. Even after all this time it was a stark reminder that Steve is no longer travelling on his motorbike in Africa. His once-clean motorbike was filthy and covered with fine Sahara sand. His black sheepskin seat that was all fluffy and new when I last saw it is now worn down by hours of riding. Steve's helmet still has remnants of his smell – albeit a little stale and smelly. :) It was good to have a part of him back, but we really want the rider back now.

Another lovely surprise this week was that Monique Strydom wrote me a beautiful email that was very heartwarming. She explained that we as a family are hostages ourselves. We could so relate to that fact, as our lives all seem to be on hold and we are trapped inside a world that is so foreign to us.

On that rather pensive note, I bid you farewell. I hope that next month will bring good news. My prayer at the moment is for Steve to be back when his sister Leigh, brother-in-law Gregg and baby Hannah come out to SA from the UK in August.

Once again, your prayers mean so much to us, and we thank you for all your messages of hope, love and light.

Remaining firm in faith,
Cath

CHAPTER SIXTEEN

Inmates & Intel

'No man is an island,
entire of itself;
every man is a piece of the continent,
a part of the main'
– 'Meditation 17', John Donne, 1623

Popular culture tells us that when the chips are down people band together and find a way out of things. By that logic, if our abduction was a Hollywood action film plot, three captives (played by Chuck Norris, Dolph Lundgren and Jean-Claude van Damme) brought together by fate, would put aside our differences and work together to overcome the odds, defeat our captors (by way of some advanced plotting and karate chops) and make it out of there alive. Years later, on the anniversary of our abduction, we would visit each other and reminisce about the bad old days when we were held by Al Qaeda.

It didn't happen like that.

When extraordinary circumstances were thrust upon us, Sjaak, Johan and I were forced to make decisions we would never otherwise entertain. With survival always uncertain, we behaved in ways that were not part of who we thought we were before we were abducted: a regular South African, a Swede and a Dutchman whose paths crossed on the road in Morocco, over beers in Bamako, and wandering around the market of Timbuktu. I have no doubt we would have been fine if that is where our interaction had ended. When we grew bored with each other's company or found someone particularly tiresome, we could simply take a walk, close a hostel door, zip up a tent flap, put on some headphones or jump on a plane and go home. We would have had the luxury of choice. When Al Qaeda took our liberty, they also took that freedom of association away from us. We were quite literally stuck with each other.

To be honest, I was surprised it turned out the way it did. I enjoy people and gravitate towards groups and conversations. I've always been a team player, in school, at work, with friends. I wanted to connect and interact with Sjaak and Johan, to get through this steaming shit sandwich fate dished up to us, together. I expected it would be us (prisoners) versus them (Al Qaeda). And while there were moments when that happened, when we pulled together and supported each other, that was only in the first few weeks. By the end of the first year, the honeymoon period was definitely over. Each of us then decided, consciously or unconsciously, on a strategy that would best serve him as an individual.

There was a specific moment when I realised the three of us were not going to be friends. We were being transported between camps, and as usual we were blindfolded. Some of the mujahideen were quite lax with their blindfold technique, so they would leave the blindfold a little loose, which allowed us to steal a peek out the bottom or side edges, and see a little of the landscape we were travelling through. Others were overzealous and tied it way too tight. On this occasion, I could feel the strap constricting my temples and digging hard into my eyeballs. When we arrived at the new camp, the guard took off my blindfold and I blinked to clear my vision. I held a hand up in front of me and it was blurred. The sand dune 500 metres away was blurry. Fucking everything was blurry. Panic kicked in – the idea of being half-blind on top of everything else was just too much. 'Guys, I can't see,' I blurted to Johan and Sjaak. 'The blindfold was so tight, I don't know if they've damaged the nerves but everything is blurred. What the hell am I going to do?'

Their response was disinterested: 'Ja, it will probably be fine.'

My eyesight gradually corrected over the next two days, but that moment slammed home for me that we all had our own problems, and each person was focused on his own survival. The situation was overwhelming for all of us. As difficult as this was to accept, this wasn't a game and we weren't a team. There was a sort of animal instinct, survival of the fittest clicking into gear. That moment set a precedent, an understanding that even though the three of us were kidnapped together and had the same set of problems, we were individuals. It was a dynamic that would last right through to the end.

Johan believed we would be executed within six months. It was not an unreasonable projection, considering our predicament. As a result, Johan wasn't interested in engaging in our hopes and dreams. For the first few months, Sjaak and I tried to stay optimistic by focusing on specific dates that held value for us and which we wanted to be home for. We would compare notes. Sjaak would say he had something important to get back to on, say, 15 December, and if I had something a bit sooner, like a friend's birthday on 1 December, we would focus on my date first. Once one calendar date came and went, we would focus on the next, and the next, and the next.

For me, the big one was always my commitment to be home for Cath's and my fifth wedding anniversary at the end of March, but there were plenty of other events before then. There was my dad's birthday on Christmas Day, Christmas itself, New Year, Cath's birthday on 3 January, my birthday at the end of January and my mom's birthday in March. I suppose deep down we knew it was ludicrous to pretend any of this mattered. There was no power in fixating on these dates, just an arbitrary whiff of hope to usher out into the universe. We knew we had no physical control over our fortune, but our thoughts were our own and we could dream about a date to be home by.

Johan would say, 'Look, this situation is going to go on for a long time. We won't be going home soon. No one will negotiate for our release. That is the way these things are done. Governments will pretend to be interested in negotiating so we aren't killed, but there will be no negotiation.' He would go on and on until his negative attitude had destroyed any glimmer of hope that we would get to live beyond this point.

In order to hang on to events, we had to keep track of the passing of the days. That's easier said than done when you are sitting in the sand under a tree for days on end. One day becomes the next becomes the next. Weekends are irrelevant, public holidays are irrelevant; the only thing you can rely on is the shadow cast by the sun as the day advances, the waxing and waning of the moon, and the changing of the seasons.

Because Adam had been sporting my watch on his arm from day one, we had to find other ways of keeping record. I started by making marks on a tree in Camp 1. I made them at the back of the tree, under a branch, because I didn't want Al Qaeda to come and see these peculiar stripes and get angry about what I was doing. Who knew what the repercussions would be? When we changed camps I obviously couldn't take the tree with me, but I would remember the number and start again on a new tree at the next camp from that number.

I knew we had been abducted on Friday, 25 November and had arrived in Camp 1 on Saturday, so I had a starting point. I began to battle to keep track of travel days and camp days, because we would travel and then stop in a temporary camp, travel again, stop in another temporary camp, and so on until we got to a 'permanent' camp where I could start making stripes in a tree again.

Untethered from the world of Google, Facebook and automated cell-phone reminders, I reverted to repeating the mnemonic of my child-hood to keep track of the months:

Thirty days has September,
April, June, and November,
All the rest have thirty-one,
Except February alone which has twenty-eight,
And 29 each *leap year*.

I was pretty confident 2012 was a leap year.

The next thing was to keep track of the time of day. It's hard to describe how frustrating it is to go from having all the knowledge in the world at your fingertips, to having nothing. Think about how inconvenienced we are when there is a power outage, or an undersea cable fault crashes the internet. Even if you go back many decades to when our parents and grandparents were young, at least they could still measure time and receive news. We had been dragged back centuries, millennia even, forced to devolve from the digital, past the analogue, straight back through medieval times all the way to Ancient Egypt, where the only tools at our disposal as prisoners were the sun, the moon and the stars, sand, twigs and camel shit.

In the evenings I would track where the moon rose over sand dunes over several nights. During the day, we'd make a sun dial outside of my hut by putting a stick in the ground and using bits of camel dung to mark off times of the day. So if Al Qaeda were doing their 2pm or 5pm prayer, we'd stick a piece of camel dung in the ground to mark where the shadow was at that time. When breakfast arrived, we'd stick a piece of camel dung down for that. If Al Qaeda came and went at regular intervals, we would mark that off too, trying to find patterns, because we wanted to see if there was a routine.

We gathered as much information as we possibly could in those early days. It wasn't just about escaping or eventually securing our liberty, although that was the end goal. It was a way to find peace in the chaos, combat the boredom of sitting under a tree or in a hut all day, and make sense of this new world.

The three of us spoke English to each other, but communicating with our captors was much harder. Some mujahideen had basic French, as did we prisoners, but Al Qaeda had few words of English at the start of our incarceration (the British recruit Abu Farida arrived later). We could not communicate well with the mujahideen who deigned to talk to us – and we were uncertain whether some of them could speak English, but chose not to so they could listen in on us talking. There was a lot of prisoner psychology at play in the desert.

In order to learn Arabic words, we would draw things in the sand but some of the mujahideen had a problem with that. Drawing animate objects like humans or animals is *haram* or forbidden in Islam; it means you seek to imitate the creation of Allah. Others argued that drawing was okay for teaching purposes, as you would with a child. For the most part, we avoided it, sometimes acting out a specific animal if that was what we were trying to learn the Arabic word for. As we pointed at things, acted them out or watched Al Qaeda kill them, our vocabulary grew. Tortoise = *fakron*, poked, stabbed and tortured till they could cut its throat. Mice = *faar*, beaten with flip-flops as they darted through camp. Monitor lizard = *laurun*, smashed with a spade.

I love the natural world and was genuinely interested in the flora and fauna – especially in keeping it alive – but what I needed most was information about where we were. It's funny how your brain tricks you into thinking you know something. Before we were kidnapped, if somebody said to me, 'Draw a map of Mali,' I would have attempted to do so with confidence. Now, trying to picture where we might be in relation to the country's borders, I was at a loss. How far were we from that colonial dividing line that drops straight down on the Mauritanian border with the northwestern edge of Mali? Were we closer to southern Algeria? Is there a bulge into Algeria or does it zigzag? There was a ridge of mountains along that border; were the mountains we could see those mountains, or another range further to the north? How far were we from towns, army bases, help of any sort? Were we even in Mali?

My only point of reference was Timbuktu, which for the rest of the world symbolises the furthest place from anywhere. That was always centred in my brain as the starting point, and my lodestone for every waking moment of the next few years, because I knew from there I could make my way home. Just where it was, though, was a mystery.

In casual conversations, if someone mentions a suburb or place and gestures towards it with a finger or thumb, they frequently get it wrong. Of course, it's not a matter of life and death in the real world when saying Notting Hill or Parkhurst is 'over there', but every time the mujahideen mentioned Timbuktu and gestured with their hands in its general direction, I agonised over it. What if they had a terrible sense of direction? What if they were only 10 degrees out? That sort of discrepancy makes a huge difference when you are fantasising about hiking 500 kilometres to safety.

In my mind, our trail through the desert sand from Timbuktu stretched out on the map of Mali like a never-ending strand of spaghetti drawn by a tireless drunken screensaver. As we looped through the desert, turned and parked and reversed and looped around again and again, meandering across massive distances and places I had given names, from The Black Mountains to The Zen Garden, The Humps, The Mounds, The Holes and back again, from below my blindfold I imagined the spaghetti drawing ever more complex Gordian knots. I was making mental notes of what I saw whenever I could sneak a peek from beneath my blindfold as we travelled between camps. Every day, every month, every year, I had to extend that piece of spaghetti to try to keep track of where we began and how many hours we travelled and in which direction.

A few of the mujahideen wore watches. Most of them were cheap watches with no GPS capability, and some were worn upside down, but even so I would get the occasional glimpse of co-ordinates.

Most of the drivers had a small hand-held Garmin GPS. Sometimes they would sit next to me in the driver's seat putting in the new camp's coordinates, and I would sit there looking straight ahead, trying my damndest to get a view of the numbers being punched in with my peripheral vision. Sometimes these digits were in Arabic and I would try to memorise the shapes to be deciphered later.

Every now and then a scrap of paper with coordinates would blow through camp, perhaps dropped from a loose pocket. They could have been coordinates for another camp, or the location of buried fuel or food, because Al Qaeda had an extensive logistics network to feed and power all their brigades in the region. We did not know, but it was a start in a million-piece jigsaw puzzle. Gradually, I started to develop a mind map of northern Mali based on glimpses and hunches, on snippets of conversations overheard.

A lot of my theories were based on knowledge from my previous life back in South Africa and my passion for outdoor hobbies. For example, having seen various types of flies in different locations across the Sahara,

I created a fly map so that when I saw a certain type of fly, I knew I had returned to a particular area in the desert.

The intelligence game worked both ways. While I was gathering as much information as I could about where we were and how our captors operated, I was also intent on dispersing my own story among Al Qaeda. From the first time we were interrogated about where we came from, kneeling in the yellow lights of the Land Cruiser, I knew from the blank looks when I said 'Afrique du Sud' that I was going to have problems. In subsequent conversations with various mujahideen, both low-level and middle management, I realised that most of them had never even heard of South Africa. How the hell was I going to convince them I was not British when they did not know the country I claimed to be from even existed? I hoped that if enough of our babysitters came to know and understand me both as the 'South African' and as the mild-mannered captive who plays by the rules, the message would eventually reach upper management. I knew full well that this was going to be a marathon, not a sprint.

Again, from a morale point of view, Johan did not help. 'Look man,' he would say, 'you've got this British Passport, you're British. End of story.' So much for camaraderie. If anybody's situation was fragile, it was mine; I was the most hated purely by association to the UK.

The way I saw it, there was a definite totem pole of privilege among the prisoners, both in the way Al Qaeda saw us and how likely we were to be killed. Johan was at the top, Sjaak in the middle and I was at the bottom. While I was the outright champion as 'Britannia' in terms of ransom value, Johan and Sjaak were probably on a par. Sweden and Holland are both liberal democracies, and both had some minor involvement in the Iraq war. In terms of on-the-ground favour with Al Qaeda, Johan took pole position, because he was the blue-eyed blonde and had the ability to grow a magnificent beard, something which Al Qaeda respect. So they liked him on appearance alone. He was also highly intelligent, and they recognised this; he became known as 'the professor'. Over time, his intelligence went from something Al Qaeda respected to something they saw as *khateer* (dangerous), because he broke their trust on several fronts, which had consequences for all of us.

Both Johan and I were 36 when we were taken; at 51, Sjaak was the elder statesman of our group. Sjaak had been a mechanic in the Dutch army, stationed in Lebanon for a bit when he was younger, so he was practical and could fix and make things. In the real world, he was very people-orientated, the funny guy in the pub being the centre of attention. At home in Holland, he was fun and silly, like a court jester. In the desert, he used to do little tricks to try to win Al Qaeda over, like balancing the butt of a spade on his chin with the blade up in the sky. As he walked around camp like this, Al Qaeda's youngsters would be falling over laughing. He would pick up a stone, throw it up in the air, bounce it off his bicep and catch it. Guys were intrigued by him because they had never seen such antics before.

Sjaak also had a short fuse and a serious temper. As time went by, he started to become more volatile. He was a tall guy and there were times that he would stand over me screaming, literally 10 centimetres from my face, with bright-red veins sticking out the side of his neck. The insecurity and stress of our situation wore us all down, and the cracks began to show.

This happened between Sjaak and Johan more frequently, and on one occasion degenerated into a full-on fistfight. Sometimes, when we still shared a hut, junior members of Al Qaeda would come past to recite the Quraan to us. As a Muslim, it's a good thing to do, as you earn points for every word of the Quraan that you read. An angel on your right shoulder keeps track of your good deeds, and marks off your Quranic recitals. The angel on your left shoulder keeps track of your bad deeds. If you spend your entire life reciting the Quraan, you get all these good points and it slowly cancels out some of the bad points you inevitably accrue.

When these young guys came into the hut to recite to us, you could see they were proud of what they were doing because they couldn't really read or write. This invasion of our limited space drove Sjaak crazy. I would watch Sjaak's fuse burn, and after about a minute he would lose his shit and go absolutely moggy, screaming and shouting at them. Some would get up and leave, others would sit and taunt him. They might leave for an hour and then come back again, and the cycle would start up once more. He got the nickname *shibani mujinoon*, which means crazy old man. For Sjaak to earn that label among a crowd where suicide bombers are not seen as crazy is indicative of the parallel universe we had fallen into.

Sjaak's and my discord was usually over me interacting with Al Qaeda. He could not understand it. He would shout, 'Why are you friendly to these guys? They have kidnapped you!' My response was, 'Mate, handle this however you want, but I have the British passport and will be the first to be killed. I have a responsibility towards myself and my family. I cannot go home a mess. Yes, these guys have stolen my freedom and so much more from me, but the minute they steal *me* from me, that is when they have really won.'

Having a British passport, I realised there was a good chance that I would never go home. Al Qaeda told me this and I was very aware that if they did not negotiate with the South African or Malian governments, I was well and truly screwed. So I figured, if these guys are ever going to show charity to anybody, let it be to me. Character is paramount in Islam, so my approach was to show good character and get along with Al Qaeda as best I could, so I could get out of there.

Part of my strategy was for Al Qaeda to think that I was slightly naive, a bit of a country bumpkin, because I figured the more innocent and harmless I was, the more likely I was to ingratiate myself with them. But at the same time, I didn't want to be a complete pushover; it was important to strike a balance. I would interact to the point that I could add value to a conversation, but not give away my secrets. I did not want them to know just how much I knew. I learned to do this from a few early interactions when I overplayed my hand.

Sitting around at night having conversations, someone might say, 'What is that star?' I'd answer too fast and too definitively, 'That's the North Star.' That would silence the camp, almost as if everyone was thinking, 'What! He knows our direction star. If he knows that, he might know enough to find his way out of here.' Sometimes I would just have to bluff my way through so it did not look like I was trying to hide something. I'd say, 'Of course that's the North Star, everyone knows that.' This game went on for years, being careful about what I knew, owning a few bits of information without seeming arrogant or a fool, and trying wherever possible to get Al Qaeda to offer up more about themselves, the area and details of our possible release than I gave in return.

When you learn a language, even if it's done via intensive immersion at gunpoint, it can take a while till you are able to pick up on a joke or wordplay. We were learning Arabic and French and snippets of other languages that popped up as camp lingo, as each day passed. The problem was, without a teacher to guide us, we were shooting blind. An example of this is the blessing, *Insha Allah*, which means 'if God wills it' or 'by the Grace of God'. It's a phrase that punctuated every conversation, prayer, meal and blessing within Al Qaeda. In the Western world we have echoes of this kind of blessing entrenched, without much meaning, into our language, our heraldry and iconography too, from 'God bless you' when someone sneezes to 'OMG!' among texting teens.

When Al Qaeda said '*Insha Allah*', they were discussing divine intervention, yet Johan with his analytical, mathematical brain was always looking for patterns, a code to crack. He became convinced that where *Insha Allah* was placed in a sentence had meaning. If it was at the beginning of a sentence, '*Insha Allah*, you will go home soon,' he decided it meant that they had no idea if anything was happening or not. If, however, it was placed at the end of a sentence, 'You will go home soon, *Insha Allah*,' then he deduced something was happening. It turned out this was rubbish. I asked Al Qaeda, subtly, and they said it made no difference, but Johan felt they were lying – even though lying is a serious sin in Islam.

I believe we all struggled with depression, loneliness, boredom and borderline insanity, but of the three I would say Sjaak became the most unhinged. I don't think he really had a strategy for getting out of the desert. Johan, on the other hand, did. The more time I spent around Johan, the more I realised that he was all IQ and almost zero EQ. He would use me when he needed me and push me away the moment I had fulfilled my usefulness, whether it was a helping hand with one of our science experiments, borrowing one of my few belongings or using the shared radio we would later receive. From Camp 2, three months into captivity, it became clear that Johan had his own plan for surviving the desert, one that did not include Sjaak and me. He started acting peculiarly, standing up in the open and eyeballing Al Qaeda as they prayed, pretending to take an interest in their religion. He was planning to convert to Islam.

This was the start of the major problems between us, and the start of the new rule: every man for himself.

CHAPTER SEVENTEEN

Cath Power

As told by Steve's wife, Cath McGown *née* Power

'Pain is your friend, your ally, it will tell you when you are seriously injured, it will keep you awake and angry, and remind you to finish the job and get the hell home' – Master Chief John Urgayle, *GI Jane*

My first therapy session was in January 2012. I hadn't felt the need up until then. My mom had been giving me some of her anti-anxiety medication, which made me groggy. I just didn't feel like getting up in the morning. I knew that this was a telltale sign; I had had a few bouts of depression in my life, but was able to bounce back out of them. My mother took me to a Nia dance class to cheer me up; I wept uncontrollably in the car the whole way home. The next month was Valentine's Day, but I did not expect Steve to be home. Steve was not a big celebrator of these sorts of things, as I was.

At times it felt like we were making progress. Ernst and Caty updated us on what was happening in Sweden and Holland. An operational HQ – the 'Troika' – had been set up in Sweden to negotiate on behalf of all three hostages. Steve being South African, not European, was a concern. The thinking was that Al Qaeda would not contact South Africa. There was talk of a media briefing to communicate that DIRCO was involved, but it had to be low-profile; if a minister was seen visiting Mali it would raise the value of a hostage. They used the analogy of chickens: all were equal and one must not be louder than the others.

A week later we had another meeting, but this time my mom attended and so did Mbulelo Bungane. He said Malian President Amadou Toumani Touré was known as a man who negotiates. He told us that Zuma was aware of Steve, but was too high-profile a figure to get involved. Someone at a lower level had to step in.

A week later we met Oupa Macou, South Africa's ambassador to Mali, at the Michelangelo Hotel in Johannesburg. He wore dark glasses and looked very different to how we'd imagined him over the phone. Oupa said things had been quiet. The plan was to get an envoy to go up to speak to the captors, and request a Proof of Life video and their demands in writing. He reiterated that Mali was always seen as a safe place to travel so their abduction was a shock.

We were asked to prepare a package for Steve. This was very motivating. I bought sunblock, eye drops, toothbrush, toothpaste, dental floss, ibuprofen, soap and Jelly Tots. I also bought him a magnetic backgammon set at Exclusive Books and wrote him a card for our wedding anniversary. Steve said I looked like a meerkat sometimes, so I bought him a card with two meerkats getting married. Very cute. It never got to Steve. It was suggested that we buy some rooibos tea for the envoy as a gift.

In early March 2012 we got a Proof of Life video. Steve was in an orange suit just like the Guantanamo guys. His package was in front of him. He looked good and spoke well. The demand for his release was five Al Qaeda prisoners. Things were looking good. I was so angry when my mom told the lady at the pharmacy what the demand was – it was confidential! I never went back to that pharmacy; the lady was a gossip.

It was hard for me to break into the speech-therapy industry as most schools already had a therapist in place. I took up a temporary locum job to help break into the market and give me some private practice experience. I was given a lovely Christian school, situated out of Johannesburg. The drive was against the traffic, and I enjoyed it in a strange way. I would pass a supermarket called Steve's Spar en route. There were days when I didn't want to look at it. There were days when I looked at it and smiled. Other days a lump would form in my throat that was sore when I swallowed.

I started off listening to Radio 702 just in case there would be news about Steve. There never was. I found this a bit heavy, so I started to listen to Christian songs. I had a few CDs and would play them again and again. There was one specific song with the words 'set the hostages free' that was beautiful.

In effect, I had two jobs. One was to start my own practice and the other was to get Steve out. I felt guilty about putting too much time into one or the other, so I divided my day up to accommodate both. It was good to work again. I hadn't worked since before we set off on our round-the-world trip. I didn't feel the baby pang quite yet, but it was constantly on my mind as I was exposed to it everywhere, through my friends and my work.

The Steve job involved sitting in front of the computer, looking for leads, answering emails and responding to friends. Someone has a friend in the security forces and they will get Steve out. Somebody else knows a guy at DIRCO. I soon hated talking on the phone, except when it was Magoo – a call from him might actually mean something was happening. Magoo and I spent so much time chasing down leads and dealing with scams.

The first scam happened when Jeremy Keenan, a professor in the UK, put us in touch with a tour guide in Mali called Guy Lancaster. Lancaster knew a local called Mohammed who said he had been in touch with the kidnappers. We sent them money to buy a satellite phone. Then we sent them money to rent vehicles and to buy fuel to go into the desert. Eventually, we turned away from Mohammed's story as the validity of the information and frequency of the requests for money became more suspect.

There was another scam, where we started talking to this South African reccie-type guy called Julius. Magoo and I arranged to meet him at the local Spur. Over sticky placemats and bottles of Thousand Island dressing he wove a compelling web. He said, 'We can do this,' implying he was going to swoop into northern Mali and rescue Steve. 'We will need to get the cash to buy guns. We need the helicopter. We need the medic.' He was talking big, but his trap was layered with little challenges to us.

He said, 'We need to be clear about something first. It's illegal to put South African boots on the ground in Mali, but we can find a loophole. Are you willing to commit?'

Julius went on about encrypted inboxes, burner phones and weaponry. What the hell did I know about this world? I am a speech and language therapist, married to a banker; my father-in-law is a businessman and a farmer. This was the stuff of movies. I was determined to look strong.

Julius went off to do some 'reconnaissance' and a month later we met him again at the same place. He looked straight at me, almost as if challenging me, and said, 'I saw Steve ... through my rifle scope. They were in the camp and were taking him out for a toilet break. They beat him.' I remember I didn't even flinch. I thought about an Afrikaans description a teacher gave me at school: *'Ek is so klein soos 'n muis maar so groot soos 'n reus.'* (I am as small as a mouse, but as big as a giant.) I wanted to show Julius that I was strong, that I could go into combat mode and do this, whatever 'this' was. I was going to show him that I could be hardcore.

I didn't know it right then, but there was no way Julius could have got anywhere near northern Mali and the Al Qaeda camps, and come back in one piece. He probably had not left his postal code in the month since we'd seen him. The man was a scam artist to his core.

In my defence, if ever there was a good time to sell me war stories, it was 2012. My maiden name was Power and my middle name is Jane, so it seemed only fitting that at least once in my life I'd go through a GI Jane/superhero stage. Mine began shortly after I got back. I started going to gym with my stepdad. He'd bought me an annual membership for Christmas and the two of us went every day. It was the perfect gift, because it gave me focus and structure.

Fun fact: there has only ever been one woman in the French Foreign Legion, a swashbuckling British super-soldier during World War II called Susan Travers. This was news to me. I looked into joining the Legion, but seeing as they don't accept women and I don't speak French, that was not an option. Regardless, I took my training seriously and trained hard. I became incredibly fit and strong. My mission was simple: I was going to find Steve and bring him home. I would run up a hill on the way to gym, imagining I was in the army – any army – and the hill was a sand dune and I had a Kalashnikov in hand. I even learned how to shoot a gun at the shooting range. It was a Beretta; I still have the paper targets.

As the months started to pass, I just couldn't imagine how Steve was going to come home. I thought that if it ever came to it, I had to be prepared. I became single-minded and stayed that way for a very long time. It wasn't just the physical side. I tried to avoid anything that brought me joy or would not contribute to bringing Steve back. I only watched Al Qaeda or kidnapping movies, I didn't see a romantic comedy for years. I had to constantly stop myself from listening to uplifting music. I didn't read any uplifting books; everything had to be about kidnapping and hostages. If I spent time online, it was to Google kidnapping, hostages, Al Qaeda and Mali.

After the initial outpouring of grief and sympathy, everybody else's lives got back to normal. For the immediate family of a hostage, that never happens. You wake up each day with the same shitty hand you had the day before. The same void where your loved one was. The same concerns about whether you are doing enough. I was concerned that, due to the media embargo, people would think I was doing nothing to help Steve. In the first weeks, months and years, there's almost a mania to your collective determination; that energy then begins to ebb. With each new idea it would peak again, and then trough, a constant yo-yo of hope and dismay.

I never envisaged the range of emotions I would experience. Sadness, sorrow, depression, hope and anxiety were all to be expected, but it was the anger that surprised me.

My therapist counselled me through this. She cautioned me against repressing any anger as unvoiced anger leads to depression. She tried to help me not to judge myself and told me that I needed to do what I needed to do to feel better. I spoke about my feelings; why had this happened? It was not fate. What had I done to deserve this?

Of course I was angry with Al Qaeda for taking Steve and deciding that he was somehow representative of the British Empire. It stands to reason that I was also angry and frustrated about the inefficiencies of the governments, and the numerous bureaucrats and diplomats who probably could help but did not lift a finger. As for the scam artists who crawled out of the woodwork to take advantage of our vulnerability as a family, well, there's a warm place waiting for them one day. All of these targets made sense, but what I did not expect was the anger I had for Steve.

My anger towards him was layered, and it lasted a long time. It was for abandoning me, but it was more than that. Financially, I could not access any of Steve's funds. We lived off my salary while Steve was an investment banker in London. We did not have a will, just the marriage contract with accrual. When I tried to access the funds, my lawyer effectively said, 'You're screwed.'

Bad things never happen until they do. Steve defaults to the positive, I look for things that could go wrong. As he prepped for his trip, I didn't think of kidnapping, I thought of accidents. Now, I was angry because I was alone, because I could not have children, and I wished he had put his affairs in order to look after me in case something happened – because something did happen. Steve is such an organised guy and he prepared so well for this trip, but he forgot one thing in all his due diligence: me.

My mom organised a family counselling session and I remember airing my anger. My brother piped up, 'Guys don't think like that. It takes away from the whole adventure.' I thought about how well Steve's dad looked after Bev, especially as she got sicker and sicker with emphysema in her last few years. I couldn't help thinking, 'Why didn't Steve do that for me?'

TOP Taken the day before I was kidnapped, Thursday, 24 November 2011, en route to Timbuktu from Douentza with my Yamaha XT600E. A 210 km ride due north.

ABOVE Outtake from an ISIS-style video made early in April 2015; it only reached South Africa in June. The Al Qaeda management felt it was 'too Hollywood'. This was the furthest south I was during my time in captivity, besides my month in prison in Timbuktu in August 2012.

TOP Al Qaeda gathered for an operation northeast of Timbuktu. This video was made to advertise their strength, and entice young Malians to join their ranks. The vehicle camouflage is a combination of water, sand and sugar, plastered onto the vehicles. It dries like cement and comes off with water.

ABOVE This photo of soldiers exercising, somewhere above Goundam, about 300 km northwest of Timbuktu, was taken after 2014 when Al Qaeda started to wear black. This area was referred to as The Holes and looked like a giant egg box. I spent the majority of my time, from July 2014 until my release, here. I encountered rabbits, owls and nightjars. The wind blew incessantly from the northeast; I used to imagine it coming from Libya 2,500 km away.

OPPOSITE On my way home! This photo was taken by Zachariah, the mujahid responsible for my release. He had just told me I was free and offered to take a photo. We stopped under a tree to take cover from a French surveillance plane. 17° 18' 47.9" N 0° 04' 20.8" E. From this point I was handed over to another rebel group to be driven out of the Sahara and handed to the Malian Secret Service.

OPPOSITE, INSET My calendar, written on the back of a milk carton. Johan (Musa) was taken from the camp 23 June; Ramadan finished Saturday, 24 June; details in brackets are my exercise routine; I showered and washed clothes on Saturday, 1 July; we had a sandstorm on 6 July.

My 40th Birthday, Mom's Birthday

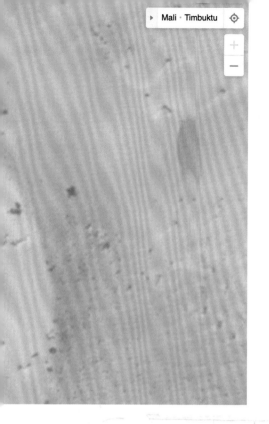

Mali · Timbuktu

LEFT I spent my 40th birthday and my mom's 67th birthday sitting in the southeastern side of this same bush at 18° 14' 30.1" N 4° 29' 12.0" W. On both days I sat by myself and watched the sunrise, 255 km from Timbuktu and 6,077 km from home.

BELOW, LEFT My reading material: a few books explaining Islam in Arabic. I created my own language library from other people's rubbish: discarded Land Cruiser service manuals, food packaging and medicine leaflets that had instructions in French, English and Arabic.

BELOW My six-year diary: initials on left are the emirs in each group, with a summary of each group, which changed every two months. I wrote in English, Afrikaans and abbreviations to make it undecipherable in case it was found.

ABOVE My Quraan, given to me by Abu Darda. It was a privilege to receive this – many Al Qaeda members didn't even have one. The Oxford French dictionary came from my mother-in-law. Al Qaeda gave me 30 pencils; I sharpened them with a razor blade and a small grinding stone.

LEFT My Arabic alphabet: I wrote this on the back of a milk carton to help me learn to read and write Arabic.

BOTTOM, LEFT I made flip cards out of milk carton boxes, with Arabic or French words on one side and English translations on the other. I stored these in small batches tied with a 'ropey' (a piece of clothing or inner tube cut into strips).

ABOVE My bag of tricks: I converted a plastic 5L water bottle using an inner tube from a car tyre, tarpaulin, a ropey and glue to make a camouflage waterproof bag. It could handle a Saharan thunderstorm. My 'toilet bottle' to do *wudu* (washing before prayers) was an empty honey bottle. Dental floss and body scrub: a torn-off onion sack. Soap was wrapped inside a cardboard milk box, inside a waterproof milk powder sachet. My scissors from Timbuktu: used for everything. A torch I made by collecting broken pieces from various camps over months. Needles were like hen's teeth and priceless. For thread I used torn clothing; three pieces of cotton would make twine.

RIGHT My Arabic: writing out some *Hadiths* which I tried to learn by heart.

ABOVE My family with Gift of the Givers at their office in Johannesburg. From left: Dr Imtiaz (Sooliman), Cath, Mom (Bev), Dad (Malcolm/Magoo) and Yahia.

ABOVE My father and I on Sunday, 30 July 2017, the day I arrived back home to my family in Johannesburg.

ABOVE At a barbecue with friends shortly after my release. Friends collected these off lampposts when news of my kidnapping and release broke.

PART TWO

Conversion

CHAPTER EIGHTEEN

Lot

'And when Our messengers, [the angels], came to Lot, he was anguished for them and felt for them great discomfort and said, "This is a trying day"' (Ayat 77)

'Ash Shadoo an La ilaha illa Allah, Wa Ash Shadoo ana Muhammadan rasoolu Allah.'

That's the *Shahada* or Declaration of Faith, the first of the five pillars of Islam. It's what you have to recite to become a Muslim. It's a testimonial that states you believe that there is no God but Allah and that Muhammad (PBUH) is his messenger. I recited it in The Black Mountains of Mali in an Al Qaeda camp on what I think was 20 April 2012.

I was not the first to convert; Johan had converted about a month earlier. I was second, and Sjaak was a few minutes behind me.

At the time, it was a survival strategy. Five months into our captivity, life had become desperate. I felt if I did not convert, I was not going to make it through. In his own selfish way, Johan forced my hand, but over time, as I came to know and appreciate Islam, I was thankful that it happened. Without Islam to turn to, I would not have come out of the desert whole.

One of the first things Al Qaeda asked us when they had us safely hidden away in the desert was how we defined ourselves in terms of our religious affiliations.

'What are you?'

It was probably the only area where I had some kind of edge over Johan and Sjaak; they identified themselves to Al Qaeda as atheists, I identified as a Christian. I was not playing games – I really was a Christian and I believed in God. To Al Qaeda, if you believe in God, even if it is the wrong one, they can at least understand how your brain works. Even if they see Christians and Jews as ancient adversaries, they acknowledge the shared Abrahamic roots of all three religions.

Hinduism and atheism, on the other hand, they do not understand.

Long before it actually happened, I thought about what converting to Islam would mean for me. I was a Christian, a bad one admittedly, but I understood Christianity. I believe that there is a greater power that created everything around us. The worse our situation got as prisoners, the more I thought that perhaps religion was the route for getting through it. But did I have to change religions? Did I want to become Peter who denied Christ three times? Did I want to jump ship?

At the same time, I did not think Al Qaeda would be gullible enough to believe that a Christian would want to become a Muslim overnight. If I was going to convert to Islam, it had to be something that I came to over time. I had to look as though I was inquiring.

After a few weeks in captivity, one mujahid called Omar started coming over to talk to us about Islam. He could speak a bit of English and a little French, and between this and the snippets of Arabic we were starting to pick up, we could converse. Omar was a clever guy and proud of his ability with languages. He used to brag that he was involved in the negotiation for Robert Fowler, the Canadian who was kidnapped before us and released.

By coming and engaging with us on Islam, Omar was engaging in *dawah,* spreading the word of Islam. Within Islam you can't force someone to enter the religion, but it's very good to encourage non-believers to wise up and follow the one true God. Whenever Omar came over, I used the opportunity to ask questions about Islam and how it compared to Christianity. There weren't many other things to do, but I genuinely was interested. In effect, I suppose I was laying the foundations for my later conversion. If it ever came to it and I had to convert to save my life, by spending time with Omar at least I had already paved the driveway up to the house of Islam.

Johan, on the other hand, believed that the mujahideen were a bunch of ignorant imbeciles who would not have a clue if he was being genuine or not. By this stage it was clear we were *not* a team, and that all of us were working our own survival strategies individually. While Sjaak and I were still hanging on to the dates that we wanted to be home by, Johan was convinced we would be dead soon. If that was part of his forecast, his behaviour when he started staring at Al Qaeda praying began to make sense.

Johan had a very mathematical, analytical approach to problem-solving. He was incredibly confident in his intellectual superiority in all matters, and never felt the need to consult others. He would analyse probable outcomes, run the numbers internally, and then make an executive decision – even if Sjaak and I were impacted by that decision. He ignored us when we said, 'Fuck Johan, stop being a dick, you'll get us all killed. What the hell kind of game are you playing?'

Johan could speak Spanish, so in March 2012 he started sitting with one of the mujahideen who could also speak the language and would share bits and pieces of info about Islam in Spanish. After doing these lessons for a while, Johan started coming back to us saying, 'I want what is best for all of us, I want all of us to survive. We must convert.'

Neither Sjaak nor I wanted to convert to Islam, and we told Johan as much, but then a few things happened that changed the situation quite drastically. The first was that a mujahid we called 'Beardman' because of his impressive facial hair came over one evening and squatted down in front of us. He told Sjaak, 'You have a good wife,' and then threw his hand over his shoulder. Not only was this confirmation that Tilly was alive after the Timbuktu abduction, but it also implied to us that negotiations had gone well for him, and that Sjaak was going home.

The following day a vehicle arrived and took Sjaak away. Sjaak's disappearance terrified me, because now my fellow *kuffar* was gone. In those early days, if any of us were split up, I struggled with separation anxiety about what it meant. With Johan busy looking to convert, I would be the most likely guy to have his head chopped off at short notice. In order to find some form of safety and send the right signals, I decided to join Johan's Islamic lessons.

This was shortly after Johan had said that he wanted what was best for all of us, so I thought he would welcome my change of heart, but his response was the opposite.

He said, 'No, you're not joining my lessons.'

I was flabbergasted. I spelled out the danger I was in, the fact that my British passport put me more at risk than he or Sjaak and how sitting in on these lessons might save my life.

Again Johan flatly refused. 'No, you are not coming with me on this.'

Up until this point, our prison personas had been pretty clear: Johan the clever guy, Sjaak the joker and me the wallflower. While Sjaak's quirks taught me to lighten up and laugh a little – one night Sjaak and I were literally in hysterics lying on our blankets under the moon, to the point that Al Qaeda had to ask us to keep it down so they could sleep – perhaps the one thing I can thank Johan for is that his selfish behaviour made me stand up for myself in the desert.

I said, 'You know what? Fuck you! You are fucking with my life here. I am sitting in on your lesson, whether you want me there or not.'

Fortunately for both of us, we did not have to endure each other's company for too long, because two days after he left, Sjaak reappeared. By now I really could not stand being around Johan. But after Sjaak arrived back, things got even weirder. For the next few days he was held separately from us under a different bush. My anxiety went into overdrive.

Where had Sjaak been taken? Why was he being handled differently than us? Why was his wife a 'good wife'? What does that mean? I had no doubt Cath and my parents were moving planets to get me home, so the only reason I could think of was that maybe Tilly was still in Mali and she was managing to talk to the relevant people to get Sjaak released. That theory went out the window when we received packages from our families in early 2012. Both Johan and I received things that had clearly been put together by people who were thinking of us – things that we needed and might find useful, like a French dictionary, sun cream and Jelly Tots for me – whereas Sjaak received an odd selection of really bland items that were probably assembled by an embassy attaché in Bamako. Nothing made sense.

In March that year, Johan converted to Islam. Even though neither of us got on with him, it was the official end of us as a team of three prisoners. He was still a prisoner, but on a different level. Now known as Musa, he was kept elsewhere. He was treated much better than we were, and some of our possessions, like my shoes and the French dictionary my family had sent me in the care package, were given to him. Was this Al Qaeda going out of their way to show us the contrast between how *kuffar* and Muslims were treated? Or, was it less calculated for them, a matter-of-fact aspect of life, like slaughtering a goat? We did not know, but life got harder for Sjaak and me.

In those first few months of 2012, every Al Qaeda camp was a hive of activity. The energy was completely different from when we first arrived in the desert. At certain camps, they were building underground concrete bunkers to store food, spare tyres, ammunition and other supplies. These were also used for Proof of Life videos. When Sjaak disappeared for a couple of days, he was taken to one of these bunkers for his video. When Johan and I appeared in ours, it was shot outside. We were left with our beards and longish hair, while Sjaak had to shave for his. The whole idea was to create contrast between how we looked, to send a message to Al Qaeda's enemies that we were being kept separately. I imagine it was to keep them guessing.

Between building bunkers at certain camps, digging trenches at others and larger numbers of mujahideen and vehicles, Al Qaeda appeared to be prepping for something. We moved to a new camp, which we called the Oasis Camp. It was a heavily wooded area in The Black Mountains alongside a *wadi*. Sjaak and I were kept on the outskirts of the main camp, in a small kraal made up of a very makeshift fence. On one side, Al Qaeda set up a screen with a parachute they had stolen from a Malian army resupply drop. (Convoys could be easily ambushed in Mali's northern provinces, so it was safer for the government forces in far-flung camps to receive supplies this way.)

I was sick with some sort of heavy fever so I was lying on the ground, trying to get through it. From the corner of my eye I could see Al Qaeda sitting in a *halaqa* (circle). Every now and then I would get a glimpse of Johan/Musa. You could feel the tension in camp; there were a lot of cars and many mujahideen moving back and forth. I was too sick to focus and do a proper headcount, but there were a lot more people than usual.

It turned out that Al Qaeda were preparing to attack the MNLA and boot them out of Gao and Timbuktu. I could hear a shortwave radio from about 20 metres away within the *halaqa*. It wasn't constant; whenever the news came on, they would put batteries in the radio and switch it on. Burning up with fever, I lay in a foetal position under this tree, listening to snatches of radio. It was a French station, so I could only make out the odd word.

The last word I wanted to hear was 'Britannia'. I wanted to hear something about the French or the Germans or the Americans or anyone else. Let somebody else be the most hated nation in Al Qaeda's world today. Or, if it must be Britannia, let it be good news, that the British are leaving Iraq, that they are putting down their guns. Don't let me hear that the British are sending troops to another Muslim country. Let America or France send their troops. Let the Brits step out of every fight in the Arab world, because if they do that the likelihood of me hanging on to my neck grows stronger.

No such luck.

Every time I overheard the word 'Britannia' on the radio, the mujahideen started talking among themselves and, as if choreo-graphed, they would look over their shoulders in my direction. It was as if they were matching the word to their prisoner. Lying there, feel-ing so sick, my stress levels continued to rise. I felt like I would go insane from the pressure.

There was this young kid named Aghmed in that Oasis Camp. He was about eight years old. He was Noah's son, so his outlook on us as *kuffar* prisoners was no doubt already tainted. While the news was playing on the radio, he was sitting cross-legged on the bonnet of one of the Land Cruisers eating a packet of crisps, listening to the broad-cast and the mujahideen's response to it. He hopped off the car rather nonchalantly, still stuffing his face with his crisps, and started walking towards our enclosure. I was lying down on the ground, and Sjaak was walking back and forth like a caged lion. I was half-hidden behind an acacia, and Aghmed appeared to be trying to peer around Sjaak.

Eventually Sjaak said, 'What is this kid doing? I think he is looking for you.'

I looked up and Aghmed pointed, 'Ah! You!' And with that he drew his finger across his throat.

It was not hard to join the dots. The arrogant little kid had been listen-ing to Al Qaeda's conversations around the radio, and he thought this would be great time to come over and inform the 'Britannia' prisoner that he was going to get his head chopped off. It wasn't a once-off. All through that day, every time he walked up the path, he would point me out to the other kids and drag his finger across his throat again. It had the desired effect. I was absolutely terrified. Eventually, I kept my eyes closed to avoid giving him the satisfaction of seeing my panic.

In the late afternoon, most of the mujahideen piled into the vehicles and left. Two of the guys who stayed behind, Khalid and Ghanda Hari, Martin's killer, walked up to our enclosure, and seemed to be fortifying the perimeter and creating a primitive alarm system around us. I called the trees surrounding us poppadom trees, because they had these big, round brittle leaves like poppadoms. Ghanda Hari and Khalid were walking around, mending the fence and kicking the poppadum leaves into the enclosure. If we wanted to escape, we would have to walk across the crackling leaves and then try to climb over the small fence.

Once they were done, Khalid came and pointed his AK-47 at us. 'Hey, sleep! Sleep! *Dormir*!' We got the message, but Sjaak, bless his fiery heart, pleaded back, 'I cannot sleep with you shouting at me!'

Everything about that camp, from the number of guys to the tension in the air, the mood around the radio, the cut-throat kid and the way they shouted at us to sleep – it was all off. I had never been so certain that I was going to be killed as I was right then. Wrapped in the fever's embrace, I closed my eyes again. The darkness was better than the light. I was waiting for the bang, the bullet, wondering, will I feel pain? It was actually something that Sjaak and I had discussed before. He joked, 'If you hear the bang, they shot the guy next to you.' I fell asleep to that thought.

When we woke up the next day, they bundled us into the vehicles and we left Oasis Camp. We worked our way over a small mountain heading north, and set up camp in a *wadi* on the other side, with a new emir in charge. This was Group Dawud. I was relieved to have left the strange tension of Oasis Camp behind. Our new camp was set up in a *wadi*, with a mountain behind us. Wild donkeys came down in the evenings and early mornings to feed on the desert melons that grew in the sand, and to drink from the half-full bucket left at the well by the mujahideen.

Al Qaeda had dug trenches as fortifications, both to defend their position and attack anyone who approached us from the other side of the *wadi*. It was a well-thought-out, pre-planned camp. Having seen a water bird or two on our way in, I was hopeful that things might even get marginally better.

Then I realised Sjaak and I were to stay in a bush, Bre'r Rabbit-style. Every time we needed to go to the toilet, we had to walk past a shaded area where Al Qaeda would be sitting, rocking back and forth reciting the Quraan. It was a walk of shame, dirty *kuffar*, doing dirty things, and their looks of disgust told the story. My fever had broken, but I still felt terrible, and my back was killing me from being stooped over, under our bush, all the time.

There was a new batch of kids in this camp, teenage Tuareg Al Qaeda recruits. They came past several times a day to insult us in Arabic or Tamasheq, and to try to get us to repeat specific words that they were saying. This was great sport to them. One of the words sounded like 'anaconda', the other like 'cockerel', and when we said them, the kids would spit in the sand, and fall about laughing. All we wanted was to be left alone in our bush. This went on for 10 days.

On one occasion, the kids got us to repeat a few phrases that they were very specific about. We mumbled our way through whatever it was, and they got very excited and ran off to fetch the emir, Dawud, who brought Musa with him. They both crawled into our Bre'r Rabbit bush, with the small group of kids in tow. It turned out that we had been tricked into saying we wanted to convert. When Dawud asked us if we were serious, we said we were unsure. Irritated that we were wasting his time, Dawud left.

The natural shape of any calamity should be a bell curve; once the terror has peaked and the adrenaline starts to subside, your situation should improve. Maybe you get hijacked, or a bear attacks your camp-site, or a truck T-bones your car – there will be seconds or minutes of unmitigated terror, your body coursing with adrenaline, but then it's over. You either die and are none the wiser, or you land up in hospital with doctors fighting to save your life. Or, if you're really lucky, like Tilly or Fokker, you walk away unscathed.

The situation I was in was not like that; the adrenaline peaked and remained at full throttle for six months. Living in constant fear does crazy things to your body and mind; you start to lose your grip on reality. A body needs to come off that terror high. All I wanted was cer-tainty, structure and to be treated like a human. Believers got treated like humans – I had seen it with Johan/Musa.

I didn't know if converting would save my life, but I had to try. I defi-nitely did not want to die, so it was a risk I had to take.

Even so, I struggled with the enormity of the decision. I was still betray-ing who I was and betraying my family, especially my wife. I was also thinking: *If I get shot right now, there's a chance that I may go to heaven, but if I convert and die as a Muslim, who gets me? Islam or Christianity? God, Allah or Lucifer?* Things like this really play on you when death is on the menu.

One of the mujahideen, Abd ar-Rahman, was walking past. Names within Al Qaeda are often quite literal or descriptive. Abd ar-Rahman's eyes looked quite Asian in shape, so he was called Abd ar-Rahman Filipini to differentiate himself from other Abd ar-Rahmans. Racist? In South Africa we are super-sensitive to racism of any kind – I wasn't going to go there with Al Qaeda.

I called out to him and said, 'Abd ar-Rahman, I want to convert to Islam.'

His eyes lit up, like he had just seen a long-lost friend. It was a big thing among the mujahideen to have a *kuffar* convert to Islam, because in effect you have saved a soul from going to hell and in return you get many points. Abd ar-Rahman Filipini was ecstatic.

He started saying, 'Repeat after me, *"Ash Shadoo an La ilaha illa Allah, Wa Ash Shadoo ana Muhammadan rasoolu Allah."*'

This was the *Shahada*, the Declaration of Faith. A part of me thought, 'If I mumble and slur my way through it, God will understand that I don't want to convert. If I do this as badly as possible, maybe even God or Allah won't understand what I've just said. Abd ar-Rahman knows I don't speak Arabic so he'll probably just put up with poor pronunciation.' As it was, Abd ar-Rahman patiently corrected each mispronounced word until I finally got it right. Once I finished saying it I tried consoling myself with the thought, 'It's lip service, I haven't changed in my heart.'

The *Shahada* complete, Abd ar-Rahman said, '*Salaam Alykum*' (Peace Be Upon You), and gave me the biggest, warmest hug. After months of the mujahideen looking at or through us with no sign of human connection, I could see life in his eyes and he was beaming from ear to ear. Because he helped me convert, from that point on Abd ar-Rahman treated me as if I was his Islamic prodigy.

What struck me most was not the hug, although later I craved human contact almost more than anything else; it was the fact that somebody was being excited *with* me as a person and not excited *at* me. To feel that I wasn't hated and was now a part of something blew my mind.

Abd ar-Rahman turned to Sjaak and asked him if he wanted to convert too. I'm not sure if Sjaak even contemplated the alternative – living in the bush on his own, being treated like shit – but reluctantly he followed suit.

Bubbling over with joy at these two unexpected blessings, Abd ar-Rahman led us out of our bush and walked us straight over to the well, where he began to fill up two five-litre water bottles. On the way there he asked Sjaak, 'What do you want to be called? How about Ibrahim?'

Sjaak said, 'Okay.'

Then it was my turn. 'And you, what should we call you?'

Steve was clearly not an option. Ever the easygoing wallflower, I said, 'I don't mind.'

There was no stopping Abd ar-Rahman now. He was on a roll. Ten points for Gryffindor.

'How about Lot?'

As is my style I started thinking, *Isn't that the guy whose wife got turned to salt and he never saw her again?* Trying to read into things that aren't there, I thought, *Is Abd ar-Rahman implying that I won't go back to my family? Maybe, if I was a better person, this would not have happened to me? Do I actually want to be this guy?*

By now a few other mujahideen who were at the well washing clothes had cottoned on to what was happening. Between them and Abd ar-Rahman the verdict was unanimous: Lot is a quality name.

It was simple and small, only three letters. There's no abbreviation for it. It spoke to my old mantra of only taking what you can put in your rucksack. I could fit a Lot into my mental rucksack. I decided: I'll take it.

Now that we were out of our bush prison, Abd ar-Rahman gave us each five litres of water and sent us off in different directions to take a shower. We were told we had to wet our entire bodies. I guess it's almost like a baptism. I had to cleanse myself of the *kuffar* I had been, Steve McGown.

I said the words.

I took the shower.

I was now Muslim.

I was now Lot.

All I had to do was grow into him.

CHAPTER 19

Islam for Beginners

*Allahu akbar allahu akbar Allahu akbar allahu akbar Ash-hadu
anla ilaha illah Allah Ash-hadu anla ilaha illah Allah Ash-hadu
anna muhammadar-rasulullah Ash-hadu anna muhammadar-
rasulullah Hayya as-salah Hayya as-salah Hayya al-falah Hayya
al-falah Allahu akbar allahu akbar La ilaha illa Allah*
– The Adhan (Call to Prayer)

No doubt many Islamic scholars will find fault with how I was taught
about Islam. All I can do is relate my experience of converting in the
desert under the guidance of Al Qaeda, which is the path my life took.
What I was taught is what they believe. Some of it I struggled with,
but most of what I learned made my life better.

Most remarkable was the immediate difference in how I was treated.
The moment I took my shower down in the riverbed and returned to
Abdar-Rahman and the other mujahideen was the moment they saw
me as a brother. By saying those words and washing myself, I was a
new man in their eyes. Lot. I was still a prisoner, but now I was human
and had a basic right to dignity and respect.

Even Ghanda Hari, the tall, fierce mujahid, turned after I converted.
When I queried this, Abu Darda told me, 'Ghanda Hari is a good
Muslim. He's passionate for the religion. He's tough on *kuffar* and gentle on Muslims.' In the months to come, before he died in a helicopter
attack in 2013, Ghanda Hari would even care for me when I was suffering from severe back pain, bringing me *habatoa soda* (nigella sativa
oil) to try to ease the pain. This from the man who had not given a
second thought to killing Martin in the street in Timbuktu.

Initially, some Al Qaeda questioned whether we had or hadn't converted to Islam. I could see it in the way they looked at us. A Muslim
should never question another Muslim as to whether they are Muslim
– this is *haram*. Allah says that if people say the words and show themselves to be Muslim, then they are Muslim. You don't need to worry

if you've got it wrong, because on the day of judgment, Allah knows everything and will deal with us then.

Converting to Islam opened up my world in the desert and allowed me so many different things. It allowed me mental stimulation. It allowed me physical movement through prayer itself and permission to exercise, and it allowed me human interaction. You can be in a coma with your heart beating, and while there is life there, you are not fully alive. That was a realisation I had after I crawled out from under that bush: life is more than a beating heart.

It did not take me long to get into the groove of being a Muslim, because I already believed in God. The structure of prayer and learning the Quraan was familiar – even though the language and some of the stories were different – and the engagement with people was a relief.

We didn't know it at the beginning, but within the Quraan, there are rules for taking prisoners. You have to feed your prisoner, give them something to drink and look after them. If your prisoner's got a broken arm, you have to fix it. It doesn't mean you can't kill your prisoner; you just have to care for them right up until the moment you make them kneel and put a bullet in their head. The whole idea about conversion to Islam is that a Muslim must carry themselves in such a way that people look up to them and want to be like them, and then convert to the religion. Muslims should always show good character.

For the first few years after conversion we were still not sure whether Al Qaeda would kill us. Some of the mujahid would come and say, 'You're now Muslim, this is good. Also now we can't kill you, you are a brother.' Johan was sceptical, convinced that Al Qaeda were playing games with us. Maybe I was more gullible, but believing in the goodness of people was also my way of controlling my fear of being killed. The more I got to know them, the more I felt my chances of surviving improved. By year four, I thought it was unlikely that they were going to kill me.

When I converted, I was purely thinking about saving my neck. I had not really thought about what it meant in terms of my day-to-day life, until I became Lot. What I signed up for was being grilled on the Quraan, waking up before sunrise, and five prayers a day – *Salat al-fajr* (before sunrise), *Salat al-zuhr* (midday), *Salat al-'asr* (late afternoon), *Salat al-maghrib* (just after sunset) and *Salat al-'isha* (between sunset and midnight).

There were things we had to get used to, like doing most things with our right hand. Sjaak was left-handed, so if somebody passed a bowl of food and Sjaak put his left hand out, they would take it back until he put out his right hand, and then they would pass it to him. In keeping with the idea that everything right-handed is good, when you go to sleep at night you must start off by sleeping on your right-hand side, with your hand under your head. You can roll over at a later stage, but you must always start that way. If you're walking into a house, you should walk in with your right foot first; when you are brushing your hair, you brush it with your right hand; and so on. Why? I don't know and, as per the religion, we should not ask. It's just a commandment from God.

Prayer and the structure and rules around it provided the foundation for our day-to-day lives. It was serious stuff. There was no talking, laughing, eating, drinking or excessive movement allowed in the prayer line, which had to face towards the Qiblah, the direction of the sacred shrine of Ka'bah in Mecca – unless we were in a sandstorm and it was impossible to tell direction.

If any emergency arose during prayer, we'd leave the prayer, take care of the matter, and complete the prayer from where we had ended. If you remembered that you didn't do *wudu* – the washing of the face, arms, hands, head and feet – you'd leave the prayer, do your *wudu*, then pray with the guard or pray by yourself. Sometime people would pass wind and leave the prayer line to redo their *wudu*. If someone left the prayer line, everybody would shuffle together to close the gap between feet. Your foot must touch the feet of the people either side of you, because Satan enters into gaps like a small lamb.

On one occasion during Ramadan, after breaking the fast, one of the mujahideen drank too quickly and too much. This was a schoolboy error. We lined up in the prayer line and began the sunset prayer. After the first *raka* (unit of prayer), this guy unleashed a projectile vomit. With that he immediately stepped backwards and out of the prayer line. I then had to close the gap to the right to fill his place. During the next *raka*, when we went down into a *sujood* (prostration to the ground), I had to quickly sweep sand over the area he had vomited on before I placed my forehead and nose into the vomit patch for the bow.

On another occasion, a mujahid had an epileptic fit in the prayer line. He collapsed and fell backwards onto the sand behind us. You cannot look behind you during prayer as this nullifies the prayer. We were in our first *raka,* so the prayer continued for a while still, with this man shaking in the sand behind us. Once the prayer was over, people began dealing with him.

Since you cannot move or look around you during prayer, you are very vulnerable. We always had a security guard, whose job was to listen for vehicles and make sure nobody came up behind us. After the French arrived in Mali, it was made obligatory by Yahia, the emir of AQIM, that all mujahideen line up their weapons in front of them during prayer in case they had to enter into a fight immediately afterwards.

Sometimes during prayer, we heard a *kashiva* surveillance plane. We would not abandon prayer as we expected that Allah would protect us and hide us from the plane; once we finished the prayer, we took shelter. On various occasions when we were caught up in serious sandstorms, Al Qaeda told us it was because Allah was protecting us from the French. They also said that the sand forced the surveillance aeroplanes to return to their base.

In Islam, everything is about intention. For example, we needed to be respectfully dressed for prayer, but if you were in a rush and about to miss a prayer because you just climbed out of a bath, you were allowed to pray naked.

Blood on a mujahid's clothing would not be a problem – the Prophet (PBUH) and his army would pray after a battle covered in blood. The only blood that nullifies a prayer is the blood from slaughtering an animal. If you got this blood on your clothing, you would have to wash it out. Urine or faeces on your clothes also nullifies a prayer – unless you don't know about it.

The Quraan appeals to common sense. It has a story or *hadith* for every scenario. If you wanted to go really left field and throw around hypotheticals, there would always be an answer within the Quraan. Eating pork, blood and carrion are well-known examples of things that are not *halaal*, but what if you are in a plane crash in the Rwenzori Mountains and all you can find to eat is a blood sausage and a dead bush pig? Islam acknowledges the need to survive.

I was surprised how angry Sjaak and Johan got about religion (even though Johan was the first to convert to Islam). I was the only one between us prisoners who actually believed in God, so I would have expected them not to care, because it was all a fairy tale in their eyes. Sjaak in particular used to fight with me on this, calling me a hypocrite and asking me, 'Why do you pray? Why do you do this? Why are you being friendly to them?'

My response was simple. 'I've always believed in God. It's one God. I'm still praying to God, I'm just choosing to miss out Jesus as the son of God.'

Was God, the Christian God, the same God as Allah? I believe so, and it is stated as such in the Quraan. Islam, Christianity and Judaism all have the same Abrahamic monotheistic roots. They just split off from each other hundreds of years ago, and kept splitting into branches and sects and cults and so on. Many of their teachings and many of their stories are shared. It's the fine print and the interpretation that makes them different; the declarations of the middlemen.

The broad strokes of what Al Qaeda taught me about Islam and the way they see the world is as follows: Islam is far greater than a religion. It is a lifestyle ordained by Allah, and all the rules for living come from the Quraan. If you are Muslim, you will be treated like a brother. If you make errors or stumble, the brothers will help guide you back to the straight path, as this is what Allah demands and what caring brothers do. Allah will not give you more than you can handle.

In contrast to Christianity, where Jesus died for your sins, in Islam, what you do is on you. You will be judged for the things you do in your time on Earth. That made a lot of sense to me.

Of course there were beliefs Al Qaeda held that I had difficulty with. Marrying children, for example. One 24-year-old mujahid, Shuaiab, got married to a nine-year-old, then divorced her because she was too young to bear him children. Another mujahid, Abu Abdilla (34) married Shuaiab's mother (55) who had already been married to three other mujahideen who had died in battle. He then divorced her after she had his child, and married an 11-year-old. From what I heard, within Al Qaeda, marriage was transactional.

What of the corporal and capital punishment elements of Sharia law (the cutting off of hands if people steal, or the execution of murderers)? In an ideal world, if everyone played by the rules and accepted the consequences of their behaviour on Earth, then these things would never have to happen. By implementing Sharia law and forcing people to live by it, Al Qaeda are on a mission to create that ideal world.

Nobody is above Sharia. In Timbuktu, a mujahid went on a rampage and shot and killed one of the townsfolk. The victim's family demanded justice, and Al Qaeda held the mujahid to account. They offered the family three options: either you can forgive him, or he can pay you money, or we execute him. Compensation would have been three years' salary, in cash, but they wanted him killed. The mujahid accepted his fate, as per the dictates of the Quraan, and was executed.

After I left the desert, I heard many people, from secret service guys to punters around the barbecue, making anti-Al Qaeda jokes, and inferring that they are a bunch of drug runners and people smugglers. From what I have seen, that's nonsense. These guys are passionate for religion and deeply fearful of God. If they came across guys running drugs, as Sharia enforcers they would burn the car and reprimand the smugglers. If they caught them a second time, they would kill them. They were the only people actually maintaining law in the Sahara, and they lived by their own rules – but do not step outside of the Sharia.

Within Islam you have God's word, being the Quraan, and then you have the *hadith* which are the words, actions and approval of Muhammad (PBUH). Together they form the Islamic Faith. Within Christianity you only have the Bible. To Muslims, the Bible is the equivalent of the *hadith*, stories of Jesus told by his followers; it's not God's word.

I learned probably 30 or 40 pages of the Quraan off by heart, and it was very difficult. When I got to the 34th *Sourat,* I started forgetting the first. I don't know how anyone learns 300 pages off by heart. Muhammad (PBUH), who was supposedly illiterate, learned it in a few different dialects.

It wasn't all smooth sailing; sometimes I fought with myself and with God. At one stage I thought, *Screw it, God, I'm done with this. I've been here long enough. I have been praying five times a day and begging for your help. When will you help me?* Two days later, with nobody else on my team, there I was in the prayer line, rekindling my relationship with God.

I converted in April 2012; by January 2015 I felt totally Muslim. It was as if I was a slow-motion chameleon, and things started to change colour as I understood the religion better. My path and Johan's diverged quite rapidly at this point. Johan became more and more arrogant and rude to Al Qaeda. It caused major problems for me because Al Qaeda still saw us prisoners as a 'we'.

I was constantly asked to explain Johan's behaviour. For one thing, I did not want to lie. Character is incredibly important in Islam, and I was trying to make the most of my situation and live an authentic life based on honesty and integrity, so that when I went home, if I went home (*Insha Allah*), I would not be a wreck. Having to explain away Johan's behaviour did not sit well with me. I told him he was jeopardising my safety and his. I did not want to rat him out, but if he continued to make my life difficult he was going to force me into a corner. On top of all that, the guy showed nothing but disdain for me, so it was hard to give a toss about him. I know he was struggling with his own demons, just as I was, but he needed to own his actions and face their consequences.

Because Al Qaeda knew I believed in God, they would come and discuss Islam with me. I learned a lot, and I believe I knew more about Islam than most of Al Qaeda at the end of my six years. By that stage many of the older mujahideen were dead, and the younger ones were illiterate, very ignorant and not as dedicated to the religion.

It was a tough decision, but once I made the call to convert, I did not regret it. One of the biggest things I learned in the desert is you've got to keep moving. I needed to keep my mind active, keep myself physically active, and have human interaction. Without those things I would not have survived. My conversion to Islam made all of that possible. It helped me understand why the hell we were all sitting out in the desert discussing God, Heaven and Earth. Without my conversion, I would never have been able to see Al Qaeda for who they were: men and boys who love and fear Allah above all else. If they put their guns down, they would be like any other dude you can sit around and shoot the breeze with. You can't have a beer with them, but you can get to know them – and sometimes be awed by their good character.

Group email from Cath, March 2013

Once again, Mali has been in the news over the past few weeks. However we've had no news at all from any of the governments regarding Steve, Sjaak and Johan (aka the Timbuktu Three).

Many of you have asked about the alleged deaths of two prominent Al Qaeda leaders – Abu Zeid, who we thought was involved with Steve's kidnapping, and Mokhtar Bel Mokhtar (MBM), the mastermind behind the recent Algerian gas plant mine kidnapping, where 37 hostages were killed. Neither death has been confirmed, which I understand is a political strategy, as it would further fuel the fire. We have been told that Al Qaeda could be using these alleged deaths as propaganda. MBM has had a few staged deaths already, so we are under the impression that the news is untrue. We received some rather gruesome photographs of Abu Zeid's body, which I felt inappropriate to include in this email. I was initially delighted to hear about his demise, but upon reflection, I realise that his death has not resulted in bringing Steve back to us. It may have even made things worse, as it has destabilised the leadership once again, but our contacts have said that only time will tell. It should not have a direct bearing on Steve for now. The French hostages' lives are more at risk at present.

As some of you may have read, the French president has said that he believes that the French hostages are still alive in the Adrar des Ifoghas mountains. The hostages' families have asked that the French stop fighting so that negotiations can take place, especially now that they are closing in on the last Mali refuge in the mountains, but the French army are not holding back. They are there to finish off the job of eliminating Al Qaeda-linked Islamists from Mali, which could have far-reaching consequences later on.

As you know, my heart and prayers have been towards the French families of late. I read a beautiful article about the wife of Daniel Thierry, one of the 'Areva Four' who were taken in September 2010 from Niger. She was initially taken with them, but released after five months on 'humanitarian grounds' as she has breast cancer. My favourite part of the article is about her joy in seeing some turtledoves take flight. For those of you who know our Steve, you can imagine how much delight he would have felt if he had shared that sight. We can only pray that he would be blessed by such moments too.

My heart and prayers also go out to the British, Greek, Italian and Lebanese families who heard yesterday that their loved ones were killed on

Saturday in Nigeria. They were taken by a Boko Haram splinter group a few weeks ago in February.

Finally, Abu Qatada is back on the scene again. He was arrested last week for breaching his bail conditions. I received a call from the British consul today to say that she can't imagine that any major decisions will happen tomorrow or in the next few days in court. We continue to hope and pray that Steve's link with him does not rear up again.

On a personal note, we as a family are still holding up. My business has taken off, which is great after a slow start to the year, although it has come with some added pressures. Nothing I can't handle though!

I have a special wedding to attend at the end of the month. Our friend Guy, who lived across the road from Steve and me in Putney, is getting married in Port Elizabeth. I am looking forward to sharing this day with him, his wife-to-be (whom Steve has not had the privilege of meeting yet), his family and our friends. It will also be a sad one, of course; I booked a flight for Steve in faith that he would be back to share the day with us. It will also be our sixth wedding anniversary that weekend, but I will be spending it with lovely family friends from my childhood days on their farm near PE, so I will be in good company. Steve's sister Leigh and brother-in-law Gregg, announced that they are expecting another little one in July, so the McGown family have something to look forward to again this year. My sister and I (as well as Rufus the basset hound) have finally settled into the flat at the back of my mom's place. We've had builders around for the last few months, which has been chaotic, but we can now appreciate some peace and quiet.

As always, we are most grateful and deeply moved by your messages and prayers that continue to keep us looking forward.

Remaining steadfast in faith and hope,
Cath

CHAPTER TWENTY

Timbuktu *Revisitée*

'Nothing beside remains. Round the decay
Of that colossal Wreck, boundless and bare
The lone and level sands stretch far away'
– 'Ozymandias', Percy Bysshe Shelley

'Ghamsa Ghamsin, Ghamsa Ghamsin, Ghamsa Ghamsin.'

We heard this a lot at the beginning of 2012. Khalid, aka 'The Milk Man' (because he used to bring powdered milk to us) was trying to reach Talha on the long-range vehicle-mounted radio. *Ghamsa Ghamsin*, meaning '55' was Talha's code name. The tall, intellectual-looking young mujahideen was now emir of Timbuktu, and Khalid was trying to ascertain if it was safe to bring the prisoners into the city from the mountains 500 kilometres away.

Like the Greeks marching on Troy and the Allied forces marching on Berlin, AQIM marching on Timbuktu was the big moment in their history. Long before ISIS claimed a caliphate in Syria, for a guerrilla force of Islamists to be coming out of the desert and taking the fabled city of Timbuktu, along with Gao, Kidal and the rest of northern Mali, was a massive statement to the world and to other Al Qaeda franchises.

It had been building for weeks. Al Qaeda was winning battles and skirmishes with the MNLA as the frontline moved further south through the villages that surrounded the southern cities of northern Mali. We moved from camp to camp under Group Ghabayb, our brigade waiting for the green light from the city to move in.

Ghabayb was the self-proclaimed youngest emir in AQIM. I didn't like him much, but he was very competent – and made sure everybody knew it. I remember once when a vehicle was being repaired in a *wadi*. The front right wheel had been removed and the axle dismantled. We were caught in a freak thunderstorm and the river overflowed. The car ended up buried halfway up to its bonnet, and the open axle was completely covered with sand. Ghabayb was furious; he completely lost his cool with his crew. The 23-year-old then single-handedly removed all the sand from the axle and repaired the vehicle back to working condition. It was quite amazing.

Another time I was walking circles in that same riverbed. I did this most evenings to clear my head. He asked Johan if I was walking out the map of Africa so that an aeroplane would see my tracks and come rescue me. He called me back under the tree and told me to stop doing exercise.

His was the group we were in while we waited to enter Timbuktu. We did not know what was going on, but sensed our minders were waiting for something. Finally, they got the okay.

The journey into Timbuktu was eventful. In one of our temporary camps on our way south, we came across other Al Qaeda prisoners for the first time. Or at least Johan did. We were doing our exercises, walking in circles, round and round, when just over the edge of a low, stony ridge Johan spotted two guys. They were dressed in tracksuit pants and T-shirts, and definitely not mujahideen. One was African and the other appeared to be Spanish. At one stage, not far north from Timbuktu, we passed the place where the internationally renowned Festival au Désert was held, and Yahia, the emir of AQIM, told me somewhat proudly that they had put a stop to that celebration of Tuareg music and culture.

We entered Timbuktu folded into the back seat of a luxurious Land Cruiser VX. It was around 9pm. We were blindfolded, with our heads pressed down behind the seats. I tried to keep track of our movements – left, right, straight, round a circle, over a small bump, through a culvert. I could hear water. We came to a stop. I heard heavy metal doors being drawn open and slammed shut again. Our blindfolds came off and we looked up. We assumed we were back in Timbuktu because of all the hype in the build up, and because of the size of the compound we were in, but there were lots of small villages on the outskirts of Timbuktu. Only when Al Qaeda relaxed a few days later would they confirm that we were indeed in Timbuktu.

We were led up a passage, walking over grey cement and through a courtyard with floor-to-ceiling burglar bars. We were on the ground floor of a three-storey building. At the end of the courtyard was a big yellow steel door, the entrance to our new home.

It was a stark, grey dual-chamber cell with the odd nail sticking out of the wall and cement dust all over the floor. We could look onto the garden through a barred window in our 'bedroom' and another in the 'lounge'. There was a tiny window in the bathroom, which had a shower and a toilet with no seat. The reason we had to wait for a green light to come into the city was because Abu Osama was still fortifying our prison in this degutted government building. He'd fitted the heavy door with a thin flap through which we'd receive our food, and stripped everything else from the room.

Breakfast would arrive every morning while we were sitting in our respective corners of the room, on the small carpets that were our beds. Abu Osama would bang abruptly into the room, head straight to the windows and give them a yank to make sure we were not trying to break our way out of his custody, all the while barking out his *Salaam Alykum* greeting.

There were a lot of firsts in Timbuktu. Some seem arbitrary, like having an apple, but when you'd been eating oily spaghetti, rice, camel and goat for months, the crunch of a fresh apple was heavenly. Lunch was meat that would come through the window in a brown paper bag with a two-litre bottle of the local version of Fanta. It was like having a party.

When we arrived, Yahia came to check up on us. Because we were in a cell, and we had no idea where the sun rose and set I asked him, 'Yahia, how is this going to work, will we do our prayers with the other mujahideen outside?' He said we'd remain inside and pointed out where east was, which allowed us to work out where south was too. That at least gave us a direction to aim for if we managed to escape. I also told him that we might not hear the *Adhan* or call to prayer, so he gave me his watch. Johan would later take this and lose it when he tried to escape. In the years since, I've thought about how cool it would be to still have the watch that used to belong to Yahia, the leader of AQIM, who was subsequently killed in 2019 by the French.

Watch and direction sorted, I was the *muhathin* (person who does the call to prayer) and Johan was the imam. Other than prayer and exercise, we tried as much as possible not to interact with one another. We each had a mat, so we took a corner as far away as we could get from the others. We each hung our mosquito nets from odd nails around the room, so crossing to the window or the door felt like a cat burglar trying to navigate lasers in a museum.

We knew that if we were going to escape, this would be one of our best opportunities; we had not been this far south since our kidnapping. If we managed to get through the bars and out onto the street, we would have to do it at night, work our way out through the back streets of Timbuktu and then the 13 kilometres to the Niger River. We would either have to cross the river or use it to float downstream. Whatever the case, it would be treacherous; we would have to avoid Al Qaeda, locals who may be loyal to them, and crocs and hippos. I was pretty sure that if we managed to get through the bars, we would split up outside. There was no way Johan and I were going to agree on what to do, and I'm pretty sure we would have been caught while arguing over the best route, how many kilometres there were to the river, or which direction was south.

While Al Qaeda were excited to be in Timbuktu, for us it was huge too. After months in the desert, this was civilisation of the highest order. We spent a lot of time at the windows, listening to city life. We heard schoolkids laughing in the streets on their way home. We tried to catch a glimpse of the outside world, both to aid us in understanding the area better for an escape and for pure curiosity's sake. One day Sjaak, the tallest among us, saw two women next door. It didn't matter that they were completely covered up. He screamed, 'Women!'

We crowded around the window, trying to see what he saw. The two women walked out of view and then returned with Kalashnikovs, swinging them around like Al Qaeda did when they were pretending to be aiming at moving targets.

'Ah fuck!' said Sjaak.

Omar (the guy who had been stationed with Robert Fowler) gave us a radio. It was a huge plastic boombox from China, about five litres of air and half a litre of mechanism. We struggled to get it to work, because reception was awful. My suggestion was to take a bit of cable, wrap it around the aerial and then link it up as high as we could onto the burglar bars. It was not 100%, but it worked. As was custom by now, Johan and I argued over the which frequency to use – shortwave versus FM. Johan claimed to know the science, while from my time on the farm I just knew what worked.

I said, 'Look, you put it on shortwave.'

He said, 'No it's not, it's definitely FM or AM.'

I said, 'Dude, it is shortwave. We have a farm in South Africa, it's in the middle of nowhere and when we want to pick up reception, we put it on shortwave.'

He said, 'That won't work,' and went into a deep dive on the science of radio waves.

I said, 'Dude take your fucking master's degree and put it wherever you want. I'm telling you, put it on shortwave and you will find the radio.'

This was typical of our fraught relationship. Johan could never admit that he might be wrong about something. With the radio on shortwave – Johan fuming, me acting nonchalant over my victory, and Sjaak looking out the window, trying to mentally escape the two of us and see any women without guns – we started to pick up the odd international news bulletin that mentioned the conflict in Mali. Every now and then we would hear machine-gun fire, explosions, and occasionally the thunderclap of a vehicle-mounted anti-aircraft machine gun firing at surveillance planes circling above Timbuktu.

It wasn't just fighting. This city had been a centre of Islamic study and trade for hundreds of years. It had been conquered and reconquered many times, but no one had tried to erase its culture – until now. While librarians managed to save many of the books and scrolls of Islamic scholarship by smuggling them out of the city before Al Qaeda arrived, the mujahideen destroyed most of the 15th century mausoleums of Timbuktu's Sufi Saints. So much ancient history reduced to rubble and sand.

Sanda, the communications guy for Al Qaeda and Ansar Dine in Timbuktu, is quoted on Al Jazeera at the time as saying, 'Ansar Dine will today destroy every mausoleum in the city. All of them, without exception. God is unique. All of this is *haram*. We are all Muslims. UNESCO is what?'

We saw quite a bit of Sanda, especially when it came to videos. One day he came to our cell and said, 'The negotiation is moving ahead. South Africa no problem, go home. Sweden no problem, go home. Holland a problem. There's a Muslim being held in prison in Holland. He did nothing wrong but the Dutch don't want to give him his freedom. But, there is an Al Jazeera interview planned for you next week. They will ask you questions. Answer how you want, say we treat you well, or not, no problem, just be honest. If you agree to do this interview, you all go home afterwards.'

Somehow, Al Jazeera had managed to get behind the frontline and make an agreement with Al Qaeda to interview us in the dunes five kilometres north of Timbuktu. Al Qaeda got dressed in their black outfits, and we were each given new clothes too.

The video was staged like a *Vanity Fair* cover shoot by Annie Leibovitz, all fluttering black flags and ominous columns of Al Qaeda cavalry. The

Land Cruisers would go out, do a loop around a tree and come back several times until the camerawork was just right. With Al Qaeda fluffing out their tails for Al Jazeera, orders rang out over the walkie-talkies, 'Put your flags up. Okay? Okay? And go!'

There was a photographer, a video crew and the interviewer, a soft-spoken Arab from the peninsula, talking to us as though we were emotionally unstable and about to collapse in hysterics, pleading for him to save us. We were actually in relatively good spirits for once, getting fed well in the cell and hanging on to Sanda's promise that we would go home. The interviewer said he was Muslim, but didn't have a beard. Whatever the case, he may have been more scared than we were, amid the beards and guns. At that stage Al Qaeda did not attack journalists, but that policy has changed.

While Sanda gave us the green light to say what we wanted, bad mouthing Al Qaeda would not be smart. So we came out in our new clothes, freshly showered and looking in great condition, and had nothing but sparkling things to say about them. So far, so good.

I was the first guy to be interviewed, and one of the journalist's questions really messed with my world. 'Have you contemplated suicide?'

I paused a moment and said, 'Yes I have.'

Back in our cell Johan said, 'I was surprised that you've contemplated suicide. I didn't think you were like that.'

This really struck me. I had made a terrible mistake. In my mind I was giving a straightforward answer, a literal one, to a literal question. Everything in the desert was literal. I had to be methodical, almost plodding with my words. If the definition of 'contemplate' in that context is, 'Have I considered my options and is suicide an option?' then yes, I've contemplated suicide. If you asked me if I'd contemplated flying by flapping my arms or playing centre for the Springboks, I'd done those things too. But am I actually thinking about doing those things? No. I never thought about killing myself either.

I really regretted that response because that was my one shot at sending a message home. If my family interpreted it the way that Johan had, then they would think that I was in a very bad place. I could not take it back; it was out there. I had dropped my guard because, as per Sanda's promise, we were going home.

Only we weren't.

Al Qaeda reneged on the deal. After the interview they stopped coming to see us, other than to feed us. We went back to jail for a week, and the week after that they sent us back to the desert. The fighting around Timbuktu was becoming too hot.

Listening to the news on our radio, it appeared that Al Qaeda was in the ascendancy. Scores of would-be mujahideen flew in to Bamako or jumped in a taxi and flocked up the tar road to Timbuktu, looking to join the jihad. The further Al Qaeda pushed south below the Niger, down towards Bamako, the more terrified I got. If Al Qaeda totally took over Mali, my worth as a prisoner went out the window. They could free all the Al Qaeda prisoners held in Mali, without a ransom. Where would that leave me?

Less than six months later, in January 2013, the urban party ended for Al Qaeda when the French arrived on the invitation of the Malian government. They came without warning in their Mirage fighter jets, flying in from France and bases in Chad, followed by ground troops. Like the cavalry of old, they annihilated Al Qaeda in two days and swiftly chased them back into hiding in the desert. It looked like a defeat and it was, if you judge victory by one-off operations. But if you are playing the long game like Al Qaeda, the French did what they wanted them to.

At the time, Yahia (Abou al-Hamman, Emir of the Sahara, Al Qaeda, to give him his full title) had this to say to the French: 'We have withdrawn from the cities in order to return with force and power. And we warn them that [President] Hollande has opened the gates of hell for the French people.'

Looking back, this had to be part of the Al Qaeda brains trust's long-term regional plan all along. Al Qaeda could not just sit in the desert forever taking the odd prisoner and launching occasional attacks. If they truly wanted to take over the country and then the region, they needed to poke the bear. France was always going to step in at its former colony to protect its own interests. By taking the north, Al Qaeda had made their statement, drawn blood and drawn France into conflict – one that would cost them, and more specifically the French taxpayers, millions of euros and some lives.

Al Qaeda's military strategy was to go back into the desert, wait for the French to get bored and go home, and then come back and fight again. And so, with the French looking for us all over the Sahara, we spent the next few years fleeing and hiding, but most importantly, being patient.

In September 2012, almost a month to the day since we'd arrived, we departed from Timbuktu. Our brigade of babysitters raced out of the city in their fleet of Land Cruisers, gunning it hard trying to outflank each other. The mood of the mujahideen was upbeat; Disney meets Mad Max, everyone in sunglasses looking very cool, as only rebels can. I looked across from the back of the vehicle Sjaak and I were in to the vehicle to our left, where two mujahideen were sitting on top of the cargo net. One was a guy called Abu Basir and the other was Osama.

Abu Basir's legs were drawn up onto whatever was under the tarp, revealing his footwear, a pair of bright-pink Barbie-branded high-top sneakers he must have picked up at Timbuktu's market. As Osama turned to our vehicle with his gun in his hand and a huge smile on his face, I saw his headgear: a pair of frog-green swimming goggles. It was almost difficult to take these guys seriously. As I used to say, the Sahara is no fashion show.

I never saw Timbuktu again.

CHAPTER TWENTY-ONE

File 13

As told by Malcolm 'Magoo' McGown

Contrary to what you might think, Steve's not a bloody idiot.

His American uncle, who used to serve in the military, warned Steve not to do the trip. I was probably less worried about where he was going and more worried about how he was doing it. Too many guys killed themselves on those motorbikes.

Steve had always wanted to do this. I understood that. When I was about 24, I went across to the States to visit my sister in New York, and decided to hitchhike down to Key West. My sister was against it, because recently two guys had picked up a hitchhiker, pulled a gun on him and shot him in the woods. My view was that the odds of that happening were very low. Life is full of chances and risks, and you haven't lived life if you haven't taken a few risks.

When Steve was in Bamako on the Monday night before he was taken, we had a long Skype talk because we hadn't spoken for quite a few weeks. I said to him, 'Steve, you do know you are going through war zones?' I was thinking of the countries that he still had to go through, like the DRC, but Steve was very clear that he was not looking to be a hero. He said, 'If it looks too dangerous, I'll put my bike on the boat or leave it behind and fly home.'

Now, the idea of him ever hopping on a plane or even a slow-moving cargo ship seemed like a fantasy.

When you need to retrieve a loved one from an impossibly dark hole across geographical, cultural and religious borders, you try everything you can. You try conventional methods and channels of diplomacy and governance, secret services and foreign affairs departments. There are people among these organisations who help to the best of their abilities, but it soon becomes apparent where their influence ends. There are people who want to help, who are genuine; and there are people who are not. There are people who claim big connections and influence, but when you call them asking for that key introduction, you realise it was all just hot air. Then, out of nowhere, the most unassuming people come forward with viable leads and generosity of spirit.

Soon, you call in the heavy hitters. You ask your most powerful and influential friends who know even more powerful and influential friends to do you a favour, to get you a meeting with so-and-so. Sometimes you get the meeting, sometimes you don't.

If I were to compile a list of all the avenues we went down and all the options we exhausted, I would never be able to complete it, because we tried so many different things.

We worked with the Swedish/Dutch Troika. We worked our own angles too. There was no point believing that they had Steve's best interests at heart, when they had their own guys to look after and their own sovereign considerations to protect.

We met the British secret service and Foreign Office, the Dutch, the Swedes and all the South African agencies and departments over and over again. The very nature of secret services is to get as much information as they can without giving you any – never mind that you are not playing silly buggers, trying to manoeuvre political pawns or make regional power plays, you are just trying to get your son home.

We met with Gift of the Givers early on, in 2012, but they were already working on Pierre Korkie's case.

We spoke to private investigators, mercenaries and hostage negotiators, human-rights lawyers like Brian Currin, and consuls like Jo Olivier of the British Embassy.

We found out that, if it ever came to it, paying a ransom is not that straightforward. You need diplomatic involvement. The Reserve Bank has to be notified for a large sum of money to leave the country.

We spoke to other people, like Yolanda Korkie and Robert Fowler, who had survived hostage situations, and to some whose loved ones had not made it home.

We pulled in all our contacts. We approached ministers and presidents, both past and current. Mbeki, Zuma, Ramaphosa, Dlamini-Zuma, you name it, they all heard from us. Former education MEC Mary Metcalfe helped us out a lot by making introductions.

We navigated scams as best we could – from people on the ground in Mali, to people in South Africa who claimed they could help us if we only bankrolled a chopper, some vehicles, satellite phones, fuel. We lost lots of money, but we had to try.

We held vigils. We commemorated birthdays and celebrated signif-icant dates for Steve. We lit lanterns and set off helium balloons. On one occasion, Steve's lantern came back and crashed into a neigh-bour's garden.

We spoke to the big bosses of South African-run gold mines in Mali, trying to see if they had leverage, if there was some angle they could work. Bottom line was they had to be careful, because if they are seen to be helping and paying for a South African hostage, their workers and other South Africans could become targets.

Our efforts went from the sublime to the ridiculous, from regular to left-field, and from diplomatic to esoteric.

One meeting in particular sums up how insignificant Stephen's cause appeared to be to the South African government. It was with Maite Nkoana-Mashabane, then minister of international relations and coop-eration. We organised this meeting at the airport, and of course it was delayed. She was on her way to China, and she arrived with all her Gucci bags. Her PA had Gucci suitcases too, and they were dressed smart as anything. Ernst was there, Mbulelo was there, I think the director-general for West Africa was there – probably eight to 10 peo-ple on the government side. On our side of the table were Cath, Sue and myself.

Nkoana-Mashabane started off. Talk, talk, talk, we are doing this and we've done that. It was a lot of bluster, a lot of listing of names – differ-ent people in the West African portfolio of her department – and none of it meant anything in terms of concrete gains. After several minutes of this, she finally stopped. I said, 'Minister, can I say something now?'

She said, 'Yes.'

I said, 'Do you have children?'

She said, 'Yes.'

I said, 'Well, put yourself in my shoes. If one of your children was gone, that is where I am at the moment. I'm not prepared to have my son put into the 'File 13' trash bin. I heard from Ambassador Oupa Macau that when the first Proof of Life came out, €1,000 was charged for it and that Holland or Sweden paid. For the second one, it was €2,000. Either Holland or Sweden paid. For this latest one, the demand was for €4,000 to be paid. There was a whole lot of hesitation before it was paid. Minister, if the government can't pay the money, you can phone me any time and I will pay it.'

She said, 'Oh no, no, no, no, we got money.'

I said, 'Then please, don't hesitate to get a Proof of Life, because if it was one of your children, that is what you'd want. I want urgency around Stephen's case. I do not want it left in File 13.'

The meeting ended and off they went to China. No doubt she had more important fish to fry, because we never heard from her again. She didn't even have the decency to phone Cath once to say, 'How are you doing?'

I get that there is much that the average citizen is not privy to. We wanted the South African government to put pressure on the Malian government, but we had no idea what high-level games they were already playing. South African companies have mines in Mali. The South African government, like any other in the African Union, has allies and enemies, and seeks to gain power and leverage. While Steve was the most important thing in the world to us, was he even a serious consideration for the government at the time? It's hard to believe that he was.

I'm sure the government eventually paid the €4,000, but the delays were unacceptable. We would find out that a Proof of Life picture or video was taken in January when we only got it in June or July.

I would get hugely frustrated. Sometimes at our meetings with DIRCO I would vent at Ernst and Mbulelo. 'You're coming here to just tick the box so if the crap hits the fan, you can say you looked after the McGowns, you were there on that date every two weeks.'

One day, as they were sitting in our living room I actually told them, 'Guys, don't take this the wrong way, but I can tell you right now, there's no one in this room that can negotiate Steve out of this. This has to be escalated far, far above us.'

We needed a specialist. Then, in June 2015, Imtiaz Sooliman from Gift of the Givers got in touch again.

CHAPTER TWENTY-TWO

Death in the Afternoon

'It is a strange feeling to have an animal come toward you consciously seeking to kill you…' – Ernest Hemingway, *Death in the Afternoon*

In the real world, we know how to navigate busy four-way crossings, how to use Excel, how to find the right emoji on our phones, how to shotgun a beer, chat someone up, how to do thousands of mundane little things. In the desert, the way people conduct themselves, how they see the world and the skill set they acquire are very different. Having lived in both worlds, I can say with confidence that the desert is more honest about the reality of life and death.

Most of the actual violence I saw from Al Qaeda was on the screens of their Samsungs. In camp, violence occurred very occasionally by way of a backhand slap when someone got a surprise. That appeared to be the golden rule among all Saharans: never walk up behind some-one unannounced, or put your hand on their shoulder. If you did this it would result in an automatic violent reaction, as the guy in question swung an arm backwards into your face. That kind of reaction makes sense if you consider that life in the desert has not changed much over the last few millennia. People creeping up on you were likely there to do you harm. Surprise birthdays are not a thing.

Al Qaeda are violent, that's not up for debate, but the way they see it, theirs is a sanctioned violence based on the rules of Islam. You need food? We'll slaughter that sheep. Steal? We'll chop off your hand as per Sharia law. *Kuffar* invaders, *murtadeen* and adultery while married? Have some death. Sustenance, punishment, the rules of wedlock – the violence always had an objective.

Dying, whether by Al Qaeda's hand or French rockets, was a constant and real possibility for the duration of my time in the desert, but the mujahideen were never overtly violent towards me. Other than being hit with my own flip-flop during our kidnapping, and being punched in the head for surprising somebody, I was actually never beaten or mistreated because my captors had a code. Until I converted I merely existed, in the sense that they did not care about my wellbeing, but as per the Quraan's rules for treating prisoners and slaves, they gave me food and kept me alive. This didn't mean that they wouldn't kill me after giving me my meal. I saw and heard first-hand, via videos shot on their phones, their joy at cutting off the heads of Malian government soldiers or executing local spies. They were totally at ease dealing with death, whether human or animal.

Much as watching an animal bleed out was gruesome for a Westerner like me, Al Qaeda were mostly adept at dispatching livestock. In Islam, the slaughtering of an animal is called *dhabihah*. It must be humane and it must be swift. When you are going to slaughter something, a task I had to take on from time to time, you take the knife and you sharpen it away from the animal. It cannot see you sharpening the knife. Then, holding the knife behind your back, you walk up to the animal (this had a definite echo with the lesson about not sneaking up on people). Again, the animal cannot see that you have a knife. You don't want to make any additional trauma. You get down there, and you must cut its throat quickly and bleed it out fast. The idea is to inflict the least amount of pain, because whatever you are slaughtering, like everything else in this universe, is going to go to Allah in the end for final judgment. (Animals, however, do not go to heaven or hell – they settle their differences and then become a pile of dust.)

When it came to certain animals, there was no elegant way to dispatch one in the halaal manner. There were two animals whose death I took particularly badly. One was a tortoise that Al Qaeda tortured with the help of Johan, trying to pull and poke it hard enough to get it to reveal its neck so that they could cut it. To watch this made me sick to my stomach.

I was not averse to eating tortoise the first time it was offered, if someone knew how to kill it quickly. Generally, with any animal we ate, the lungs were the worst part (they tasted like bath sponge) and the liver the best part, the bit the mujahideen prized over anything else. Tortoise liver tasted like other animals' lungs. But otherwise, the meat was fine, if tough – not worth all the pain and suffering the animal went through to die. I'm no Islamic scholar, but what I saw was not a swift death, and we had enough food so there was no reason to do it.

The second death was that of a baby camel.

It was early days, January 2012, and we were camping in what looked like a stadium-sized volcanic crater. At times I would pretend I was going to the toilet, climb up over the edge, and just sit there to clear my head and take in the view. The vista was astounding; the land fell away beneath you down onto perfect sand dunes and far off into the distant mountains. Sometimes, from this vantage point, I could see the odd camel, and I noticed that there was one with a human on it. Just a speck, he kept his distance, about 700 metres away. I could see that he was on one of the big male camels, a *jmal*, sitting on some sort of throne-like saddle. Any hopes I had that he might send word back to civilisation were dashed when he came to speak to Al Qaeda. He approached slowly on his majestic camel, pausing on the edge of the crater so that he could be seen. As he came towards us, his *jmal* made a lot of noise. That's a pretty good rule of thumb in the desert: if you can hear a camel moaning, it usually means there's someone on it.

The Arab clearly knew Al Qaeda, because they asked him for food, livestock specifically. It was a big camp with a lot of mujahideen to feed. He disappeared again and returned a day later on his *jmal*, with a baby camel in tow. We watched them walking in, the big camel majestic with is slow, loping stride, the juvenile all neck and legs bouncing alongside. The Arab climbed off, had a conversation with Al Qaeda, got back on his camel and then turned around and started to disappear, with Al Qaeda holding on to junior. It looked confused and terrified. It was being separated from what we assumed was its father. The only other creature like it, its family, its security, its everything, was leaving its world.

As with the goat in Camp 1, for Al Qaeda handling this camel was just the practical transition of foodstuff from the metaphorical farm-yard to the larder. Laughing and chatting, they brought the young camel to its knees. There's a technique to tying a camel's leg so it can't get up. Completely trussed up, the camel sat there, ten metres from us, for about a day and a half, in the sun, looking around with its big brown eyes, calling out to its family, to us, to the mujahideen, to the world, anything and anyone. I related to this poor camel. I looked at this thing and my heart broke for it. I thought, *It's like us.*

The way Al Qaeda slaughtered it was traumatic. Five guys came up on it and held it down as the camel threw its head around trying to bite them, grunting and moaning, hanging on to life. They grabbed it by the mouth, pulled its neck back over its shoulder and after saying,

'*Bismillah, Allah Akbar*,' one of them began to stab it at the base of the neck with a knife. All sorts of horrendous sounds were coming out; it roared and moaned and bleated and bled. With a goat or a sheep you can cut the throat relatively easily, but the skin on a camel is very thick, so they had to stab it again and again in the same spot to make a gaping hole in the jugular. Once they got in, they tried to cut across to make it bleed out quicker. All the while, the camel bleated and fought as blood gushed from the wound. You could see it start to get weaker. As its head stopped fighting, the guy with the knife moved to the back of the neck and severed the big flat yellow tendon that holds the head up. It was like tearing your Achilles tendon; you lose all control over the limb. With its legs trussed and its neck now useless, the mujahideen straightened the camel's neck and laid it on the ground over the puddle of its own blood as the light drained out of its eyes.

They then proceeded to dismember it. They chopped the neck and head off and put them to one side, then the legs; then they worked their way up from the back, cutting down the spine, over the hump, skinning the animal and cutting the meat into strips. Because there is so much meat on a camel – more than enough for one camp – Al Qaeda would quite often load some of the meat into one of the Land Cruisers to take over to another camp. Judging the length of time they were gone, we started to get an understanding that there were often other Al Qaeda camps in relatively close proximity to ours.

The strips of meat were hung over a small acacia tree to dry out. I called this the Tree of Death. It looked like a Christmas tree, but *The Nightmare Before Christmas* version. Instead of baubles and ribbons and stars, we had strips of camel. There were several Trees of Death in the desert, depending on how often we slaughtered a camel or goat, or had excess sheep meat that needed drying. If we ever needed to move camp while drying meat, the Tree of Death would be dismantled, the meat stuffed in a sack, and re-hung in a new tree when we got to our next camp. Usually a layer of grass was thrown in the branches above the meat to protect it from direct sunlight. The idea was for the wind to dry out the meat; the sun would only make it go off.

If meat wasn't cut into strips, it would go off within a day in summer. Even so, flies and maggots would appear in no time. In winter, you wanted a nice breeze blowing to dry it out, but often you would get hit by a sandstorm, and then you'd have sandpaper meat and would have to wash it in a bowl of water before use.

Typically, the head gets taken away and cooked overnight, basically slammed into the hot sand of the fire. The next morning, whoever was in the kitchen making breakfast would call in his mates and they would eat the head, the brain, the nose, the ears, the Adam's apple. In the early days, we ate everything.

While I never enjoyed taking an animal's life, in time the visceral nature of it became less shocking. Like Al Qaeda, I'd see it as just another aspect of life. I slaughtered about five goats or sheep myself over the years. As for the macabre Tree of Death, it was simply a larder or biltong cupboard. Juniors in camp would often run up, snap a piece off one of the strips, and run off gnawing on it. Unlike suburban kids with Woolies Snapsticks or a piece of droëwors, at least these kids understood exactly where their snack came from. We stalk the grocery aisles and jump on the skinless chicken breast, but we don't want to know about the animal that died to feed us.

In a place as ancient in custom as the Sahel, the death of an animal is as normal as opening a tin in your kitchen.

CHAPTER TWENTY-THREE

Imtiaz

As told by Imtiaz Sooliman, Gift of the Givers

When Malcolm McGown came to me, he was distraught. Here was an old man whose wife was sick, and who didn't know if he was ever going to see his son again. I knew that as Gift of the Givers we had the capability and the experience to deal with the kinds of people who had taken Stephen. We had done so before more than once, and it's pretty much the same group. I told him that I couldn't do it now, but when I was finished with Pierre Korkie's case, I would help Stephen.

One of these cases is complicated enough and requires all your focus. If you make a mistake, a hostage can die and it is on your head. Malcolm understood that. When I told him that I would look into the case, I did explain that there was one major problem: where his son was taken, I had no leverage. I knew nobody in Mali, and nobody there knew Gift of the Givers. In Korkie's case, it was easy; everyone in Yemen knew us, because when we go into a country we make sure everyone knows who we are. We send in containers, we provide aid and we are visible in the media. In Mali, I did not even know where to start. I told Malcolm that was not an obstacle, just something we would look at when we got to it.

The first time we got involved with something like this was in 2011, when Bruno Pelizarri and Debbie Calitz got taken in Somalia. We first intervened in that country in 2007 with a massive famine programme. While we were there, family members of Bruno came to us and said, 'Can you help?' All we did was check around and ask questions. It comes down to this: people trusted us, because we delivered aid. We had leverage. That really is the key word in all this. We had hospitals, we had medical staff and we were sending aid. All the tribal leaders and all the different groups were sending their families to us for treatment. We were not asking them questions about whether they were Al Qaeda or transitional government. You're sick? You need help? We help.

2

Within 72 hours, we got feedback on the group that took Bruno and Debbie, which area they were taken in, who they were sold to, where they were moved to, which area they were in. We passed this on to the family; they carried on, the Italian government got involved, and whatever happened thereafter was up to them.

The second case was the following year. The Taiwanese government called us because 26 of their sailors had been taken in Somalia. Same thing: we made enquiries and got back to them 12 hours later with the news that their sailors had been released. Somebody had paid the ransom, but the government didn't know about it yet. They confirmed it the next day.

Then Pierre Korkie's case came about. How we approached Korkie's case helps Stephen's case make sense. I'd opened an office in Yemen in August 2012. I went to Syria in October 2012, and in April 2013 I took a team into that country. I brought a Yemeni guy with me to Syria; first because he is Arab and speaks the language as well as English, second because he was starting with me so he needed to learn the international scope of the work we do, third because he is a journalist, and fourth so that he could help us if we got caught in the Middle East by talking about the work we were doing in Syria.

About a month after we got back from Syria, around 28 May, my Yemeni employee called to say, 'Do you know there's a South African couple taken hostage in Yemen? Do we do anything?' Our organisation's motto is 'Best Among People Are Those Who Benefit Mankind'. Helping Korkie fitted in with that. What did we have to lose? Governments say they won't talk to terrorists, but we can do something. People know us in Yemen, so we started building leverage in the country. Everywhere we did our distribution we asked, 'Does anyone know about this South African couple?'

You see, you don't find Al Qaeda; they find you. All the lessons we learned with Korkie, we later applied in Mali with Stephen, because we were dealing with exactly the same group with the same mentality. If it was somebody else, it would have been a problem, but we understood how they think and what they were going to do.

In Yemen, it took eight months before Al Qaeda's intermediaries called us to say, 'Are you the guys who keep announcing in the media that they want to meet? Tomorrow come to a certain place at a certain time.' And because of that experience of how they dealt with us, I knew we could apply the same logic in Mali.

While we were working on the Korkie case, I made one or two calls about Stephen's case. My office manager Allauddin was going to visit his son who was studying in Mauritania. While he was up there, I asked him to go to Mali, meet with spiritual leaders, teachers and the tribal people, and see if we could get some information. Malcolm was very excited, but when Allauddin got there it was December; nobody was around and it was a total dead end. He could not find anybody to assist us, and nobody knew who we were. I'd tried to give Malcolm some hope, but it didn't work.

We were going to get Pierre Korkie out of Yemen on 6 December 2014, but then the American Navy SEALS went in and he was killed during the raid.

In June 2015, I was sitting in the lounge watching TV and I saw this video of Stephen and Johan. They were sitting outside under a tree, with the Al Qaeda guys in their big 4X4 with guns. I looked at this video, called Malcolm and said, 'These guys are talking. They want to negotiate. I am taking the case.' This time we were going to make it work.

Malcolm was very excited. A day later, we put out a press release that said Gift of the Givers had been asked by the McGown family to intervene in Stephen's case. But in that press release, I did something very unconventional. I said, 'We are getting involved in Mali, but we do not know anybody in Mali. Is there anyone of Malian origin, who is a Tuareg, who knows the tribal leaders and who is willing to go there to be a hostage negotiator?' Two hours later, Yahia Diko walked into our office in Fordsburg.

I wasn't there at that time, but my guy called me to say, 'There's a tall guy here and his name is Mohammed Yahia Diko. He's a Tuareg who moved to South Africa 15 years ago and he said he has come to help. His family is involved there, he knows the area well and he doesn't want any money. His wife has told him he should help South Africans because South Africa has been good to him.'

We have a spiritual teaching that you can make out a person by their voice and by their face. I told my guy to put Yahia on the phone. I spoke to him for a couple of minutes, and told him he is the right guy for the job. I did not meet him, I did not see him, I just heard his voice. The next day, another guy came in with the same story; that he came to us to help. He also got put on the phone, but after a few minutes I could tell he was a chancer, so he was thrown out of the office. We went with Yahia, and it was not a mistake.

The first thing we had to do was introduce Yahia to the local media in South Africa. We put a few articles up on our website announcing that he was going to Mali. It was important that his picture was all over the show. This part of the strategy would make sense later.

The brief I gave Yahia was, when he got to Mali, to announce loudly what he was there to do. Nothing hidden, nothing undercover. He had to be visible, from Bamako to Kidal. The point was to let everyone see and hear him. Wherever he went, he had to announce, 'I am Yahia Diko, I am from Gift of the Givers in South Africa. I am looking to talk to someone who knows where Steven McGown is.'

Yahia set off on his journey and started making his own connections, who told him to go to Point B, then Point C, then Point D, and so on. It was very hush-hush, nobody spoke much about hostages at that time. Eventually someone sent him to Niger to meet a possible Al Qaeda intermediary. The connection in Niger said, 'I could have helped you, but because Stephen was taken in Mali, there's a protocol here. The Mali people should help you. I will put you in contact with the right person in Mali – he was actually just here 48 hours ago.'

They made the connection and things started to happen. What none of the governments or secret services could do, from November 2011 until July 2015, we did in six weeks. We connected with the guys who were connected to the negotiators for Al Qaeda.

CHAPTER TWENTY-FOUR

Predators

'He who is cruel to animals becomes hard also in his dealings with men. We can judge the heart of a man by his treatment of animals'
– Immanuel Kant

Most of the animals in the Sahara had never seen humans so they showed no fear of us. They should have, given Al Qaeda's trigger-happy ways.

Despite the laws of Islam about how animals should be killed, Al Qaeda did not always do things the right way. If they saw a wild animal, nine times out of 10 they would try to kill it, usually with their AK-47s, but shovels, sticks, rocks and flip-flops would do too. While I had to get to grips with the visceral matter-of-fact nature of where our food came from, I still spent much of my time in the desert trying to convince Al Qaeda not to kill every wild animal they saw.

Every living thing in the desert just wanted to survive. Because it's such a difficult environment to live in, animals would frequently come into my hut for shelter from the sun, the rain or sandstorms. Often, I'd be sitting in my boogie, and a bird would fly in and sit next to me with its eyes closed, rocking gently, because being outside was just too hot. When a sandstorm hit, I would sit up in a foetal position in my hut, arms around my knees, completely wrapped up – including my eyes – to try to keep the sand out. Wasps would come in and take shelter under the arch of my foot or fly up my trouser leg and sit in the crook of my knee till the storm passed. They weren't there to harm me; they were just looking for a safe place to wait things out, so if I didn't forget about them and move in such a way that put physical pressure on an insect, I would not get stung. We were all on the same team.

While I was in prison in Timbuktu, I began a list of all the animals, trees, birds and bugs that I saw, a list that grew as the years passed. I made this list because I was passionate about animals, but I also realised that knowing where certain animals were found might help me identify where I was when I returned, blindfolded, to an area I had been held in before. I created a fly map of Mali based on the different flies we found in different areas. If you have ever walked into a fly-fishing shop and wondered if any of those crazy designs and colours actually exist on this earth, they do – in the Sahara.

Along with camel dung, the only other thing we found absolutely everywhere in the desert were flies, and it was one creature, along with the ubiquitous mosquitoes, that I would gladly kill. They land on you in swarms of hundreds. I would take my scarf off, fold it into a fly swatter and self-flagellate to get the flies off my back. Those things would drive you crazy, dive-bombing your eyeballs for a drink of water. When we slaughtered an animal, it would take a day for flies to lay eggs in the meat, and then we would get little maggots crawling everywhere. At times it appeared that the sand was alive with maggots; soon there would be a fly infestation of biblical proportions.

In the winter, the flies got sluggish due to the cold, and in the early morning there would be hundreds sitting on the grass roofs of our huts. Each little blade of grass would have 10 flies sitting in a row, and you could literally walk up to them and flick them one by one, poek-poek-poek. It was almost like a war had been declared between man and fly in the desert. Man's only opportunity was to attack at first light. For the rest of the day, the flies were unstoppable. The three of us would sit in the hut, waving our arms and flapping our hands like lunatics. When it got too much we'd unite for a five-minute flip-flop flap to see how many flies we could nail, and end up with a heap of corpses.

While I hated the flies, some bugs I loved and some I found fascinating. In one camp there was a tiny fairy-like midge. It reminded me of a long-tailed widowbird. Around four millimetres long, with a black body, translucent wings and white, wispy tail feathers, it really looked like a little fairy. I'd never seen anything like this before, and when it flew past me like a dandelion blowing in the wind, I followed it to get a proper view. It would land on a piece of grass, and then lift up again and drift off like a helium balloon. It was incredible to me that such a delicate thing could survive in such a harsh environment.

In terms of things that could hurt, sting you or bite you, there were scorpions, spiders and camel spiders, which look like a nightmare scorpion-spider lovechild. Then there was my old friend the *misnuna*. I found these bugs pretty incredible – until they bit me. They are big as bugs go, up to three centimetres, and they have a little trunk like a mini elephant. When it bites you, it's like being jabbed with a giant needle – you go from lying down to standing up in a split second. In the outside world, it's called a kissing bug or a Chagas beetle, and it gives you Chagas disease. The weird thing is, it's not meant to be in Africa. When I came out of the desert I spoke to the bug experts in South Africa, who said you only get this bug in the Americas. 'Trust me,' I told them. 'You get it in the Sahara. It bit me a number of times.'

According to Al Qaeda, within Islam, there are certain animals that you must kill. These include crows, kites, mice, scorpions, snakes and geckos. Some camps would get a lot of mice and jerboa, the cute kangaroo-like mouse endemic to the desert. I once found a jerboa digging a hole under my sleeping mat. I lay there in the morning, watching him. He would pause, look at me, have a think and then continue with his work. Gently, so as not to scare him, I'd help clean away the sand from behind the hole he was digging.

Al Qaeda were vigilant about mice raiding the rice sacks. I wasn't too fussed about it. One night, there was a nice big moon out above the dunes, and the sand around my boogie shone so white it looked like a ski resort. I had some biscuits on me and I was alone, so I fed these little mice. They would run around full of energy, play-jump on each other and scrum for crumbs. Some of them ate out of my hand. As long as Al Qaeda didn't see me, I figured I wouldn't be judged for my actions and the mice could be my companions. The next night, this youngster called Abd al-Hayy started killing my mice. He was running round the camp, using his flip-flop like a boomerang, and when a mouse ran past he would either hit it with his hand, flatten it with the flip-flop, or use it to knock the mouse's feet out from beneath it. Angry and disgusted, I went off to bed. The next morning I woke up to 15 dead mice all over the camp, all on their backs with their legs up. I blamed myself; they probably got comfortable with people because I was feeding them, which led them to the slaughter.

For the most part, our diet was really straightforward: rice and spaghetti swimming in oil and tomato concentrate, small biscuits, sugar, green tea, milk powder, a concentrated milk called Gloria, and a South African powdered drink called Jolly Juice. We had onion and potatoes for two months of the year, and sweet potatoes once. Our salt came from the mines at Taoudenni, and we had sardines from Mauritania and Western Sahara – from the same factories I'd zoomed past on my way south, a lifetime ago. For protein, we ate goat, sheep, camel and, once, beef. As much as I hated watching that camel die, eating it was relatively straightforward.

Rabbits were common in The Holes area, while gazelle were near the mountains. These were a favourite Al Qaeda target for the pot. They would first be shot, then have their throats cut halaal-style. I saw a striped polecat, that African Golden wolf, Fennec foxes, and a striped hyena – all of which Al Qaeda chased in Land Cruisers and tried to shoot. We saw three honey badgers; one was killed but the other two got away.

There were also bats. If we found these I knew I was heading south, because they would roost in the arak trees (the roots of which we used as toothbrushes). Abd al-Khalak caught one and kept it with a string tied around its wing, so he could throw it around and pretend it was flying, to scare his friends. I pleaded for him to let it go; I heard it scream softly as he broke the bone in its wing tying the knot too tight. Half an hour later it was discarded under the tree. These moments in the desert I found particularly difficult. What a pointless waste of life.

I had a thing for *fakron* (tortoises). In fact, I had a thing for animals in general, and Al Qaeda found it odd how I always wanted to see the animals and the birds and keep them alive, but the tortoises were the closest I got to a pet. Al Qaeda were terrified of tortoises. One guy confided how much he marvelled at the amount of blood that came out of a tortoise after he swung it repeatedly against a tree. If they found a tortoise in camp, everybody would stand around looking at it. If it moved towards them, they would literally run away screaming.

Once, when we were staying in The Holes, Al Qaeda brought me a tortoise as a gift. On arrival in our camp, they took a hot knife and made a small hole at the back of his shell and attached a small rope so he was on a leash. It was early morning and they tethered it to a post. At around 9:30am I left my hut, and found the tortoise in an absolute state trying to get towards a small mound of grass – not because it was terrified of people, but because it was terrified of the Saharan sun; it must have known that the day was warming up. It was frothing at the mouth and because it was tied up, it was stuck in its place and its legs were just digging it down into the sand. I untied him and dug a hole in the side of a sand dune. He made a beeline straight into the cave and disappeared for the day. The following day I found him walking around, and as the morning warmed up, he came into my hut and found a place next to me, where he dug down a bit and stuck his head into the grass wall of my hut.

Al Qaeda were insistent that I had to take him far away, up over the top of our hole and into another hole altogether. I pointed out – while the tortoise unhelpfully plodded towards them, mouth agape – that this thing is harmless and eats grass. It didn't matter what I said, they were having none of it. I promised to keep the tortoise close to me, but one night it got out of my hut and walked 100 metres across the hole. You could see the perfectly spaced tracks leading all the way to where the mujahideen were sleeping under the stars. It landed up snoozing in a tuft of grass a metre away from two of those guys and when they woke up they went fucking mad. Eventually, I took the tortoise away and placed it at the edge of our hole. I pointed its nose south and gave it a pat on the shell, and the diminutive 4X4 took the hint and left, going straight up the steep part of the sand dune.

Generally, reptiles were not looked upon kindly. People reacted really badly to snakes and desert monitors. Little critters like the long-footed lizard (*zulzil*) were merely caught for sport. Once in Group Dawud, in February 2012, I was helping Bashir in the kitchen. We were sitting under a tree together, close enough to touch knees while breaking spaghetti, when a snake dropped from the tree above and landed on Bashir's lap. Before I had any idea what had just happened, Bashir was already at full stride and five metres away. All over the world people are scared of snakes, but in desert communities far from medical help, a venomous snake means death; Islamic *hadiths* dictate that the snake must die. There is, however, an additional clause that must be adhered to if the snake is found inside your house: you must ask the snake three times to leave, because it may be possessed by a spirit; if it does not leave on your third request, you can kill it.

The mujahideen were deathly afraid of geckos. One *hadith* states that Abraham was put into a big fire and 'It (the gecko) used to blow on (the fire of) Ibraaheem'. This indicates that the gecko is innately evil and harmful, but that's not the only reason for killing it. Another *hadith* states that it spits into vessels, as a result of which man is exposed to a great deal of harm.

While the geckos were in attendance, blowing on the flames, creating a bigger fire, frogs were also there, spitting water, trying to put the fire out. So it is *haram* to kill frogs but halaal to kill geckos. We would get these big black geckos in the trees, and Al Qaeda believed if one drop of lizard saliva fell into your cup and you drank it, you would die. They believed that gecko saliva was more poisonous than an adder.

Another story was that if it bit you on the ear, you had to cut your ear off. This was not because it was poisonous; it was because it would never let go. I asked them why you could not just chop the gecko's head off and then open its jaws rather than cut your ear off. They looked confused at this logic and did not have an answer. I had never heard of venomous salivating lizards before, but when every guy has the same story you wonder whether they know something you don't. I never picked up or touched those geckos.

The same thing happened with snakes. Some of Al Qaeda believed that horned vipers did not bite you; instead, they would stab you with their forked tongues and sting you with their tails. After several years of these stories, I started to question my own education. Everything about my existence was so odd and upside down, who was to say that there isn't a venomous lizard in the Sahara?

Of all the animals I saw in the desert, it was the birds that tugged at my heartstrings the most, probably because I envied them their ability to fly away. I would often daydream about being a bird, soaring up, and getting onto those thermals and soaring home.

I saw hoopoes in the south, sand grouse, rollers, starlings and yellow-billed kites, all of which indicated to me that we might be near people, water, food and therefore transport. I'd hand-feed crickets to the wagtails from the shade of my boogie. At times we saw white storks, the same type we get in South Africa. When they set off in flight, they would come up from between the dunes and start catching thermals. They would float up higher and higher until they were just spots in the sky, 15 or 20 in a holding pattern, and then all veer towards the southeast and disappear.

One night in group Abu-Hamza Chinquetti, at the end of the rainy season, it was a full moon. I was lying down among the sand dunes when seven or eight white storks came past, silhouetted against the sky, flying so low I could hear the wind through their wings. It was such a beautiful moment, and then it was gone. I was left with the deafening silence of the desert and my thoughts again.

It was the swallows, swifts and bee-eaters that absolutely captured me. I watched the migration of these birds, back and forth, back and forth for six years as they followed the summers. I started documenting their movements, writing down first and last swallow of the season, and the day I saw the first bee-eater. With swallows, it would generally start in mid-February; and two weeks later, you would get your first bee-eater. The migrations would last until April, and then you would see the stragglers coming through. The return trip would begin in August and end in October. I was absolutely in awe of those birds.

For nine months of the year, the wind came from the northeast, and for three months it came from the south. When it changed direction, summer began. It was on the 1 June, or a day either side; you could set your watch by it (if you had one). I used to lie on my back and watch the high-level clouds come from the west to the east like huge trains dragging water in off the ocean. The searing-hot low-level winds came from the northeast, blowing over thousands of kilometres of sand. April was probably the worst month of the year for me, because the winds literally felt like a blowtorch. It was such a strange sensation that I would have to open my eyes and look at my arm to make sure that my skin was not rolling off, like paint from an old piece of wood.

When the winds blew into the desert in summer, bringing with them the rains, they would sometimes blow birds off course too – birds that had no business being in the desert. Many mornings camping in The Holes, I heard the unmistakeable cooing of a pigeon. It took me back to being a youngster on our farm in the Eastern Free State, where we had Cape turtledoves and laughing doves sitting in the big pine trees next to the dam. I'd lie there in the grass, with not a care in the world, listening to these birds singing on a beautiful, fresh summer morning.

Back in the sand, I wanted to find that pigeon, because if I did not, it was going to die. My heart broke for it, because it became a prisoner like me. It was easy for them to fly in on the cool southerly winds, lulled by the rain and the fresh-seeding grasses; the problem was summers were so hot, and they did not realise that the door was closing behind them. These birds were not designed for the desert; they would get absolutely exhausted. I could literally walk up to a bird and pick it up. I'd put it in some shade next to my hut and give it water in a small tomato purée can buried in the sand. I'd go up to the *mauna* and boil some rice to give them something to eat. Without winds to carry it the 300-odd kilometres back to where it was meant to be in the savannah, this bird would not survive. At one stage, I was even keen to pack the pigeon up in a small box to take between camps, but Al Qaeda would just not see the point of lugging a bird around. When we loaded up and drove away from camp, I heard the bird cooing and thought, *Well, I did my best, but I know you're going to die.*

I also found a spur-winged plover that got blown in on the strong summer winds. I woke up in a temporary camp hearing kek-kek-kek. We were camped under a lone acacia tree in the middle of nowhere, just sand around us, and here was a water bird. The plover kept walking around in the sun, coming close to the edge of the shade, but he didn't want to come under the tree because of all the people. As we moved out from under the tree and started packing the vehicle, he came into the shade, but Al Qaeda, being the kind of guys that they were, thought it was funny to chase him back into the sun. I always found that sort of thing incredibly difficult. There's life in trees, there's life in animals, there's life in birds, everything's got a spirit and everything just wants to survive, so why make its life worse?

The plover flew off 10 metres away into the sun, and then gingerly begin making his way back to the shade, because it was so hot. This happened a few times until we drove off, the plover still calling kek-kek-kek, sitting under a tree, with no grass, no insects for it to eat, nothing.

It was going to just go kek-kek-kek until it fell over dead.

That bird was as lost as I was.

CHAPTER TWENTY-FIVE

Prey

'Bonjour, you cheese-eating surrender monkeys!' – Groundskeeper Willie, *The Simpsons*

In my mind, it felt like the cavalry had arrived. When French and Malian forces pushed Al Qaeda out of the northern cities of Timbuktu, Gao and Kidal in early 2013, the wave of jets, surveillance planes, choppers and military vehicles acted like a big broom sweeping Al Qaeda out further into the sands above the Niger River. It was like they had been knocked down the food chain by a bigger predator. Ever elusive and believers in a greater cause, the mujahideen were still a hugely dangerous force in the greater Azawad region, but the dynamic in the desert was markedly different.

The impact on us and our babysitters was that now, with the French applying the pressure and their surveillance planes visible almost every day, we moved more than before and we had to be more vigilant than ever.

To avoid the reflection giving our location away, our vehicle would be parked, bonnet-first, into a bush or tree to cover our windscreens. The vehicle would be plastered in a matte mixture of sugar, sand and water. In camp, we would cover the vehicle with a tarp, and the tarp with sand, grass and *sabaya* branches. Occasionally we would dig a rectangular hole and bury the entire car. For a long time we built our camps at the bottom of one of The Holes under a lone tree, but that tactic changed over time with us mimicking the locals and building our huts in the open on the slopes of holes.

Off the back of that initial French push, we moved camps in an anti-clockwise circle to the furthest extremes of the desert in the western side of Mali, far from the hot conflict areas in the south and the east. From 5 to 11 March 2013, Al Qaeda convened and convalesced in The Holes for six days at what we called 'International Camp'.

It was a massive gathering of many vehicles and mujahideen who had signed up to fight when AQIM took northern Mali. These were battle-hardened mujahideen, who had fought in the Battles of Konna and Timbuktu and had faced the French. Those who made it to International Camp were the survivors, the walking wounded, and the mood was understandably grim.

We could hear the French Mirage jets flying some distance away, and there were food and water shortages. The logistics required to get every-one together, feed and fuel them while on the run must have taken great coordination. This camp was basically Al Qaeda's last big powwow, a chance to work on their strategy for the next few years against the *kuffar* invaders. They knew that the French would not keep it up; they just had to outlast them. Buckle down, hide, run, wait and then attack, sucking the life force out of the alliance, creating a drain on the French taxpayer and making the war even more unpopular back in France. As per Yahia's prediction, Al Qaeda would endure and outlast the French and win in the end: the Quraan says that jihad will persist until the day of judgment.

We'd had an experience in Group Adam with a Mirage fighter jet in January 2013. Adam's group had just arrived in camp, looking dusty and completely shell-shocked; they had come from the frontline of the war, where they got blasted by Tigre attack helicopters and Mirages. One guy had pieces of splintered rock embedded in his head and elbow from when large-calibre bullets pulverised the rocks around him.

We were camping in The Black Mountains, in an area where the *wadis* flowed out of the mountains off these flat, black stones. There were a lot of acacias, and we had our vehicles under the trees. Suddenly we heard a deep, earth-shaking roar as two Mirages came screaming over the *wadis* from miles away.

Adam yelled at us to spread out and run for the trees, the idea being that they can't shoot everyone in the camp if we split up. I landed up behind a tree with a mujahid called Abu Mariam. I asked what we should do if the planes came back. Abu Mariam said if a Mirage fired a missile at us, we would probably be okay as long as it was not a direct hit, because missiles sink into the sand with a muted sound, and when they blow up they leave a small crater. If you had the luxury of a good vantage point, his advice was to watch the missile as it leaves the plane and judge which direction it's going in. If it's coming straight towards you, then run towards it and try and get past it, or run left and right, but don't run backwards. If you could get just 10 metres from the point of impact, he said, you would be fine.

If, however, the Mirage dropped a bomb, we'd be fucked, because that unleashes a massive, fiery explosion that scorches absolutely everything. His theory was, if they drop a bomb, your best chance of survival was to hide behind a tree and cover your head because the flames are just going to engulf you. He'd experienced this before and had survived by doing just that.

Of all the French weaponry, Al Qaeda feared the Tigre helicopters the most. As prisoners, we were also always very scared of seeing a helicopter, mainly because of Johan and his experience playing Xbox. He said the pilots would stay a good kilometre away because they were scared of getting taken down by RPGs. From there, they would circle the camp and just blast the crap out of us. When we asked Al Qaeda about how the choppers behaved, it turned out that the Xbox veteran was wrong. They had missiles and massive machine guns, and were relatively stealthy compared to the jets. They could cruise up a *wadi*, pop over a mountain and destroy a camp; you would hear them coming, but AK-47s had no impact on them. When they found a camp, they came in close, hovering right alongside so as to destroy everything. While we never saw the helicopters ourselves, the *makan sakhen* (hot areas) were not far away. In 2016 there was a helicopter attack just 16 kilometres away from us, in which mujahideen were killed and vehicles destroyed.

Now as I stood there, cowering with Abu Mariam behind the tree, the raw scream of the jets echoing off the walls of the *wadis*, reality felt momentarily suspended. I was taken back to air shows I attended as a kid in Johannesburg, when it seemed like the planes were roaring dragons flying around in the sky. I could feel my heart beating in my chest as the penny dropped: this was not an air show, this was not a game – this was a war, and the folks in those planes were here to kill me, not save me. Like everyone else, I was being hunted. It was a major epiphany, because up until that moment I still thought the French might somehow swoop down and snatch me up. Now I knew that a Mirage or Tigre pilot, seeing a bunch of bearded guys in local gear running around under some trees at a distance, would not think twice about pulling the trigger.

It turned out those Mirages were on their way to bomb another Al Qaeda camp about 50 kilometres away, but my realisation about the French stayed with me. In time, I grew to resent them. Not only did Al Qaeda tell me that the French had interfered with my negotiations

– this may have been propaganda, but I knew for a fact that French prisoners kidnapped around the same time as me went home long before I did – but the French presence in the north only made us change camps more frequently.

The giant square-winged *kashivas* always arrived from the south and did huge oval loops, around and around again. I used to think of them as the pirates of the sky; they flew so slowly, and materialised as if out of nowhere from behind the clouds. With all the technology on board and the hope they gave me, they were useless. I wondered if the crew were all sitting back drinking coffee; they didn't see a thing.

When we were living in London, Cath thought I was going deaf, because she would talk and I wouldn't hear her. In the desert, some-what bizarrely, I had wolf-like hearing. I would be the guy in camp who would hear everything first. Al Qaeda would come to me and say, 'Hey Lot, did you hear something?' I'd say, 'Yes, there's an aeroplane to the east, but quite far off,' or 'There's a vehicle to the south, but it's driving southwest and not coming this way.' Of course, I battled with this. Why on earth should I help these guys? They can listen for their own enemy planes. At the same time, I was trying to form a rapport, and the planes never saw us anyway. All that happened, time and time again, was that we had to pick up our stuff, leave camp in a hurry and walk 20 kilometres through the desert with five litres of water until one of the mujahid could double back, retrieve a Land Cruiser and eventually fetch us, only to make camp and have to do it all over again half a day later. My brain bubbled with anger towards the French. They were not on my team.

Perhaps the only thing Al Qaeda feared as much as a helicopter was something that was intrinsically linked to the arrival of a helicopter: *jasoos*. When it came to spies, Al Qaeda were vigilant and ruthless. While they had plenty of allies among the local populace – after all, many of them came from local families – they were not universally popular in the region. There were many other groups in the area, from rebels to smugglers (of people and drugs), and Al Qaeda, as the self-appointed Saharan policemen, had made plenty of enemies. Like in any war, loose lips sink ships, so if somebody informed the Malian army or the French Special Forces about the location of an Al Qaeda camp, it would result in a devastating loss of life for Al Qaeda. Al Qaeda could hide from French hardware, but not from the French-paid *jasoos*.

Whereas the French – armed as they were with high-tech equipment – had no first-hand knowledge of the areas they flew over, we never went into an area that was completely unknown. Regardless of where we stayed, there would always be somebody within our brigade who was from that locale. They knew that five kilometres in that direction was a well, seven kilometres to the south an area with good grazing, a friendly *shibani* over that hill who would sell us a goat, and 20 kilometres to the east was a truck route that occasionally sees some military convoys heading up to Taoudenni. While this was good for Al Qaeda's defensive strategy, it also made it very difficult for us to try to escape. If some of the mujahideen were local, the people in the area were either Al Qaeda supporters themselves or not dumb enough to turn a blind eye to an escaped white guy running through the sand.

Try as we might not to leave any signs, there were always vehicle tracks or the smell of cooking, or the occasional gunshot from hunting rabbits. We often camped in high areas and weren't allowed to have fires at night, because you could see flames from miles away and the smoke would carry. If anyone came to the vicinity of the camp unexpectedly, we were told to hide in our boogies no matter what. If the person was not immediately recognised by our local mujahideen, they could quite easily be *jasoos*.

There is an established etiquette in the desert when it comes to greeting strangers. There is an understanding within Arabic culture, especially in the desert, that everyone is having a tough time just trying to get by, so you are obliged to greet them. If we spotted someone, generally riding a camel, two mujahideen would head off, greet the guy, sit down and make tea.

A little cooker called a *virna* would come out, loaded with a few chunks of *harmoom* (charcoal), then some dry grass, lit with a match and placed in the path of the Saharan winds. When the charcoal began to glow like a smelter, they would make Arabic tea (*chai*) served with sugar (*sukr*) in a shot-sized glass teacup.

Beyond tea, Muhammad (PBUH) said Muslims must greet everybody by being friendly and offering food. Quite often, if someone approached our camp, it was just because he was hungry. Al Qaeda would go to the *mauna*, open up a 50-kilogram bag of rice and fill up a plastic bag for him.

Of course, over and above being good Muslims and offering charity, Al Qaeda weren't there for the tea party. What they wanted was to find out who the guy was. Sitting in our boogies, we could often hear the questions. If the guy did not know any locals or was not familiar with the area, or did not know any of the mujahideen's brothers, friends or family members, we would change camps immediately.

Osama Bin Laden made a *fatwa* (declaration) against beheading people on camera, but AQIM still had no problem executing *jasoos*. If they caught a spy, they would only kill him once he admitted that he was a spy. They would intimidate the guy to such a point that eventually he confessed so as not to spend an eternity in hell. Having confessed, he would get a chance to repent and then he would be executed. I saw the videos. They would make a public thing of it, get dressed in their full camo outfits, go into the village market and perform a public execution. The guy had to kneel down with a bunch of mujahideen behind him. They would declare his crime, recite the relevant parts of the Quraan and basically tell the entire market that if anybody is caught being a *jasoos*, this is the punishment. Then they would either shoot him in the back of the head or cut his head off and march it around the market.

Harsh, but necessary in their view. If you are hiding under a tree in a country the size of France, the chances of *kashivas* actually finding you were incredibly low. But if a goat herder pointed out where you were in exchange for a reward, it was a different story altogether. A case in point: shortly after 'International Camp', a large group of mujahideen were hit in a helicopter attack at a well. Adam the baby-faced kidnapper, Ghanda Hari (Martin's murderer), Abu Osama the Afghan war vet, Ghabayb, Dawud – some of their finest fighters – all died. In the privacy of our boogies, we prisoners smiled. It was a devastating loss for Al Qaeda, because they were already wobbling after the battles in the south. You could really feel how that helicopter attack affected the morale of the men who remained.

How it came about, whether through surveillance or informants, I am not entirely sure. But there certainly were some other very opportune, very accurate helicopter attacks on very prominent Al Qaeda members well off the beaten track, and these were definitely not a result of surveillance.

CHAPTER TWENTY-SIX

Scavengers, Science & Suicide Bombers

'Like sands through the hourglass, so are the days of our lives'
– Macdonald Carey, *Days of Our Lives*

In the modern world we are spoilt for choice. From Netflix to radio, podcasts and books, we are constantly offered distraction, much of it vapid entertainment that crushes our brains. When you are tired of staring at the TV screen (while simultaneously second-screening on your phone), you can always turn to your friends and family and have a conversation. You have options. In the desert, which feels like a different age altogether, we had none of that. And boy, were we bored. At one stage I even tried counting sand, just for something to do.

The only form of entertainment were Al Qaeda and, later, ISIS videos of jihad, beheadings and other violence that the mujahideen would watch on their phones. Everyone seemed to have a Samsung; iPhones were not popular, because there was a story about the iPhone having a secret camera that took photos of a Mauritanian man's naked wife and shared them on the internet.

Other than the occasional jihad movie, being in the Sahara was like going back in time 2,000 years. Not only were the animals not scared of us, but we had to figure everything out from scratch. There was no way to Google an answer or pop off to the DIY store down the road; we had to become self-sufficient. To do that, we needed tools, and that meant scavenging.

Some of the things we found were properly ancient, others more recent human detritus. There were fossilised mussels, plants and sea snails from the ancient oceans that used to cover the Sahara. We came across strange melted sand called fulgurite in the shape of straw, where lightning hit the sand. There were ancient bits of broken pots, grinding stones, beads, stone flints, rusted arrowheads, ostrich egg shells and

animal horns. Sometimes we would come across old vehicles abandoned by people trying to cross the Sahara to get to Europe.

I used to lament that the desert is the world's biggest rubbish dump.
While each emir would designate a specific area in the camp as the
poubelle (dustbin), there was so much crap lying around, it boggled
my mind that the surveillance planes never saw us. The sardine cans
alone must have looked like a solar farm reflecting out of the sand.

Rubbish was opportunity for us prisoners. Think about life in the
modern world, how much stuff you have. Entire rooms filled with
clutter, garages heaving with the extraneous flotsam of a life spent
accumulating. In the desert, we literally had nothing except for the
clothes Al Qaeda gave us, so we had to scavenge everything. A sardine can lid? That's a makeshift knife. Empty milk cartons? Paper
for writing or drawing on. Fibres from a sack, the hem of your
clothing, a discarded piece of rope or the drawstring stitching from
a sugar sack? That's thread for dental floss or sewing any number
of things, from backpacks to blankets and clothes. My two most
prized possessions were my needle and a pair of scissors with a
half-melted handle; but razorblades, inner tubes for making ropies
(to tie down the roofs of boogies) or pieces of tarpaulin for sun-
proofing were all treasures.

Milk cartons were especially valuable to me. Breakfast was always
made by Al Qaeda, brought to us in the mornings along with a bowl of
milk. It was powdered milk, mostly from Argentina or Canada, and it
would come in small carton boxes. We used to collect the cartons, tear
the sides and bottoms, and that was writing paper. I ended up keeping
a whole stack of these things, tied together with a rubber ropey cut
from an inner tube, like a giant deck of cards. These also provided
reading material – I had nothing else other than my French dictionary.
This was how I learned Arabic, improved my French and picked up a
smattering of the other languages in camp.

Whatever packaging came into the kitchen, I would hang on to it, so
I could learn new words. Quite often the inner pamphlets, doses and
listed ingredients had English and French or Arabic side by side. The
problem was that these pamphlets were written in a dialect of Arabic,
while our captors mostly spoke Hassaniya.

Scraping together whatever we could to use as tools or entertainment, we tried to keep busy with projects. I made backpacks, fixed
radios, and created a rudimentary sprinkler system in my boogie that

would drip water on my face in the heat of the day. One of my big hobbies was to make self-cooling water bottles, and I became known for having the coldest water in the desert. This was something that worked for me and against me, because guys would always come and ask me if they could drink my water. As a good Muslim this was fine, but the problem were the dicks who would come and drink my entire water bottle. All my cold water, which took an entire day to cool, gone.

To make it cold, you use your scarf as an initial layer around the water bottle. Then you take some old clothing or a hessian sack, which is even better, and wrap it again. Come Ramadan, everybody wants cold water, because hot water just does not quench a thirst. So, you prepare your water the night before and keep it in the shade all day. Being able to bring out a cold bottle of water when you broke the fast in the evening was a celebration.

In fact, Al Qaeda joked that I was 'Boutique Lot' because they would come to me to either borrow my things, which they would inevitably break, or to get me to fix something they had already broken. I built a torch from rubbish discarded by Al Qaeda. It was a short torch, because they're normally made for two batteries, and it had an on/off switch. It was handy in my boogie when I got stung by a scorpion and needed to find the little bastard.

If Al Qaeda broke a GPS or shortwave radio, they would bring them to me. I would get them to open up a Kalashnikov bullet. I put the head of the bullet in the fire to melt down the lead. I'd heat my scissors in the fire, open up the device, find the loose connection and then do some soldering using the scissors and the bullet lead.

I also made bags for my tools, my milk carton cards, letters from my family and any other belongings I had, ready to rumble if the planes came over and we had to abandon camp. By stitching together 50-kilogram sugar sacks with flour sacks, I made a five by five metre patchwork quilt as a way of creating shade. The problem was that the sun would still go through it, and even indirect sun is a huge problem in the desert. To get around that, I would collect Al Qaeda's discarded clothing and stitch them in from the four corners of the quilt. It weighed a ton, but I could fold it up and take it with me from camp to camp, throw it over my boogie, cover it with grass and create some good shade.

Keeping order in the camp could be a challenge. When we woke up one morning, there was a turd, a large, fresh human one, 10 metres in front of the small tree we were sleeping under.

This was a clear sign of laziness or disrespect. We had converted eight months earlier, and while we were not about to march down to high command, we wanted to nip this kind of behaviour in the bud. There were defined toilet areas near each camp. Somebody literally did not give a shit about us.

Lesa jayed, lesa jayed. 'Not good, not good.' That was Abu Laith's response when we told him. As deputy emir of Group Abdel Kahar, he called a meeting and warned the brigade that this was not on. The culprit was not expected to step forward – in Islam it is not good to humiliate someone. So, like Sherlock Holmes and Dr Watson – but with less friendly repartee – Sjaak and I started working on the crime. We looked at the tracks, and narrowed down the possible suspects based on tread and shoe size until there was only one person it could possibly be: Solomon!

Solomon was a Malian from down south, and not altogether there at the best of times. A few months later, he forgot to put the safety on his AK-47 and almost shot a hole through his foot while he was walking. (As prisoners we found that hilarious, because it was not as though we could get revenge on him for the deposit he left on our doorstep.)

When we told Abu Laith that it was Solomon, he did his job and had a word with the man, but you could almost see the eye roll. Abu Laith was a simple, scrawny guy from Western Sahara who had strong opinions about the militant groups there fighting the Moroccans. He was a very organised person, and a control freak. He did not really know how to manage or delegate, so he would take on all the work himself. Here he was, trying to run an orderly camp in service to Allah, and some Bambara country bumpkin from the south craps on his well-run operation. This was not what he signed up for.

A few months later, Abu Laith blew himself up. On the day it happened, I heard the explosion – a deep rumbling boom that came through the soil. I asked a mujahid if he also heard it, and he had. A few months later, that same mujahid returned to our camp during a group change. He asked me if I remembered that day with the explosion, and told me that Abu Laith had done an operation northeast of Timbuktu at a temporary MINUSMA (United Nations Multidimensional Integrated Stabilisation Mission in Mali) army base. Later, the mujahideen showed us a video, which revealed that our old deputy emir was behind it.

In Azawad, everybody knows if a beige Land Cruiser drives towards your camp and the driver is handling it like a maniac, it's probably a suicide mission – so get the hell out of there. The video opens with Abu Laith saying his last words in the cab of the car. Behind him in the back of the Land Cruiser were four 200-litre drums filled with explosives. Final *salaams* done, the vehicle careened off into the distance, twisting and turning, towards a gathering of trucks and tents. Finally there was a massive explosion, and we saw what looked like bodies and car parts flying through the air amid the smoke and dust. It was a successful mission by Al Qaeda's standards. An old broken Land Cruiser and €100 of explosives for a number of helicopters, trucks and many human casualties. I found it strangely sad that Abu Laith blew himself up.

Al Qaeda insisted that the city was 200 kilometres away, but I struggled to reconcile the fact that we were hearing and feeling an explosion from that distance. I pondered the science behind it. It was like those impossible maths questions you would get at school: if a suicide bomber is travelling at 70 km/h with 800 *l* of explosives in his one-ton Land Cruiser on a windless day, will the sound of his detonation carry 200 kilometres?

When it came to storms, we would see lightning and count until we actually heard the thunder. The highest count we got to was 52 seconds, which worked out to around 20 kilometres if we were basing our calculation off the speed of sound, which is 360 metres per second. Then there was the speed of light, which is basically instant. This stuff was important to us, because a 20-second count would mean the storm was much closer and all hell was about to break loose. Planning in advance was important; the alternative was to sit and bear it.

Abu Laith's suicide bombing led to a bunch of theories about how we could hear a bang from 200 kilometres away, but not thunder from more than 20 kilometres way. Maybe this bang was the movement of sound waves through the ground, like a ripple effect through the sand. We spent hours trying to figure it out.

Johan created a star map to work out angles between stars. It was a highly scientific thing involving pins, cardboard and the lining up of multiple points. We worked on it for months – it was one of the few times we collaborated and got along. We used to sit up at night, calculating angles. I could see Al Qaeda thought we were up to no good. In the beginning Johan didn't want them to know what he was doing, but eventually he decided to take the poison out of his project by simply telling everyone what he was up to.

The problem was not many mujahideen understood what he was

talking about. Johan was a very good mathematician, so not only was this higher-grade stuff, but with Al Qaeda we were dealing with a bunch of guys who believed that the world is flat. I once told them that the moon was not a physical lantern, but a ball of sand and rock lit up by the sun, which was how we saw it. I then asked them how they thought the moon waxed and waned; they said that Allah physically added or took away sand every day to make it bigger or smaller. We were coming at each other from different worlds.

Of course, so were Johan and I. Once he got what he wanted from me, Johan told me, 'The next part of this project does not require two people.'

CHAPTER TWENTY-SEVEN

Prison Break

'The only way to escape the abyss is to look at it, gauge it, sound it out and descend into it' – Cesare Pavese

'RED ROVER RED ROVER, SEND IBRAHIM OVER.'

Of all the things I would land up doing with my life, playing Red Rover and soccer with a bunch of Al Qaeda mujahideen in a *wadi* in northeastern Mali was never on my radar. Yet here we were, trying to explain the nuances of the offside rule. They were useless at soccer; only the Bambara from the south knew how to play; the Tuareg and Arabs from the desert just liked kicking the ball as far away as they could until it fell apart on thorn trees. Red Rover was more their style, because of the running and wrestling involved.

Muhammad (PBUH) used to wrestle. It was reported that he was very good at it and never lost. Dawud, the emir of that group, did not trust the prisoners and the guards engaging in such frivolous carefree behaviour, and he cancelled our games pretty much immediately. I wasn't too upset about this, because while I liked the social engagement, the games were a little too risky for my dodgy back.

Years ago, back in Johannesburg, I hurt my back playing in a jumping castle with a friend's kids. One of them, a five-year-old called Max, was wearing a Velcro suit. I'd pick Max up and throw him at the wall of the jumping castle and he'd stick like Spider-Man; then he'd peel off and I'd catch him, and we'd do it again. On one of the throws, I stepped backwards, twisted awkwardly, and something went in my lower back. I've never in my life experienced such pain. I limped my way back to our car, with massive spasms shooting through my body, and spent a week in bed.

It happened again in London. I was having a French-baguette sword fight with a girl at a house party, and at one stage I thought I'd go in for close attack and try to hoist her over my shoulder. It was an error. The doctor gave me options: block the pain with an epidural, have an operation, or manage the pain with exercise.

I didn't like the idea of locking in the problem with screws, so I opted for exercise. That's what I've done ever since, which is why exercise was a big thing for me in the desert. The idea of my back going out was a massive psychological issue. I didn't think Al Qaeda would put a bullet in me for slowing them down, something that supposedly happened to one of the French hostages who was sick; I simply could not fathom the idea of travelling with Al Qaeda in such intense pain.

In the early days, we created a track in our area. We walked this track from breakfast till dinner, wrapped in scarves to protect us from the sun and from sandstorms. The repetition of walking in a set pattern was a great way to distract yourself from the reality of being captive, so we filled our days with walking in circles.

Once we converted, our exercise routine metamorphosed into something far greater. All movement was classified as exercise, and this became more important after a few years, once my body started to atrophy and I lost both strength and size. Standing was better than sitting, walking was better than standing, and running was better than walking. It also became custom after the 4pm prayer to leave the hut and begin moving around; any time before this was too hot in summer. All exercise was done barefoot, and I would often end up with blisters under my feet. Early mornings were an issue; the sand was icy-cold and it felt like walking on broken glass. In winter we could exercise almost any time of the day, but I was still very anxious about sun exposure.

If Al Qaeda felt we were getting too strong, and potentially planning an escape, exercise would be cancelled. Al Qaeda did very little exercise, so it was a fine balance to get the benefit of exercise without Al Qaeda becoming suspicious. Johan seemed more interested in sport than Islam.

Since he found it easy to learn the Quraan off by heart, Al Qaeda felt Johan should learn the entire book. They would remind him that it is better to focus on the Quraan and learn Allah's word, as every word you read gives you points for the day of judgment.

Shortly after conversion, I realised that exercise was a marathon and not a sprint. I got into a routine of doing regular push-ups and sit-ups – although I hated sit-ups because they hurt my lower back. Each time I went to the ablution, I would drop down and do 20 push-ups before heading back. Using sacking as thread and Al Qaeda's old clothing, I created sandbag weights, stitching up one end of the arms and legs to make a sack. My tin mug held exactly one kilogram of sand. (I figured that out by making a balance inside my hut, a cup of sand on one end and two 500-gram packets of spaghetti on the other end. It balanced out perfectly.) I used this measure to make three-kilogram, five-kilogram, 10-kilogram, 15-kilogram and 20-kilogram sandbags. Al Qaeda was not keen for too much strength work, so I told them the sandbags were for placing on top of my hut during a sandstorm to keep it from blowing away.

Johan and I found that we only really got along during exercise, probably because we had a common goal and couldn't speak when we were out of breath. We created a three-day cardio routine: one day we ran for one hour, the second day we did sprint training on a figure-eight track, and the third day we would do a kind of boot camp.

At night I would take my five-kilogram sandbags and create a 10-metre track behind my hut, on the dark side in the shadow, away from where Al Qaeda sat around the fire drinking Arabic tea. I would walk up and down my track until dinnertime, then again up until prayer time and bed. I would imagine myself swimming at Ellis Park, rolling my arms and walking out an individual medley, butterfly, backstroke, breaststroke, crawl. This gave me exercises as well as a mental holiday. I used this to remember myself as a teenager, when life made sense; to remember what it felt like to be confident and carefree, and to have heaps of friends around you, laughing and joking. I used this time to remodel myself back to the days when I felt I knew who I was.

As Johan's and my relationship was tumultuous, our exercise routine was on again, off again. Towards the end of our time in the desert it was off, because we openly loathed each other.

Using acacia branches that I incorporated into my hut design, I made my structure wide enough to do push-ups and sit-ups inside, with sidewalls that lifted for ventilation. I also used my two sturdy branches for my doorframe. Those branches came up to shoulder height and would connect to my hut three-quarters of the way up the branch. At night I would dig a small hole between the branches in my doorway, place a sturdy branch across the top of my doorpost, and with bent knees do pull-ups in my doorway. I could also use my sturdy doorframe as a bench-press stand. I was quite proud of my mobile gym.

My grandfather was a POW during World War II in Italy. I thought of him often in the desert. He escaped twice and hid out in the Alps, where he and some other soldiers lived in a cave through the winter.

They would go down at night among the farms, where some of the Italians gave them food, but things got really bad. He had horrible stories about having to catch and eat people's dogs. They couldn't make fires up in the mountains and it was cold; sometimes the snow was literally chest-deep and they had very basic gear.

I had huge respect for him because he escaped. I had no idea how, but the terrain they were in was vastly different from where we were. He was also a soldier who knew how to use a gun and had been trained for combat. Sjaak, Johan and I discussed escape all the time, but it always felt like an impossibility. Johan and I were in our late 30s/early 40s, Sjaak was in his 50s. Al Qaeda was a bunch of teens and guys in their early 20s who wrestled and did flick-flacks and ninja kicks for shits and giggles; in comparison we were old and malnourished.

That didn't stop us discussing all the possible ways we could escape. One option was to overpower the mujahideen, take a vehicle and head south. That sounds simple enough in principle, yet for us there was so much at stake and so many variables. Even if I got my hands on a gun, I would not necessarily know what to with it. I'd be the old guy walking around going, 'Hang on hang on, don't shoot me, my gun has jammed, just give me a moment.'

If we overpowered them, we would have to kill all of them, because just tying them up would not last for long. Assuming we managed to get hold of a few guns, and assuming none of us died in that process, were we capable of shooting all 20 of our guards, from the teens to the battle-hardened veterans? If we did kill them, would all that gun-fire not alert the mujahideen at other camps? Would at least one of them not manage to get away and alert a nearby camp? If we did not kill them, they would definitely go for help. If we damaged the other vehicles so they could not drive, they would still know how to find the closest local with a cellphone or satellite phone to alert others in the area. At best, we might get 100 kilometres away.

One idea I had was to steal a grenade and drop it into the hut, then go in afterwards with an AK-47 to sort out any survivors. But what if the grenade didn't detonate? A banker, a mechanic and an IT guy would not stand a chance against them. Johan had done his military service in Sweden, but he opted to be a fireman, so it was not as though he knew what he was doing, no matter how many hours of Xbox he had under his belt.

While my read of the desert told me escape was not an option, just talking about it made me feel like I was free. I would lie on my back, watching the clouds roll by, and fantasise about running out of the desert like in Super Mario Bros, hopping from cloud to cloud, only dropping down once I was far from Al Qaeda.

The reality was that it was impossible. The longer we stayed with Al Qaeda, the more we realised there were often other camps in relatively close proximity to us, so there was a high probability that if we escaped we would wander off in the direction of another Al Qaeda camp.

Even if you got out of camp, if you were on foot you would leave tracks. Everything in the desert leaves tracks. To track a snake or a mouse or a camel or a human was easy, you just follow the tracks through the sand. Your only chance would be if a sandstorm hit at just the right time.

Water was a major consideration. Without it, you would not last a day. To walk the 400–500 kilometres we would need to make it to a settlement, or even the 100 kilometres it might take to get to a vehicle route, we would need lots of water. There is only so much you can carry as one person, plus the more you carry the more you get weighed down as you plod through the thick sand under the blazing sun. If you walk at night, you run the risk of losing your bearings, stepping on snakes (a common threat in camps) or getting more lost.

For a logical, mathematical guy, Johan had some bizarre ideas of what he was capable of. He swore he would be able to cover 100 kilometres per night. Not even a camel could do that. When you're born into an urban life, you know how to turn on a tap, you know how connect to WiFi, you know how to read and write, but do you actually know what the human body is capable of? Do you know how far you can walk in the desert, and with how much water, before you physically fall over and begin dreaming about vultures circling? These are the things that we don't know.

I might have been ever so slightly better prepared than Johan and Sjaak, because of growing up on the farm and being in nature in South Africa, but even I had no idea. I was not a mathematician, but I had worked in risk and I knew how to evaluate the odds. No matter if you were a Navy SEAL or a ninja, a marathon runner or strong man, what I knew for sure was that if you wandered off into the desert you would die.

The night Johan escaped was a normal evening towards the end of winter, in February 2013, so it was still quite cold. We all went off to our various places to sleep. We were quite far from each other, up

to 30 metres apart, which is exactly how Johan had this opportunity –
because he put himself right on the edge of the camp.

The next morning I woke up, and I heard the clap, clap, clap of whoever
was in the kitchen making bread. (The bread was baked in sand; Al Qaeda
would dig it out and beat it with their hand or scarf to remove the sand.)
I walked over to where the guys were bringing out their blankets. We sat
down, somebody started making the tea. We broke bread, said 'bismillah',
and started eating. The sun was up and it was all very comfortable.

Someone asked, 'Where is Johan?'

I said that I did not know and looked towards where he'd been sleeping. I had been trying for some time to emphasise to Al Qaeda that we
were not a 'we'. That I was not responsible for Johan, that we didn't
speak for each other.

One guy got up and went to where Johan was sleeping. He returned
two minutes later and said Johan wasn't there. By now, a slight urgency
had crept into the scene. Al Qaeda asked the group if anybody had seen
him that morning. Sjaak looked at me, I looked at him. There was a
wry smile on our faces. We were both thinking, *Shit, maybe he's done it!*

Johan had stuffed a whole bunch of things under his blanket to make
it appear that he was there, and left a note on top. Johan's plan was
to write a letter to them saying, 'Dear brothers, I feel that as a Muslim
I will have a bigger impact going back home to my family in Sweden
(to spread the word of Islam). I know you may not be happy with my
actions but this is something that I feel I must do.' It was a fail-safe in
case the escape didn't work. A way of saying, 'my intentions were pure'.
But in the dark he couldn't see which piece of paper he pulled out of his
sack; instead of leaving his letter on his bed, he took it with him and left
behind some random Swedish notes by mistake. Johan's a perfectionist,
so I can only imagine how much he beat himself up over this.

With emir Adam clearly rattled, we packed up and moved camp,
driving straight off into the sand for about 45 minutes. We arrived at
another camp and immediately were treated like criminals again. We
were pulled off the car and told not to move.

This one big Moroccan guy kept saying, 'Lot was sitting with Johan
yesterday, Lot knew this was happening.'

I defended myself saying, 'Don't look at me. I was not involved. We
were learning French behind the vehicle'

This is what really irritated me; while I wanted nothing to do with
Johan, I still got dragged into his stupidity.

As it was, Johan did not get far. A hunting party, led by Abu Laith and staffed by locals who knew the area and a few guys with tracking skills, went out in a Land Cruiser; about three hours later they came back with Johan. With the French advancing north, his plan was to walk south at night as far as possible, hoping to get closer to the area that the French were active in, and then set fire to a tree to attract a surveillance aeroplane. He had tried to walk on the black stones as much as possible, but eventually these small islands of stones would end and he would have to walk in sand again. All Al Qaeda had to do was drive around the stones until they picked up his footsteps. Al Qaeda found him sleeping under a tree about 30 kilometres away at around lunchtime. They drank all his water and all the milk he had stolen, loaded him up into the vehicle and drove him back to the new camp. He bragged to us that had walked 50 kilometres and was just getting warmed up, and if he'd had just had a little more time he would have been away.

His escape attempt would have consequences. In the short term, it meant that our exercise privileges were curtailed and many of our possessions were taken away, like our water and flip-flops at night. Being punished for Johan's reckless and futile move drove me nuts. It was a major tactical error on his part, because by trying to escape after he converted to Islam, he not only betrayed their trust in him as a sincere convert, he reaffirmed his brazen disregard for them and their faith. In their eyes, he became *khateer* (dangerous) and not to be trusted. After some time, our privileges like exercise were reinstated, but he had lost their trust forever.

Once, driving in far north in thick orange sand dunes, we came upon a grave made from boulders. This truly was the middle of nowhere. We looked at this thing and it felt like we were lost in time – it could have been a week old or 5,000 years old. Heaven only knows where the guy who did the burial found the boulders. In my mind, I imagined guys on camels on this ancient salt route going up to Morocco. One of them dies. His companion digs a hole, buries him and then walks a huge distance to find stones. If you died there, you would be forgotten by absolutely everybody, save for the person who buried you. It would almost be like you never existed.

That's how I felt about trying to escape into the Sahara. If you were lucky, you would be caught. If you were not, you would die, your location unknown by anyone who cared about you. You would spend eternity alone, lost in the sands.

CHAPTER TWENTY-EIGHT

Finished

As told by Cath McGown

'If you don't have answers to your problems after a four-hour run, you ain't getting them' – Christopher McDougall, *Born to Run*

During the time Steve was away, I met someone else. It's not something I planned or something I am proud of, but if that period taught me anything it's that a lot of things in life do not go according to plan, no matter what your intentions.

When we get married, we all have these romantic ideals of 'until death do us part', but Steve and I were not parted by death. Nor was it something tangible like a prison sentence, with a beginning and an end. It was like my husband got swallowed up by the Sahara. Even though we got occasional Proof of Life videos, negotiations seemed forever stalled or set back. Our hopes were raised and let down time and time again. The reality was that we never knew if Steve was coming back, which somehow almost seemed worse than death. Only once you've been in a situation as bizarre as having your loved one taken away like Steve was, for so long, is it possible to understand what this was like.

I met Nick in 2014, the year I hit rock bottom. That June I ran my first Comrades marathon and I finished strong. I've always been a runner. Steve and I actually ran the Berlin marathon together in 2007, the year we got married. I beat him by a good half hour. After he was taken I threw myself into my fitness, initially because I wanted to get strong, and then because it became both a distraction and a release. When I was running I was happy. At the same time, I wanted to push myself to the absolute limits of pain, so I could feel a bit of what Steve was going through. I guess that's what made me successful as a runner at the time – I could push through pain barriers.

In September 2013 I entered the Otter Trail run, and much to everybody's surprise, mine included, I finished third. It was an extra-special run for me because the route was marked with yellow ribbons, a symbol for the release of hostages or the safe return of troops from war. I always ran with a yellow ribbon on my CamelBak, which I could often see blowing in the wind when it unravelled. When I told the Otter organisers about the ribbons, they arranged for two trees in the marquee to be tied with massive yellow ribbons, which they later handed to me when I collected my award. We tied those ribbons around two trees in Steve's folks' driveway.

Buoyed by that run, my New Year's goal was to run the Comrades Marathon. Most people take a few years to train to the level they need to run the Comrades. I decided six months before the race that I was going to do it, even though I'd not done enough training. Running the Comrades was an amazing experience. I wore a yellow ribbon for Steve and on the day, Olympic legend Zola Budd was running wearing a yellow ribbon for Pierre Korkie, the South African hostage held by Al Qaeda in Yemen. Most people assumed my ribbon was also for Pierre, because we still couldn't publicise our cause. Tragically, six months later, as Pierre was about to be released thanks to the work of Gift of the Givers, he was executed during a botched raid by American forces.

That run was probably one of the best days of my life. I ran well, and the crowd support was amazing. My mom, my stepdad and my sister were there at the end, with my running club. The following day I felt good. I actually wasn't even that stiff. Then two weeks later I caught flu, and the depression set in in a big way. I could not shake the fatigue that took hold of me. All I wanted to do was sleep. I got so frustrated with life. This was the lowest I had ever been.

That July, we were cycling the Freedom Ride for Mandela Day. As usual I had my CamelBak with my yellow ribbon, but while Steve was always in my mind, I decided that that ride had to be for me. It was about setting myself free. I had reached a point of desperation where I needed to move on. It did not mean I did not love Steve – far from it. It was just that I had to live my own life and have goals for myself, because I had come to accept that Steve might never come back.

Before I did that ride, I took my wedding ring off and I put it away with Steve's passport in a little go-bag I always had packed with essentials like a change of clothes and toothpaste, just in case I got called to go to the airport if Steve was released. I did the ride in the morning with a friend, and that afternoon I invited Steve's dad and mom around for tea. My mom also joined us. That's when I told Magoo and

Bev what was going on for me. I said, 'I just can't continue this journey any more. It's too much, I need to move on with my life.'

Steve's mom completely understood. She actually said she expected me to say that to them that day. As a wife, she knew what I was dealing with. I think it was harder for Steve's dad. He said, 'We love you,' and gave me a big hug. I have no doubt he was being sincere, but he was disappointed and sad for his son. Through this whole thing, Bev and Magoo were amazing, the best parents-in-law I could have ever hoped for.

I also told them I couldn't carry on going to all the meetings, to be a part of all the dead ends and other efforts to try to get Steve back. Those meetings took so much time and emotional energy. I would have this expectation that something *must* have happened, that there *must* be some movement of some sort between this faction of Al Qaeda and that leader that they wanted to swap for these prisoners; and *if* Sweden came on board and *if* Holland played along and *if* France agreed to these terms and *if* the UK did their bit, then maybe, *if* the South African government were accurate in their assessment, just maybe, we *might* have a chance of getting Steve back. For years I would sit there taking notes, writing everything down as I always do, but eventually I could not do it any more. There was just no news. We would just be sitting there, having tea, going through the motions, and the government officials would ask us, 'How are you doing?'

The thing is, even though I told Magoo and Bev that I wanted to stop attending all the meetings, I still continued to go. There was no way I could not. Even though I was trying to take a path of self-care to look after my own sanity and health, there was a part of me that still couldn't step back.

The last thing I said at that meeting with Bev and Magoo was that I wanted a divorce. I actually said the words. Like saying I wanted to step away from the meetings, what I said and what I did were different, because I never followed through with it. In terms of a legal precedent, I could get our marriage annulled on the grounds of abandonment or 'substituted service' or some other legal term for when a spouse disappears. One of the wives of the 'Baghdad Four', a group of South African security contractors who were abducted in Iraq in 2006 never to be seen again, got an annulment this way. Steve was a member of the 'Timbuktu Three'. We were still getting sent the occasional Proof of Life video, so while it seemed like I would have to take a similar path, our situation was a bit more complicated. Steve was not dead; he was gone.

I worried what people would think about me wanting a divorce, but almost everyone supported me and I did not feel judged. The first couple I chose to share the news with was my pastor, Leigh, and his wife, Irene, who had stood by me since the beginning. Leigh understood; he had lost a wife in a car accident when he was young, so he knew loss. Irene implored me to spend time reading the Bible. She didn't realise how bad things were – I could no longer read. My brain could not concentrate or comprehend what was on a page. I felt literally useless. I was of no use to anyone.

It got so bad I couldn't work. I'd been working at the Talk Shop, a specialised preschool for children with speech and language difficulties. Barbara, who headed up the preschool, had lost her husband and daughter in a car accident. She came to my rescue, arranging for someone to take over my caseload until I was up and running again.

That August, I started spending more time with Nick, who was in my running group. In my mind, he wasn't my boyfriend. I was still Steve's wife. Nick was just a guy that I liked hanging out with. In retrospect, he was several steps ahead of me about what our relationship was, and I went along with it.

Word soon got out to Steve's mom that I was seeing someone, and of course it broke my heart that they heard before I could speak to them about it. Steve's parents handled the news very well, but I could see it was hard for them.

One of the biggest goals for Steve and I coming home to South Africa was to start a family. I needed to think long and hard about whether I would ever bear a child. I had to ask myself if it was still on the cards for Steve and me as husband and wife. Did his abduction mean both our futures changed? Would we have children together? Would we both be childless? Would we be stepparents to another partner's children?

Years had now passed with no end date in sight for when Steve would be home, and I had put off going to see the gynaecologist since my return. I didn't want to face up to the dreaded reality that I was not getting any younger. I was very aware that my fertile years were behind me, but there were lots of stories of women falling pregnant after 40. I assumed I would be one of those. Working in the paediatric therapy world, I was also exposed to many children with a range of special needs. I was full of admiration for their parents' stamina and dedication.

Two years earlier, a friend of my mother's suggested I consider freezing my eggs. I dismissed the thought immediately – I even deleted the email with the details. In mid-2015, I decided to explore my options and booked an appointment at Medfem Fertility Clinic.

I went to the appointment on my own. The waiting room was very quiet, which made me feel even more alone. Steve should have been there with me. I filled in the standard forms. On the first page was a line for 'husband/partner'. I just couldn't write Steve's name down. A wave of anger welled up inside me again. *I wouldn't be here if it wasn't for your African adventure!*

In defiance, I left it blank.

When Dr van Schowenberg asked what he could do for me that day, I burst into floods of tears. I couldn't talk. I just managed, 'Stephen McGown, the South African hostage, was my husband.'

It turned out he also attended Rosebank union church. He said, 'I know who you are. You are doing the right thing. Let me talk you though the process.' He was so kind and gentle, and I was so relieved. I didn't need to talk. He sent me downstairs for blood tests and told me to call in for the results in a few days.

When I did I was nervous, but Hanlie, the nurse, was gentle. Among all the statistics I heard 'normal', but then 'below average' I felt a stabbing feeling in my throat. I asked if the results could improve in any way. She said that my thyroid was easy to treat, but my egg reserve number could not be treated. Diet could help. Once again, I felt my life was out of my control. Then that quiet voice from above came to reassure me. *Everything is going to be okay.*

I changed my diet to include less sugar and caffeine. I was advised to reduce my exercise. Until this point, I had been pushing myself to keep up with my running friends, but I was depleted. At least I could control this. This got me feeling a lot better too.

When I went back to see Dr van Schowenberg in the new year, he commented on how well I looked. I was emotionally and physically ready to have my eggs harvested. I had saved up, so I was financially prepared too. Steve's parents kindly offered to help fund the process, but I declined. These eggs were mine for now. Steve's contribution could come later. My mom came with me for the procedure. The doctor was pleased with the outcome. I had nine eggs. This was not a lot, but it was enough, and more than he expected. My nine little eggs were frozen and stored. Bev said she would wave hello to my stored eggs every time she went to Sandton Clinic, which became a frequent trip for her as the years went by. My mom and I would do the same when I went to visit her in hospital, wondering what would happen to them.

Like everyone else, they were in the dark, waiting.

Meanwhile, from about August 2014 till the first half of 2017, Nick was in my life. We broke up a few times, but I kept on going back to him. He was a good guy. I couldn't fault him in any way. He was just not Steve. My counsellor said he and I developed a co-dependent relationship.

I had been in a very dark space on my own, anxious, depressed and suicidal, so being with someone created a routine and gave me support. At the same time, I found myself craving alone time and started pushing Nick away more often. He found this hard, but always respected my needs.

Things started to get really bad in May of 2017, after Steve's mom died. Nick wanted more than I could give; all I wanted was more and more space.

My heart was always with Steve; losing Bev just reinforced that. It brought me closer to the McGown family again. I spent more and more time at Steve's dad's place.

When Johan was released a month later, it threw me off completely. I took a week off from work, stayed in my flat printing out emails and collating photographs, preparing for Steve to come home.

The problem was, there was still no guarantee that he was coming home.

It all went quiet again.

CHAPTER TWENTY-NINE

Oasis of the Mind

*'Bad luck ... It's got to land on somebody. It was my turn, that's all.
I was in the path of the tornado. I just didn't expect the storm would
last as long as it has'* – Andy Dufresne, *The Shawshank Redemption*

If you worked for the CIA or the NSA's eye-in-the-sky satellite divisions
circa 2016, and you happened to be zooming in on a small brigade
of what you thought might be AQIM mujahideen camped in the far
northwestern reaches of Mali, there's a good chance you saw a man
with long hair and a ginger tinge to his beard halfway up a sand dune,
arms open, trying to embrace a massive thunderstorm whipping in
from the forests of West Africa.

That was me. Music is *haram,* but internally I was singing, my heart
was dancing and my mind was surfing the wind, free. There were two
songs in my mental jukebox. Somewhat predictably, considering I was
standing in the rains in Africa, one was Toto's 'Africa', while the other
was 'Break My Stride' by Matthew Wilder.

These thunderstorms were so enormous and so much greater than
I was that it felt exhilarating to be alive, so small and insignificant in
the face of Earth's power. At that stage I was about 80% through my
self-imposed rehab. Standing in a thunderstorm, just so I could feel
something, anything, was a legitimate part of my process.

I realised early on in the desert that I had an indefinite prison sentence. I decided that if Al Qaeda did not kill me, then I had to go home
a better person, complete in myself. I began to consciously rehabili-
tate myself.

Of all the things that I have EVER done, this was the most satisfying
yet emotionally challenging. For most of my time in the desert, I struggled with depression and anxiety. In fact, these two things had been
omnipresent since my early 20s, from my time in Johannesburg right
through my London days. My journey home was supposed to set me
back on course and allow me to find myself again. Then I was taken

against my will into the desert, and for a long time I was completely overwhelmed.

I knew that I needed to get some kind of control over my situation. I realised I actually had to figure out who the hell I was. My conversion helped me with this; it allowed me a more 'normal' environment with fewer moving parts. Then, as I came to grips with who I was – or at least who I wanted to be again – I had a choice to make: either I could fight what Allah/God/fate had dished me, or accept the situation and heal.

My battles with anxiety and depression were things the other two prisoners knew nothing about. I kept them very close to my chest. My mom and I were very similar. Her depression and anxiety attacks, made worse by going though typical South African crime situations like being held at gunpoint, were so debilitating. I would sometimes be reduced to tears thinking about the pain she had to endure.

I sent out a silent prayer for her on my 40th birthday, up in The Holes in Group Abdul Aziz, on 28 January 2015. We all woke up for the morning prayer, and then everyone went back to their hut, lay down and went back to sleep as per usual. At this stage it was dawn and the horizon was starting to get light. I walked back to my hut and made a small fire in my *virna* burner, which I'd made from a pineapple can with holes punched in the side for ventilation. I boiled some water, made coffee and sat there by myself, next to a small *sabaya* bush, watching the sunrise and thinking about Cath, my mom, my dad and my sister.

My mom's birthday was a few months later on 20 March, when we were in Group Khalid, also up in The Holes. A surveillance plane flew over our camp mid-morning. After it completed two loops above us, I noticed a small silver pinprick behind it. This turned out to be a Mirage fighter jet, so we had to abandon camp. We walked five kilometres northeast, dashing from tree to grass clump to *sabaya*, until Khalid arrived in the Land Cruiser to pick us up so we could reconvene at another camp. We drove about 20 kilometres northeast and happened to land up in the same camp where I had my 40th birthday.

For my mom's birthday, I ended up sitting next to the same bush. At this stage, I had run out of coffee. Again, I boiled some water, and this time I made some Arabic tea. It was quite profound that I spent both my 40th and my mom's birthday sitting in the same camp next to the same bush, looking at the same view. On both occasions, I wasn't interested in talking to anyone else about it; this was for me, sharing thought with my family. It was beautiful watching the sunrise and the sky going pink before the day heated up.

Depression is something you cannot reason with. It moves in and takes over, wiping aside all logic and determination. Without an arm or without a leg you can still function, but when you are not in control of your mind, you feel desperate, full of fear and anxiety every moment of the day. Without a clear mind, it is difficult to say that you are actually alive.

Although my wife would say that I am friendly and fun, and everybody around me thought the same, inside I felt out of balance. Until I found equilibrium inside myself, until I felt complete, it was irrelevant what people saw from the outside. I had to be able to live with myself.

In the first two years of my captivity, I was broken down by fear to a mere skeleton of who I had been. I had those stupid Hollywood sayings running through my head, like 'break them down to build them up', but I really had been broken. I felt that there was nothing to me. I began to stutter again. I truly had nothing left to lose. I saw myself as a blank canvas; I could decide what picture I would paint on it.

I liked the person I used to be, the person God intended me to be. My rehabilitation was about reconnecting with the complete person I was before I sold my soul for money and became somebody that society expected me to be. Me before my depression. When life was about passion. I was going to reprogram myself to be that person again.

I wrote down my goals on a piece of milk carton. I kept this scrap of milk carton inside the top pocket of my *kamees* (shirt). I would bring it out and literally spend hours reading through my list. If I felt I had achieved one of my points, some of which would take a few months, I would cross off that point and add a new word to my list. I reprogrammed myself through reading those cards and living out the words in my everyday actions to create positive habits.

I had zero passion for anything, but I used to love the outdoors, birds and animals, people, so I started to force these things on myself, hoping that I would reignite that flame. A bird would fly past my hut and I would make myself get up and have a look at the bird, to recognise things in it that I used to find beautiful. Often I would look at the bird, shrug and return to my hut – I felt nothing.

The part of me that I had lost was buried very deep. But with time – and it was slow – I began to see the beauty in that bird. It gave me a joy that would literally bubble inside my chest, knowing that I was finding myself again. I could feel the flicker of the passion that I used to feel for everything and anything, no matter the situation. I could begin to see the best in the very mundane, and I knew that I was on the path to re-finding myself.

I'd force myself to stand in thunderstorms, hunt for things in the sand – beads, fossils, and ostrich shells – and learn Saharan 'things', like how to milk a camel, milk a goat or make rope from grass. I figured that if I saturated myself, or even forced myself into things that used to inspire me, my passion would begin to reappear. It took a while, but I began to feel life starting to flow back into my being.

My kidnapping and rehabilitation were too perfect not to be part of God's plan. I was kidnapped with two very different people, who played a big part in my rehabilitation. Sjaak saw the lighter side of life and was quick to be silly and laugh, and this reminded me what it was like to be carefree and fun. Johan was structured and robot-like, and taught me how to stand up for myself. It took him walking over me in the beginning for me to push back against his overbearing nature.

In the beginning, Johan was known by Al Qaeda as the Professor, Sjaak was the Comedian, and I was Britannia, the quiet guy. I knew that I had to throw some personality into the mix to get a name for myself with Al Qaeda; if they liked me, they were less likely to kill me. My rehabilitation was imperative to my survival.

There was another part of my rehabilitation that ran parallel to me re-finding myself: I suffered from panic attacks. It was absolutely irrational and I had no control over it. A grey mist would appear in my head, and I would not be able to think or make conversation. I would sit in the presence of someone, overwhelmed with anxiety. As part of my rehab, I would plan a conversation and then go over to Al Qaeda and speak until I had exhausted my topics. When the grey cloud returned, I would crawl back to my hut.

Sjaak and I had a few fights because I got close to Al Qaeda. I told him that he could handle his situation however he wanted to, but I wanted to go home a better person. I did not want to be a further burden to my family once I was released. He could not relate to this, but he did not know what I was struggling with. Had I spent six years being an angry recluse in my hut, I would have come out of the Sahara a very different person.

Sometimes I felt like I was making progress and the grey cloud was not so thick. Other times my mind would just seize up, I would forget everything I wanted to speak about and I would sit in front of one of the mujahideen in a very awkward silence. Al Qaeda, through Islam, showed good character, and every day was like Groundhog Day with them; today I could embarrass myself, but tomorrow would be a fresh start. I got to try again and again until I got it right.

My growth would be two steps forward, one step back. The reason for this was that we changed groups every two months; by the time I got used to people in one group and found it easier to make conversation, we would change groups and I would begin again from the bottom, where I could feel the grey cloud come in. But the trend of my growth-graph was upwards; I was making progress.

Time truly does heal. I was held captive for five years and eight months, and slowly I believe my chemical balance started to change. I am not a doctor, so it may never have been chemical, but with time I could see I was getting better. At this stage I felt that I had progressed far enough to work on the next stage of my rehabilitation. I needed to learn how to laugh again and make silly conversation ... I was too serious. I would make an effort to smile and laugh. In the process I learned that we are all a product of our environment, and beneath the weapons, death and religious fanaticism, we are all the same.

Over the better part of four years, I finally got free from the grey cloud that had always haunted me. Somehow I had managed to reset my mind, become that guy I enjoyed again. After about five years and three months, I felt that I had reached the top of my Saharan schooling and it was time to graduate. Five months later I was released. The whole situation was too perfect. I believe God has a plan; we may not understand it or like it, but there is perfection in it. Everything happens in God's time; we just need to be patient and trust.

Group email from Cath, April 2015 (Easter Monday)

I didn't think I would spend Easter Monday writing one of the soul-baring emails that seem to have become part of this journey. I was oblivious to the fact that a rescue operation for Sjaak was taking place. The news of this hit me as though it was Steve who was rescued. It bounced back to hit me harder with a series of emotions that ranged from utter joy to disbelief to hope to disappointment and so on. I am sure that those of you who received the news also felt a wave of bittersweet emotions.

The news has been unnerving. We have been through the motions of having other hostages in Mali released, so we are familiar with the process. In our desperate search for something to ease our pain and not feel so alone in this ceaseless nightmare, we would research these hostages and 'keep track' of them on the internet. We knew their names, faces and other details about their lives. Sjaak's release is the closest we have got to date, so everything seems a little more heightened.

I was alerted this weekend to another hostage who was taken in Burkina Faso, and then taken into Mali to possibly even join up with Steve and Johan. Al Qaeda were no doubt thanking Allah after their victorious capture – the news of Sjaak's rescue mission must have come as such a blow to their brand-new success. The problem is that they often retaliate by kidnapping other hostages, or worse, killing them, but in our case, Steve and Johan are seen as precious diamonds worth millions. My first thought was that they will add extra security and he will have less freedom to walk around or do whatever he is allowed to do. As has happened in the past, they may have gone into hiding, further up into those rugged mountains.

Another possibility is that, because a few militants were also taken in the raid, there may be a prisoner swap. Once Sjaak has been debriefed we hope that he can give us important information. He will also reveal details of how they lived and how they were treated, which may not be what we envisioned. Because we know so little about them, we hang on to anything that is revealed, even if it is small. We were told that they communicated with their captors by drawing in the sand. How we cherished this information.

Many of you know already that we have had a rather rocky start to 2015. It started off with Bev falling and fracturing her hip, which resulted in a hip replacement op. Well, Bev came through almost stronger! She has, however, found the last few weeks very hard on an emotional front.

On my side, the cloud of depression has lifted a little to reveal some blue skies. What a relief! I am still not able to run to the extent that I ran last year. I had to surrender my Two Oceans and Comrades Marathon entries for 2015, which was very hard. I am acutely aware of how lucky I am to be able to put on my running shoes and pound the pavements or trails. Running became a definite escape for me; the runner's high was so appealing. Loneliness has been my enemy, yet I seek to be alone through my most difficult times. It is only through facing reality head-on that one can really grow.

We were blessed with a visit from Vicky Gustafsson, one of Johan's many sisters. It was so good to go down similar thought paths with her. She was a ray of sunshine. It was also good to find out more about Johan – who was once a stranger to Steve, now a fellow hostage and no doubt a saving grace to him. I can imagine they would have formed an extraordinary bond.

Now, some sad news: my beloved stepfather Allan passed away unexpectedly from an aggressive leukaemia that was only diagnosed the week before. This all happened on Steve's 40th birthday. My mother is brokenhearted. It is so hard to see someone you love so much in such agonising sorrow. I now know how many of you felt when my grief was so acute. Allan was very special to me too. We had a special unspoken understanding, which is very rare, as I only really got to know him since coming back home after the kidnapping. He took me into his home and stood by me in every decision I had to make.

A few weeks later, we had another loss: my outstanding grandfather, Barry Peiser, passed away. My poor mother has been hit by the loss of a husband and a father within less than a month.

A few weeks on, we are feeling a bit bruised and tender, but ready to carry on with this one life that we are given. We still receive your messages of strength and support and thank you for them. The 'forgotten hostage' is certainly not forgotten by you all. One would have thought that you would have been depleted of your words of kindness, but that tank of sympathy overflows with such love.

Yours in grief and hope,
Cath

CHAPTER THIRTY

The Flying Dutchman

'All animals are equal, but some animals are more equal than others'
– George Orwell, *Animal Farm*

In the weeks leading up to Johan's attempted escape, the fights between him and Sjaak grew more frequent. There was no team spirit from the beginning, but their fighting had started to escalate from the verbal to the physical. At first I tried to broker peace, but as things got out of control I just stayed out of it.

We all knew how to push each other's buttons. Sjaak challenged Johan's macho, all-knowing, self-sufficient view of himself; Johan belittled Sjaak's intelligence and grip on reality.

Pre-escape Sjaak said, 'Johan you're a little boy, all talk. You will never do this, you are going to wet yourself when you get out there. You don't have the balls for it.'

Shortly after Johan's attempted escape, we moved northwest into the big desert. We were in a hut we had built, and they were at it again. Johan goaded Sjaak, who jumped up and grabbed Johan by the beard. Now, Johan had a very impressive beard, which Al Qaeda really respected. We used to joke that the biggest insult in Islam is probably beard pulling, and here these two were, like two warring, emaciated garden gnomes. I went and sat outside in the sun.

At this stage the French were in the ascendancy, and a lot of the Al Qaeda guys had been killed. There were water and food shortages, and thanks to Johan's attempt to run away we had been reclassified as proper prisoners again, so there was a lot of stress in camp. All the shouting drew Abu-Hamza Chinquetti, the camp emir, to find out what the noise was about. He asked me what was going on.

Trying to be seen as an individual for the thousandth time, I said, 'I don't know, talk to them. I'm not involved.'

Four months after that, in February 2014, we were split up. We were sitting in our hut, and a mujahid came in and told Sjaak to pack his bags. He made a gesture with his hands implying Sjaak was out of there. This had happened before, when Sjaak was moved elsewhere for Proof of Life videos, but this time he didn't come back. Living up to his nickname, the *shibani mujinoon* had been acting more and more crazy, so whether they were taking him away to separate him and Johan, or whether it was because of his negotiations, we never knew.

For a while we would ask the guards were he was, and their eyes would glaze over. As good Muslims they could not lie to us, so it was better not to respond at all or claim ignorance. Trying to out-game them, I asked, 'How is he?' or 'Tell him I say *Salaam Alykum.*' When they said he was fine or okay, we knew he was still in Mali.

In the middle of 2015, someone let slip that the French got him out. Bit by bit, we managed to piece the story together. When he left us, Sjaak was kept in a camp in the mountains with a French prisoner. The French guy got released in January 2015, and in February the French rescued Sjaak in a night-time helicopter operation.

The way Al Qaeda told it, it happened by chance. Earlier that day, one of their surveillance planes was on its way to its start point far at the end of its range. What they would do is fly out and then work their way back to their base, flying in big, concentric oval loops. On its way out, the plane flew right over the camp, but instead of doubling back and doing loops it marked the spot and carried on its way. The mujahideen saw it, but because it did not linger, they made the fatal error of not abandoning camp. Later that evening the French special forces units walked in. It must have been terrifying. I've only heard of two successful rescue attempts – generally, everybody gets killed, including the hostages. Sjaak, dressed in desert clothing with a tan and beard, would have been hard to differentiate from the mujahideen. He got incredibly lucky.

After Sjaak's rescue, something changed among Al Qaeda. I think their confidence was rattled. If the French could do it once, what was to stop them doing it again? Al Qaeda didn't want us to know, I suppose because of prisoner psychology, but you could tell from the mood in the camps that something was up.

With Sjaak gone, it was just me and Johan, and our relations were worse than ever. Even on the bare basics, he did not want to engage. 'I have a house in Sweden and a house in the Sahara,' he would say, 'and in my mind I want to be as if I'm at home in Sweden. I don't want to have to say good morning, good night, please and thank you.'

This pattern of negativity had gone on for so long, that even members of Al Qaeda started apologising for Johan's behaviour. Abu Darda came to me once to commiserate: 'I'm sorry Lot, you have it difficult with Musa.'

We would be stuck with each other for another two years.

CHAPTER THIRTY-ONE

Yahia

As told by Imtiaz Sooliman

Nobody gets connected with Al Qaeda directly. You get connected with an intermediary, who gets connected to another intermediary, who gets connected to another intermediary. It's a long chain. That way you don't actually know who the last guy in the chain is.

When Yahia went back to Mali after six weeks, he met the intermediary at his apartment in Bamako. An hour after the meeting, Yahia got a call and the intermediary said, 'Al Qaeda have a problem with me talking to you. You are not on the website? How do they know who you are?'

Before Yahia left, I had made sure that everything was on the website, but for some reason it was not clear enough for Al Qaeda, so I phoned my website manager and said to put his face up there. From articles with Yahia's photo, to the letter from Gustafsson's family and the McGown family, we plastered everything all over that website. Twenty minutes later the intermediary called back to say, 'You have been accepted. It has been agreed that you will negotiate on behalf of Gustafsson and McGown.'

That's how it started. The next thing was to actually build that leverage. Ramadan was coming and the second Eid was coming so I said, 'Let's slaughter some sheep, give some food, get involved in feeding, help with some wells, rebuild a section of a mosque.' We started doing all of that in different parts of Mali. Word started spreading. You could see the guys were getting more comfortable talking to us. At the end of the day, you can do all those things, but they still want money. What providing aid does is keep the negotiations open.

There are two types of Al Qaeda people in that region. There are the Arab nationals, the Algerians, the Libyans, the ones who come from outside the country. And then you get the Tuareg. The Tuareg are much softer, gentler, more merciful and more compassionate. The elder generation of the Tuareg were willing to let Stephen come home, but the new generation was radicalised after having foreign troops in their land. They were against Stephen coming home with no payment or negotiations. We could probably have got him out much earlier if there was no interruption from the younger generation, or no conflict between the Arab and non-Arab component.

These groups don't represent the religion in its entirety; what they do is actually against the religious teaching. If it were part of the teaching, the whole Muslim world would support them, which is not true.

Later, I told Stephen, 'It's very nice of them to say that you are their brother and that you are accepted, but they also know the rules. If you are their brother, then they cannot hold you captive. They have to let you go. It's not about paying ransom then. Their own teaching says, "Free a slave, free a captive." In the first place you can't take innocent people captive, so what kind of nonsense is that? It doesn't make sense, it's a warped understanding of the religion.'

The negotiation process continued. Al Qaeda were giving us outrageous ransom figures. I told them, 'This is not Europe, this is South Africa.' They brought the figures down, the money kept on dropping and then they said we don't want money any more, we want a prisoner exchange. The problem with that was that our government would then owe the Mali government something. At one point Al Qaeda wanted only hostages, then they wanted money, then they wanted money and hostages. It kept changing all the time. Eventually their intermediaries said, 'Look you guys can only go to a certain point, beyond that it's not even your business any more. Your government has to talk to the Mali government, your state security has to talk to their state security, and arrangements have to be made with the military for the safety of the hostage.'

DIRCO was with us, the Malian government was with us, the state security agencies both here and there were with us – they all knew, and they were all in the loop. Right from the beginning I said we want nothing under the table, we want everything transparent, open, public.

The fact that so many hostages have been released means that obviously governments do get involved. Over a period of time, there's public pressure, there's media pressure, there's family pressure. The problem is if you pay. People want the hostage out, but at the same time the public doesn't want a ransom to be paid, because other people will be taken hostage. My question is: if you know it's a high-risk country, why go there? The fact of the matter is, whether you pay ran-som money or don't pay ransom money, they will keep catching guys as long as they go to those areas. It's not going to change anything. It's like the coronavirus. Unless you take positive action to stay away from the virus, you are going to get sick by going into the wrong area. In the same way, if the wrong nationalities go to the wrong country, expect to get taken. Whether you pay a ransom or not, Al Qaeda have 15 or 16 other hostages at any one time. So if they don't get from the one, they get from the other 14.

I was on SAFM and a listener phoned in. Sitting on his high horse, he said, 'Bloody hell, you guys are helping terrorists.'

I said, 'When that guy's son gets taken hostage, he is going to phone me to help get him out.'

I have seen the suffering of the families of hostages. I've seen how people have battled in that situation. Every time we say we are not going to take these cases on again – it's a headache, it takes a lot of time, you neglect your family, it's high-risk, there are too many public questions to answer, it involves ransom and terrorist groups and it's bad for your image. But then another hostage's family approaches you.

At this point, Al Qaeda said, 'You have done all you can, and the most important thing is you have connected the South African and the Malian governments and state security. They know how to work through the intermediaries and the final arrangements will be done between us. What they give us or what they don't give us, that's not for you to know. It was just for you to make the connection, and if the connection is made properly, within 10 days you will have your man.'

Then we never heard from anybody. More than three weeks passed, and then it just happened suddenly. We don't know exactly what hap-pened with the last stages of the negotiations and release. We know they were waiting with a plane for a few days in Bamako. We sus-pected something was up, because 24 hours before it was confirmed we got a call from state security to tell us congratulations. We didn't know what they were congratulating us for. We assumed that maybe Stephen was out, but they did not say it directly.

We tried hard, but we couldn't quite get Stephen home before his mother passed on.

Another year has passed. So much has happened. So little has happened. The fact that Steve is not home makes one think that we have made no progress. But so much has changed. For one thing, Imtiaz Sooliman and his team at Gift of the Givers (GOTG) have been working tirelessly for us.

I have attempted to update you all a few times this year, but haven't been able to finish them off for various reasons. With so many disappointments, one gets to a stage when one has nothing more to say. One would have thought that I would become wiser, more sceptical with each disappointment, but that has not been the case; a thread of illogical hope gets reignited each time. Hope can override any logic. Just like faith.

Now that GOTG is involved and the ransom has been done away with, we have been able to approach the media more freely and speak more openly, which is a relief, as we have felt so restricted and powerless.

In summary, GOTG have now gained the trust of the Malian community, which includes the spiritual leaders, tribe leaders, elders, etc. Their only stumbling block at the moment is the youth. These young men comprise some of Gaddafi's soldiers who had to flee Libya; many joined Al Qaeda branches. They have dug in their heels and are holding tightly on to Steve and Johan. With the end of Ramadan in August, GOTG donated over 350 cows and sheep that were slaughtered for the people of Mali and surrounding areas. This is a yearly religious event called Kurbani. GOTG also helped provide water for them by building a well. Our latest attempt is to renovate a mosque in the area close to where Steve and Johan are being held. This additional goodwill task will hopefully trigger their 'shame', which is a large factor in the Muslim religion. This is not something that Christians or Westerners understand; we are rather driven by 'guilt'. It is a complicated concept, but basically touches on disrespect and dishonour. It has nothing to do with our South African 'Ag, shame' saying — if only it did, we would have Steve and Johan home in no time! So our aim is for an unconditional goodwill release. Something I struggled to see as being a possibility, especially with the large amount of ransoms that have been paid in the past. I always felt uneasy about a ransom payment as it would fuel further kidnappings and terrorist attacks around the world. I would hate to carry this burden.

At present there are four other hostages in Mali: an elderly Australian doctor, a Frenchman, a Swiss nun and an American. The Mali elections have resulted in further strife in the region, making it difficult for negotiations to take place, which is a major reason for the delay in these kidnapping outcomes.

As a family, we have tried to remain positive. Bev has had four emergency hospital stays this year. She has thankfully come out stronger after each one, but it has not been easy for her and Malcolm. I am always greeted with loving hugs, warm smiles and lighthearted laughter when I see them. On the whole, I have had a far better year than last year. I know that this is not the case for many of you. I know that recent world events (Trump, Brexit) have added to the stress and uncertainty of the year ahead. There are a few of you in particular who have had to deal with tragic family losses. I realise that there is nothing much one can do or say to ease your pain – I now know how you have all felt with us. I recall that time when no words or amount of love could dull the pain, when I was in that dark place.

I now have a little saying. It's nothing mind-blowing, but it got my attention and it worked itself into my heart, soul and mind. This little saying came up on a few occasions at various car-park pay stations – a tiny sticker with 'EVERYTHING IS GOING TO BE OK'. Every time I have seen it, I've been in a different phase of this journey, and it always struck me with light beams. It has set me on the right track when I felt that I was going down onto that road of depression again. There are of course many biblical verses that I hold on to, but at the time my brain could not even process a passage in the Bible. I would lose concentration and fall asleep or zone out, but those days have now passed.

I'm not saying that I am completely out of the woods. I am no longer a running racing snake or a social extrovert. I've had to learn to manage my reduced capacity and reserves. This has frustrated me no end, as I have wanted to accomplish so much. I do, however, hold more peace and contentment in this uncertain world we live in. So I'll close this email on that note, until my next one, which we all hope will be the last. But if I have to continue writing, so be it.

From a more contented Cath

CHAPTER THIRTY-TWO

The Pale Arab

'I had dropped one form and not taken on the other, and was become like Mohammed's coffin in our legend, with a resultant feeling of intense loneliness in life, and a contempt, not for other men, but for all they do' – T. E. Lawrence (aka Lawrence of Arabia)

Having accepted my lot in life, I worked hard to find joy and meaning in each day. This approach had a profound effect on my depression and mood. Towards the end of 2016, I felt like I was close to graduating from both my Saharan schooling and my overall rehabilitation.

Over the years I had picked up a ridiculous array of skills and knowledge, from making rope out of grass to lighting a fire from a torch cone, slaughtering and butchering animals and making sausages from the *omasum* (one of the stomach chambers) and fat (you don't want to know more), milking camels and goats, creating a cool bed from wet grass, jacking up a vehicle in soft sand, push-starting a car by putting a rope around the tyre and pulling, filling a flat tyre with bread dough, starting a car using camels, fixing electronics, using wind direction and sand corrugations to navigate on a cloudy day, and making sundials to tell time. I could track and hunt rabbits, call out to and get a response from a polecat, dig a well, and hundreds of other things. I had even learned passable Arabic and gained control over my stutter again from reading the Quraan and reciting passages in a large group.

I did things just for the joy of it, like trying to help small trees in camps I might never come back to. I became a gardener in the desert. I found one small acacia growing completely cockeyed. I don't know if it was stepped on by a camel, but it was in the middle of nowhere on a sand dune. I built a little splint, dug a hole and tied the tree against the pole, so that it would have an opportunity to grow straight and true. It felt like a good thing to do. Al Qaeda sat there watching me working with the splint and my ropies. Later, they said, 'In 20 years' time when we come back to this area, we are going to park and seek camouflage under that tree. It will forever be called Tree Lot.'

I now felt so habituated to the Sahara that I saw myself as a pale Arab. I was starting to feel complete again, and I felt that God would send me home. Al Qaeda had long since stopped seeing me as a threat, a *kuffar* and possibly even a prisoner. I knew this because of the way they relaxed around me, and how they spoke about securing my release. They also asked me to join jihad – I politely declined – and didn't think twice about handing me their weapons. I was not *khateer*.

Getting into the car one day, Abu Farida, Al Qaeda's British videographer and communications guy who I had taught to use a camera, was faffing, trying to carry a few too many things. Needing a spare hand, he passed me an awkward bundle, which turned out to be his homemade suicide belt. It was as if he had handed me a slithery snake. It looked like a kidney belt, had a little core with a detonating device at the end, a button to push when the time came. I had seen another mujahid, Ibrahim, who was blind in both eyes – he wore dark glasses, had a young kid as a 'guide dog' and was missing a hand; he was supposedly their bomb expert.

I said, 'Abu Farida, dude, put this thing in the other car! I don't want to sit next to your suicide belt. What do you know about making these things? You gonna blow us up.' We both laughed, but it was a very peculiar moment.

Once, as we ran from the surveillance planes, I reluctantly helped carry RPG rockets. Thabit, a tall Al Qaeda youngster with huge hands and feet, was lagging behind, trying to carry his Kalashnikov, the RPG launcher and four RPG rockets through endless dunes of soft sand, so the emir of our little breakaway party, Ghabayb, just gave me the order as if I was one of the mujahideen. I shouldered the rockets. At times like these, it was difficult to reconcile who I had been as Steve McGown, London banker, with who I had become, Lot the Lonely, walking over dunes, hiding behind bushes till the planes were gone, carrying RPG rockets and trying to convince Al Qaeda to not kill animals.

While I had changed, Al Qaeda had also evolved as an organisation. I watched boys grow into men, I saw Al Qaeda go from being a group of extremely strict zealots to a bit more relaxed as more southerners joined, and the older Arab and Tuareg guys who started the cause were killed off. I watched as they started to allow certain forms of jihad music when before all music was *haram*. I even saw how diet trends filtered into Al Qaeda as certain foods like sugar were banned or restricted.

In Group Sayid in October 2016, we were camping high up in The Holes when at around 2pm I started hearing the drone of a *kashiva* to the south. I told Al Qaeda, and we all remained in our huts to wait it out. The sound persisted, moving back and forth from southeast to southwest, all through the afternoon. It was unusual for it to go on so long, and in the desert anything out of the ordinary created cause for concern. The call was made to move camp.

It turned out that the American Jeffery Woodke had been abducted the previous day in northern Niger. Because northern Mali was known as the place where Al Qaeda hid their inventory from across the region, the skies of Azawad began to crawl with surveillance planes.

As we abandoned camp, everyone took their five-litre water bottles and a few supplies. Al Qaeda loaded up the ammunition and weapons they could carry, and we set off on foot, leaving everything else behind. One mujahid stayed behind to drive our vehicle away from the camp, the idea being that he would later collect us; the rest of us began to walk. I went north with Sayid and another guy before turning west, while Johan went directly west with another group. For a long time, we walked parallel to each other about 500 metres apart, the plane a constant droning threat to the south. We stopped to do our sunset prayer and then continued again, our two groups joining together as we started to lose the light. We walked for hours on end, up and over and around.

It was a big moon, so we could easily see where we were walking. About 10pm I saw a big black object on the ground at the side of one of the holes. I shouted out, thinking one of the guys had dropped his rucksack, but as I walked up to fetch it, I realised it was an enormous tortoise, at least 60 centimetres long, travelling at night through the desert sands. It blew me away that here, in a place that literally defined 'the middle of nowhere', there was life; an ancient tortoise doing his thing, looking for a blade of grass to eat. It was like seeing that unknown grave up in the north; this was the unknown tortoise. I squatted for a few seconds, my hand on his shell, marvelling, thinking, *He's got life. He's perfect in creation and he's got purpose.* I jogged back into line and didn't say a word about him.

While mankind was killing itself and destroying the world, this tortoise was oblivious to all this, just doing what a tortoise does. Yet soon enough its life would be affected by man's greed and its by-products: pollution, deforestation, climate change … What a nasty creation we are!

As much as they prayed for my release and told me they wanted me to go home, by this stage, it was clear that Al Qaeda were exasperated by the lack of movement with our cases. They could not understand how my country could leave me for so long. Al Qaeda started saying, 'Lot why are you still here in the desert? You're a Muslim, you're a good guy, we want you to go home.'

Abu Darda the Mauritanian scion said, 'I wanted to ask Al Qaeda management for your release a year ago, but there was an imminent negotiation that we thought would be successful, and that you would be going home. I give you my word that if this current negotiation fails, I will get a petition together and get all of senior management in Mali to sign this, asking for you to be given away for free as a Muslim brother.'

There were even suggestions that I stay in the desert and marry the Swiss missionary being held captive for the second time by Al Qaeda. I declined, reminding them that I had a wife and a family to go home to, *Insha Allah*.

In November 2016, in Group Abu Walid, I wrote Cath a letter I knew she would never see. We had been chased by a surveillance plane and we ended up in a small hole further south. Apparently we were about 20 kilometres south of where the Swiss woman was being held. I was about 40 metres from the Al Qaeda hut. We all got to choose where we wanted to build our huts. I was under a small tree called a *tashtaya*. Using my milk carton scraps, I wrote my letter to Cath. It was a diary of some of the things that were going on, how long I had been there, how much I wanted to get back to her and my family, and how I was not sure if I was ever going to come home. I had a small plastic soft-drink bottle, which I figured would be waterproof, and put the letter inside it. I dug a hole right next to the base of the tree my hut was built against. I dug it deep, about an arm's depth, through the dry sand and into the wet sand. I screwed the bottle up tight and put it in the hole. I layered tins of Gloria, plastic biscuit packets and sardine cans on top of it – my plan was to make it as stinky and disgusting as possible, so nobody would ever come and dig around it. I had the GPS coordinates of the camp, and I thought one day I could return with Cath and dig up this bottle.

In December 2016, a vehicle arrived driven by a mujahid called Abd ar-Rahman. He was excited because he had a letter for me 'from my family'. He gave it to me on his phone. It was in colour, possibly downloaded near a cellphone tower in the south.

It was dated August 2016, and the letterhead said, 'Top Secret: Confidential from the Minister of Internal Affairs.' It started with, 'Dear brothers…' which, if they knew anything about Al Qaeda, they would have known was a mistake. The mujahideen did not go in for African Ubuntu. Hell, before they kidnapped me, many of them did not know South Africa even existed. The only people they considered brothers were other Muslims like them.

'Stephen McGowan's mother is critically ill and could die imminently. We are asking for compassion that you give him away for nothing.'

Johan was eavesdropping as he always did, while Abd ar-Rahman was looking at me expectantly.

'What does it say?' he asked.

It blew my mind that he had probably driven a huge distance to deliver this to me, had come to me in good faith, but that he had no idea what it said. He thought I would be over the moon to get a message from my family.

'The letter is from my government. It says my mother is about to die. And it is asking for *rahma* (compassion) from Al Qaeda.'

I could see that he did not expect this. His expression changed, he got pensive. By giving this devastating news, they had given a prisoner a reason to be unpredictable.

It took me to a sad place, and then I got angry.

There was the usual anger at myself for everything that had happened, for not being there right now for my mother, for not even knowing if she was still alive.

I was also incensed at the incompetence of my government who could not even be bothered to spell my name right – they wrote 'McGowan' and not 'McGown', which I took as an indication of how important I was to them.

Al Qaeda were no better. They were always going on about me being a Muslim brother, and how Muslims look after each other and want what is best for one another. Well, now Al Qaeda knew that my mother was about to die. If they truly wanted what was best for me, a Muslim, they would let me go. If they didn't, and that was the feeling I got from Abd ar-Rahman, then they were hypocrites and everything they had taught me was lip service.

My mom could already be dead. Why did it take them four months to deliver such important information? Al Qaeda had already taken everything away from me. My freedom, my family and very possibly my future. In a heated debate with Abu Abdilla, who I considered a friend, I swore that if I ever returned to South Africa to find that I had lost my family, my wife and everything else, I was going to come back to the desert to leech off them for the rest of my days. I was a part of the *Umma*, the Muslim body, and they had a responsibility to look after me. He just laughed, which made me more incensed.

Among the mujahideen, prayers for me to go home were redoubled, but they also got a bit more creative with negotiations. In January 2017, they said they had one more route they wanted to take to try to negotiate me out of the desert. It involved two Qatari princes who were visiting the Sahara. Much to Johan's dismay, I was to be the test case for this approach. A Proof of Life was shot at very short notice, popped onto a memory stick and delivered to the Qataris, who were at a camp nearby.

I believe that this was the moment Johan realised he had really screwed up, by being so arrogant, aloof and difficult. He spent hours trying to suck up saying, 'But I also want to go home. I don't want to be here for the summer, it's hot.' He became the sweetest, most syrupy person, and everybody could see right through it.

In the end, somewhat ironically, Johan actually went home before me, on 23 June. The Swedish government must have finally come to the party. A vehicle arrived in Camp Noah, a meeting was held, and later that afternoon I saw Khalid driving out of camp. He waved out the window and said, '*Salaam Alykum* Lot.'

I had no idea Johan was in the car. It was the second-last day of Ramadan, so later that afternoon at sunset, I went to break the fast. As I sat down with the mujahideen to eat the customary three dates, I asked, '*Ayna* Musa?' Where is Musa?

There were a couple of awkward blinks before someone said, 'Ah Lot, you didn't know? Musa has gone home.'

You may have all heard the news about Johan's release by now as it hit local and international headlines with a bang on Monday. The news seemed to fizzle out as the week progressed, as is so common for any hostage story. Johan's family specifically asked for some privacy so that they could welcome their son and younger brother home. Johan has five sisters, and now a lot of nieces and nephews he has yet to meet. I've been in regular contact with the family, especially Victoria, throughout the week.

I've waited to write this email as I felt that I needed to gather more information in order to make sense of what happened, how it happened and why our Steve was left behind. As you can imagine, we have been in a frenzied state since we received the news. As with most things in life, what we dream up in our heads or anticipate does not always pan out the way we envisioned it. Sjaak's rescue on Easter Monday three years ago caught us all by surprise and now … Johan's release.

A multitude of unexpected emotions arose after receiving the news. My good friend Jonathan, who has stood by me for years, broke the news. I was driving at the time and I thought that he was just calling me for a social chat. I will never forget his calm tone of voice, which I think saved me from crashing into a lamppost at Zoo Lake. I veered off onto the side of the road in order to digest this news. My sister confirmed it from Germany, where she's attending a conference. She experienced the same blow I did. What about Steve? With that little thread of hope we cling to, we scrabbled to find out whether Steve was also on a plane back home. I did a quick summary of all the things I needed to do before Steve's arrival at the airport. I'm amazed how quickly our brains can function if put under stress, but when I realised Steve was not coming home, it shifted gears somewhat. I phoned Malcolm, a contact at SAPS, and then Imtiaz from Gift of the Givers. Neither of them had news of Johan's release, which just added to the confusion and the unexpected rise in fury.

Once the news had settled somewhat, the reality of Steve on his own hit, and hit hard. It almost seemed okay that he was with Johan, but now that he was alone it felt unacceptable. From all the hostage stories I have read, the feeling of isolation and abandonment is hardest to endure.

I spoke to Victoria late on Monday night. The government provided a 'safe house' for a few days, where the family could escape from the media. She said that they were only given news of Johan's release once he had boarded the plane on Sunday evening. Victoria said that Johan and Steve have been together all this time. Johan was called aside last Friday by his captors and taken away from Steve. He was driven across the country to the border, where he was handed over to the Swedish authorities. They didn't get to say goodbye. Yolande Korkie was also snatched away from Pierre with no explanation or warning. This is a form of torture in my mind.

Victoria said it has been a whirlwind since Johan arrived, with lots of heightened emotions. She added that Johan could not stop talking. He apologised repeatedly for putting his family through this ordeal. She said his accent and mannerisms have changed somewhat. I spoke to Johan on Skype. He said that Steve is physically well. He thinks Steve will be treated even better now that he's on his own. He said Steve misses us all, and wants Malcolm to retire – he is riddled with guilt, as this message to his father in a way signifies. If only Steve knew what a busybody his father is and that he is nowhere near to retiring!

We met with the South African government on Tuesday. We thought it went well. They are really positive, although they couldn't provide us with specific information. We bombarded them with questions. Top of mind was whether the Swedes and South Africans had been in contact over the past few months, as we have presumed all along that they were working together and would bring Steve and Johan home together. They said that they have been communicating all along, but they had also been working apart in order to create more opportunities. The frustrating secrecy has been hard to accept, but one can understand why they have to protect their sources. The question of the ransom always comes up. As Malcolm says, 'Just bring back my son. We don't need to know how you arranged for him to come home.' We both have renewed energy to bring Steve home now. It is time.

I will end with my usual thanks for all your messages of support and continued prayers, and another apology for my need to take shelter during this time.

Renewed in energy,
Cath

PART THREE
Home

CHAPTER THIRTY-THREE

Exodus

'Movement of Jah people' – Bob Marley

My release came as a surprise to me. Of course I knew it was possible after Johan had gone home, but I had learned over the years not to get my hopes up. Sjaak had been rescued years earlier, and the Swedish and South African governments were completely different entities, so who was to say that I would ever be released? I had learned to live in the present, to focus on what I could control. Dreaming wild dreams of being home in Johannesburg with Cath and my folks was just going to set me back. If and when it happened, it would happen, *Insha Allah*.

On 21 July 2017, we were in The Holes in Camp Noah, near the Mauritanian border, when a vehicle arrived driven by Abd ar-Rahman. He sat conferring with Noah on the edge of camp for a bit, and then called me over. He told me I would be leaving with him and, *Insha Allah*, I will be going home. I felt a surge of excitement as I always did, but reminded myself that I had heard this many times before, so better manage my expectations. As a test, I asked him what I should bring, because if I was told to bring everything, it would mean I was not going anywhere other than another camp.

Abd ar-Rahman said, 'Whatever is important to you.'

Unsure if I was going to make a Proof of Life or move to another camp, I packed my sack, my blanket, a short pole and my gym equipment. We started driving around 10am and drove till 4pm. Our route took us south past two wells, *Haasi aghmar* (the red well) and *Haasi sheikh* (the sheikh's well), and then entered an area of long valleys that ran from the southwest to the northeast. On Google Earth they look like giant drainage veins that run across the desert. We drove along one of these veins for hours, getting stuck in a colossal sandstorm, the sky turning orange and low-level winds buffeting the car. The heat was intense and we got multiple punctures. Unusually, it was just me, Abd ar-Rahman, and one other mujahid travelling in a single vehicle, so there was no support if we got stuck.

We arrived in an Al Qaeda camp, where we were greeted by Salah, a mujahid I knew from previous camps. Salah was quite dramatic and liked to gossip. I'd been burnt before by him implying I was going home and it never panned out. This time he was winking and saying, 'If you come here, you are definitely going home. We saw Musa a month ago. *Au revoir*.' While they refuelled the car I did my afternoon prayer alone and once I was done, a new guy, an Algerian named Zakaria, took over driving duties. We set off again, arriving in another camp, which had about 30 kids in it, at 9 pm. We spent the night there. The next morning we left in a convoy of three cars; with all the banter and excitement from the kids running around the camp, it was like heading off on a field trip.

Over the course of the next day and night, we made our way east towards the mountains and stopped in an area alongside the Tilemsi, a huge drainage system that captures floodwaters out of the mountains. It was incredibly green, like a giant golf course with trees, fairways and bunkers. From Camp Noah we had covered 800 kilometres.

The north-south Saharan truck route ran down the one side of this green. Along the way we spotted a striped hyena (*dhuba*) and a porcupine (*thorban*). When we finally pulled over to camp under some trees, I could see that this was a well-established area used by truckers. There were wells, and people walking past tending their goats. It felt positively biblical compared to the hell of the desert.

We spent the next couple of days there. I had to stay hidden. Cars came and went to meet with Zakaria. Once, we drove out from the campsite, past burnt-out vehicles and ammo boxes from a recent battle, to an area with a cellphone tower, where we met up with five other Al Qaeda vehicles. The drone of a surveillance plane came from the east where the mountains were. We were definitely close to a hot area, but the mujahideen were incredibly relaxed because we were in civilian territory on a trucking route.

In my heart I hoped that this really was it, but I was sick to my stomach at the thought of it not being my release. Hope can break you. Every sinew thought I was going home, but I had to manually override it.

We waited and waited. There had been lots of cars coming and going – maybe these were bringing information about my release? To pass the time I played chess with Zakaria. I won twice and then he said, 'If you beat me again, you won't go home.' I thought, *Maybe Zakaria is that kind of guy and I should let him win?* It turned out we got distracted and never played the third game.

It was 25 July.

When the changeover happened, it was all a bit odd. A vehicle drove in from the northwest and everyone looked confused. It was a Land Cruiser that looked exactly like one of theirs, so to me they were being ridiculous. The vehicle drove past across the 'golf course' fairway. When it came to a stop, Zakaria told me to get my stuff together, we were going for a ride.

I picked up my tattered black rucksack, my home-made sleeping bag, pillow, tin cup and water bottle. Zakaria told me to leave my blanket under the tree out of sight of surveillance planes. In my mind that meant we were going somewhere to come back. We were travelling light, traveling fast and travelling hard. Then he lobbed my prized tin cup out the door, saying, 'You can get another one of these at your house.'

At my house? Did I hear that correctly?

We drove across the golf course and parked next to the other vehicle. After a brief conversation, the other vehicle did a U-turn and started bombing it south. We followed in hot pursuit. The pace was fast and the terrain was hellish as we traversed fields scattered with termite mounds like speed bumps. Then we hit a graded dirt track, with the occasional boulder-sized milestone that appeared to be from *Asterix & Obelix*. It was the national road.

At 8am we left the national road and drove a short distance east to an area of small ponds. Zakaria parked under a tree, so the reflection of our windscreen could not be seen. I saw a sweet paper floating in the water; we were getting closer to civilisation. At this stage I still had no confirmation what we were doing there. I stood under the tree for about 25 minutes, waiting. Zakaria called me over to join him. He said, 'Can you hear the airplane?' We were looking through the leaves of an acacia, trying to spot the plane. Looking, looking, looking – eventually I sighted it, and pointed it out to Zakaria.

He asked me which direction the plane was heading. It was doing circles as always, but it was drifting towards the east.

Zakaria said, 'That's good.' Thirty seconds later he nudged me with his elbow and said, 'Hey Lot, you are free to go now.'

My expression must have prompted him to speak again.

He said, 'If you don't believe me, walk, but if you don't want to walk, when this airplane goes away, that other car is going to come and take you away.'

In Islam, raucous laughter is frowned upon, and when you smile you are not meant to show your teeth, but right then Zakaria had a huge smile on his face. I stood there, trying to compute what this meant. In the hostage release videos I saw in the desert, they showed prisoners and cash changing hands as one guy, the hostage, walks off to a vehicle and drives out of the Sahara. This was nothing like that. Because I had no information, I had had almost no emotional transition from being a captive to being free. In my mind I was still being taken to see the boss, or shoot a Proof Of Life, only to be returned to another camp deep in the desert as had happened so many times before.

Zakaria gave me a three-cheeked hug goodbye, gave me his cellphone number to stay in touch and a new set of clothes. I got into the other Land Cruiser, sandwiched between the driver and the guy next to the window. I was told that I was a Tuareg businessman and that my companions, two guys who looked like Al Qaeda, were my chauffeurs. Zakaria said I was going to be handed over to the Malian government. There would be a lot of military and police roadblocks. I was not to talk to anyone until Bamako. The drivers and the government guy would do the talking.

We pushed south-southwest and approached the city of Gao, the seat of government when the MNLA ran Azawad. Approximately 30 kilometres before Gao, we stopped and changed cars again. The new car was a white Toyota Hilux Double Cab with tinted windows. There was a third guy in the car, called Musa. I did not know it yet, but he was Malian secret service.

We worked our way through roadblocks past the airport and the military base, through the centre of town, until we crossed over a large bridge. This was the Niger River, the fabled border between the north and the south.

As we moved through the outskirts of a settlement on the southern side of the river, the car slowed to pull over onto the dirt edge. Escape was still on my mind, and I was still not 100% sure if the two chauffeurs were Al Qaeda or not, because they were smoking cigarettes and listening to music, but they dressed and carried themselves like Al Qaeda – and both had AK-47s beside them. I was thinking, *If I have not been released, I should climb out of this vehicle and run.*

We pulled up next to a shack with Coca-Cola signs and adverts for food, drink and cellphone networks. Musa climbed out and said, 'What do you want to eat or drink? Coke?'

I stammered as if he had asked me something in Martian. 'Fanta.'

Musa brought out some cash, paid the guys at the shop, came to my window and handed me a plastic bag with a two-litre Fanta and some kind of a meat schawarma.

As if it was normal.

Just the same way those two mujahideen slaughtered the goat on the first day, just the same way Zakaria said to me so casually, 'You are free' – all of them conducted themselves as if it was business as usual.

I had not seen a tar road for six years, let alone a cold drink. Open your electronic window, here's your drink, here's your schawarma. In a plastic bag, served with a napkin.

It was too much to take in. That morning, I had woken up a prisoner of Al Qaeda, and in the space of a few hundred kilometres I had travelled between geologies and worlds, across time and space, from 2000BC to AD2017 – and now I was given this package of food, prepared by someone other than Al Qaeda, like it was nothing. My body and mind could not comprehend anything, not even the sensory feeling of the ice-cold drink in my hand or the addition of spices and sauce on the schawarma.

In that moment, as the tears streamed from my eyes and six years of stress lifted from my shoulders, both the schawarma and my desert existence fell apart.

The game was over.

I was free.

CHAPTER THIRTY-FOUR

Home

'But sing no more this bitter tale that wears my heart away ...'
– Homer, *The Odyssey*

When we arrived at Lanseria airport, I was this guy walking through customs with a big beard and long hair, wearing Arab gear with a turban over my shoulder. No one gave me a second look. There was something really special about that; how South Africans are so mixed we don't bat an eyelid at what someone looks like.

I went through normal commercial passport control. I had my South African passport, which Cath had given to the South African Secret Service. We were standing in line – two big Secret Service guys, a little white guy with a big beard, another big Secret Service guy, and a female agent who was my principal handler. Out came their red diplomatic passports and in between was my green passport, the passport I should have been caught with. I don't know if the passport control official had been prepped, but she looked at my passport photo and then at me, two different people from two different worlds, stamped my little green book and said, 'Welcome home.'

Getting to that point took a lot longer than I expected. From Gao I was driven west across the country. We overnighted in Douentza – after getting authorisation to enter the town, where an overnight curfew had been implemented. The two 'Al Qaeda' chauffeurs went to a hotel, while Musa and I slept on the pavement off the main road; apparently going into a hostel with a white man dressed as a Tuareg would attract too much attention. As for my chauffeurs, it turned out they were from one of the rebel groups in the area that worked with Al Qaeda from time to time, but judging by the smoking and the music they were more relaxed on the religion front. I'd spent the day talking to Musa in broken French, while trying to help translate a few things with the chauffeurs in Hassaniya; after they left, it dawned on us that we both spoke English.

A day later, after many roadblocks, Musa and I changed vehicles, getting into a dark-blue Toyota RAV4 driven by Musa's boss, who worked under the director-general for Malian Intelligence. That car took us all the way to Bamako, to a secret service safe house.

I spent the next four days getting debriefed by Musa, eating things like fruit and getting reacquainted with the marvel of a flush toilet. I was not allowed to speak to anyone or contact my family back home, but I did receive a beautiful, heartfelt message from the Malian president.

On 29 July, I was driven to Bamako airport, where a private jet hired by the South African Secret Service was waiting for me. It had apparently been there for over 10 days, at a cost of R500,000 per day. I boarded the plane and met the SASS team who were working on my case, the pilot, and a young Afrikaans air hostess who offered us champagne. I accepted orange juice instead. She and the SASS agent were the first women I had spoken to in six years. As she smiled and joked, I realised that I was free, heading home to a place where I was safe and loved. I began to cry. The next few days were full of tears.

It was only once we took off, soaring high up into my Super Mario Bros clouds like the white storks and the crows I had envied for so long, banking southeast towards the equator and South Africa, that I felt a wave of relief. I truly believed I was leaving the horror story behind. But it was still an anxious night.

A new door of worry swiftly opened up: I was still being kept in the dark about so many things. What was I going home to? Do I have a wife? Is my family angry?

The Secret Service agent was tucking into her dinner. I asked, 'What am I going home to, is Cath okay, how is my mom?'

She avoided giving me a straight answer. 'I've only dealt with your father.'

A few hours later I spoke to another member of the SASS, who was sitting in front of me. I said to him, 'I haven't spoken to my family in almost six years, can you give me an idea what I am going home to and what to expect? Will there be a large crowd of journalists at the airport?'

He replied, 'Wow, this dessert is good.'

After six years of Al Qaeda prisoner psychology, now I was getting it from my own Secret Service. They were giving away nothing, and my time in captivity had conditioned me not to push a point. What should have been the most incredible night of my life was a complete disaster. I felt like I was going home to a train wreck.

There was no one there to greet us after we cleared passport control at Lanseria. I was okay with this – I wanted to avoid a noise – but having watched French presidents welcome back emaciated hostages with champagne amid red, white and blue fanfare, it wasn't what I expected. Instead, I was led outside to a waiting black minivan. We drove out through the boom and into the traffic.

It had been nine years since I had been in Johannesburg. Even so, the route they were taking to get to my folks' place seemed a bit odd. I offered to guide them, but the Secret Service insisted they knew the way – plus they had GPS.

While we were driving, my handler said, 'Should we call your father to let him know you are coming or just arrive?'

I was amazed that this was something they had not already done. The man was over 70 years old; surprising him with his long-lost son could give him a heart attack. Was she being serious?

She was. She dialled my dad, spoke to him for a bit and then hung up. She paused for a moment before turning back to me again and saying, 'Your father is both very happy and very sad.'

I said, 'What does that mean?'

She said, 'He is very happy to hear that you are home, but he is very sad because he does not know how to tell you that your mother has passed away.'

Just like when Adam dragged me from under the table in the Alafia Hostel, everything slowed down again. There were no guns this time, but it was the same blurry fuzz, all sounds and sensations muted, the world on pause.

We were 10 kilometres from home. How was I supposed to react? My mother was dead. What else was waiting for me? Was I still my father's son? Was I still Cath's husband? I did not know if I had brought shame on my family, if I had bankrupted them. I had no idea what else was waiting for me.

We were driving along Witkoppen Road, and even through my haze I could see that they were taking a really strange route to the house. I left them to it. A few minutes later we pulled up outside a house I had never seen before and they said, 'We are here.' It was the wrong house. Right street name and number, wrong suburb. Seriously, could they have handled it any worse? I began to understand why it took them almost six years to get me out the desert.

I directed them to the right suburb and the right house. The gates opened and my father walked out. I had to grit my teeth one more time: was I still my father's son?

When he walked up to me and gave me a hug, six years of worry began to lift. I was home with my family, safe and alive with the people I loved. I had beaten this.

About the only thing the Secret Service did right that day was stick around on the patio of my parents' house while we spoke to each other and I got a grip on things. There was so much to talk about, but I was still very raw, stumbling for words. My dad and I did not discuss my mom. We did not even discuss not discussing her. We both knew, now was not the time.

In my head I had three tick boxes – my mom, my dad and Cath. I had one box left to figure out.

Cath and I had been married for four years. We had known each other for five. We had been apart for six. The situation we had been put through was insane. So I knew that, whatever came through that door, I could not judge her.

It's funny how strong neural pathways are. When I heard the unmistakeable sound of keys opening the front door of the home I grew up in, it took me back decades through a thousand greetings, hugs and kisses.

I got up and rushed towards the entrance hall, to Cath.

CHAPTER THIRTY-FIVE
Lot's Wife

As told by Cath McGown

'And Lot's wife ... was told not to look back where all those people and their homes had been. But she did look back, and I love her for that, because it was so human' – Kurt Vonnegut, *Slaughterhouse-Five*

On the morning Steve came back to us, I had gone for a run with some friends. I was not in a good space and was taking a cocktail of pills to deal with my depression and anxiety. As I swallowed this fistful of pills each day, I would literally talk to them, saying, 'Just do your job.' It had been a month since Johan was released, and after the initial excitement and hope that Steve would be released too, things had gone quiet again.

I did not want to do the run, but my friends were insistent. They knew, as I suppose I did, that it would do me good to get out the house. The night before I even slept in my running clothes, because even though it was cold, I thought, *If all I have to do in the morning is put my shoes on, then I might just make it out the door*. It worked. I managed to do the run. After we had finished, I got a voice message from Steve's dad.

He said he had had a visit from the Secret Service early that morning and they were still at the house. They would not say whether Steve was being released or if he was dead, but something was happening. Bottom line: 'You need to come now.'

Driving to Magoo's house, I was convinced that it was bad news, that this was the end. It sounded urgent and Magoo did not sound very happy, but I guessed he didn't know what was happening either.

When I got to the house, Magoo was nowhere to be seen. I saw the Secret Service guys sitting on the patio and I identified myself as Steve's wife. I asked them what was happening, but they wouldn't or couldn't tell me anything, other than that Magoo had gone to shower. When I knocked on his bedroom door, Magoo opened it, put his hand on my shoulder and said, 'Cath, he's coming home.'

These were the words I had longed to hear for years. This day that I had played out with so many different imagined scripts was finally here. This was real, it was not imagined.

All the right feelings were in place. I felt good. I felt ready to receive Steve. I didn't feel the blood drain from my body, which had become a familiar feeling for me over the years when dealing with shock or disappointment. A warm rush of happy endorphins, which I must have had in reserve from my 14-kilometre run that morning, swept through my body. My heart was pumping, but I did not have the sore throat I usually get when anxiety rises or I get bad news. This was a great feeling. I was on a high. Even though my thoughts were racing, my mind felt clear.

In the 20 minutes or so it took from the time Magoo called me till I arrived at the McGown house, the Secret Service had told him that one vital piece of information we had been searching for for so long: Steve was coming home. As we came to accept, they wouldn't say just how he was going to be coming home. We didn't even know if we were going to be flying up to Mali, or meeting Steve at the airport. They just kept saying they were waiting for a phone call.

I was still in my running gear, so I asked if there was enough time for me to go home to shower, change and get my overnight bag. I had a bag packed at all times with my passport, my wedding ring and a long black dress and headgear, just in case I was called to go to Mali at short notice to fetch Steve. Even now, that seemed like it might be a possibility; we had no idea how things would play out.

The Secret Service agent told me to hang on while he went outside to make a call. He came back in and gave me the go-ahead to shoot home quickly, but he wanted to take my phone – they were scared that I was going to phone my mom, call the press or whoever, and reveal that Steve was home. For some reason everything had to be hush-hush – we found out later it was because President Jacob Zuma wanted to announce Steve's release to South Africa when he was good and ready.

Magoo intervened and assured them that it would be fine for me to keep my phone, that I wouldn't call anyone. I shot back to my apartment, which was only 15 minutes away. I had the quickest shower ever and got changed. I admit I took a few minutes to blow-dry my hair too, because I wanted to spruce up a bit for Steve. Never mind that he had probably not seen a woman in six years.

When I pulled back into the driveway at Steve's folks' place, there was a third car there, where before there had been only two. Something had changed since I left. I had my own keys, so I let myself in and said, 'Guys, I'm here.' I could hear voices coming from the patio.

I tore from the entrance hall into the lounge, and there he was. My husband. Steve.

With long hair and a long beard, he was still dressed in desert gear, brown robes and a blue bandanna-type thing around his head. No shoes. He looked more like a lost hippie than the Steve I knew. It took me a moment to process that this figure really was my Steve.

My bag fell from my hand. I half-turned and dropped into a crouch. It was as if my body could not trust my eyes, like it had to challenge gravity, to test the fabric of the world, to confirm that this time it wasn't a dream.

Steve came to me and held me in his arms. I clung to him. His shape was familiar, but thinner, and he smelled different, a potent mix of sweat and livestock.

He said, 'Your hair is so long.'

I said, 'But yours is longer than mine.'

The rest of that day was a blur.

Steve showered and put jeans on, which made him look more like the Steve of old. After that morning's run and all the excitement, I was famished, so I offered to make breakfast. I started frying some eggs and bacon. In a way, this was a big thing for me because before Steve was taken I was a vegetarian, something he struggled with a bit. While he was gone, I had changed too; I'd started eating a bit of meat. Not quite lamb chops, but biltong, chicken, bacon, mince and what have you. Earlier that morning, before Steve arrived, one of the agents said, 'You need to prepare for him to be different. He's a Muslim now.'

When Steve saw what I was cooking, he said, 'I don't know about the bacon.'

I said, 'Ah, of course. That's the Muslim thing?'

He put his arms around me and said, 'There are so many good things I'm going tell you about Islam.'

He ate the bacon.

Later that night, after the Secret Service agents eventually left Magoo's house, Steve and I went to bed in one of the spare bedrooms. It was incredibly surreal to be there, to be with him again after everything that had happened. From the Sahara to Sandton, across space and time, Steve and Cath, husband and wife.

I jumped in the shower. As I came into the bedroom and was drying my body, Steve sat on the bed and averted his eyes. It was awkward, but by being there with my bag packed for the night, my ring on my finger and getting changed in front of him, I was trying to show him *I am still your wife, I am still here.* I'd had dreams about Steve rejecting me, my subconscious twisting itself into hypothetical knots over whether he would accept me as his wife again. And here he was, dealing with his own demons, struggling to even look at me. We were going to have to get to know each other again.

So much had passed in the last six years.

I got changed and we got in to bed. When Steve hugged me, I told him then and there that I had been with someone, but it was over.

Steve said, 'All I want to know is are you with me? Is it really over?'

'I'm with you,' I said. 'It's over.'

CHAPTER THIRTY-SIX

Lot McGown

'There was no division I could see between the essential teaching of all Prophets and wise men of religion' – Cat Stevens/Yusuf Islam

I think of the time I spent in the desert as a black hole, but even the days when I got back home are hard to remember that well. My memory from those first few weeks is poor. I had to go to hospital for a bunch of issues, from encephalomyelitis to malnutrition. I lost 16 kilograms in the time I was in the desert.

Even while I was in the hospital, it was hard to get away from the noise. Government wanted press conferences, as did Gift of the Givers, who had played such a vital role in getting me out. I heard about all the people who prayed for me, and felt incredible gratitude.

Then came the press and the embassies, the secret services, the families of other kidnapped victims; I even heard from an Oxford professor doing research into sandstorms.

We finally met President Zuma (after he cancelled on a few occasions). He was the reason I could not tell anyone I had been home for a few days – it needed it to be his announcement. Zuma was charming, as everyone predicted. He related his own stories of what it was like when he got out of prison and asked me, 'What's it like to see women again?'

I was *gatvol*. I hadn't said 'no' to people in six years, because I'd been bullied by teenagers with Kalashnikovs, so now with everyone wanting a piece of me, I was torn. At first I helped, then I felt overwhelmed, then angry. Did this publication or that secret service lift a finger to help me? Then why should I help them? I had a six-year black hole that I was trying to make sense of, and everybody was exploiting me because of it. It only made sense to share information when another hostage's safety was at stake.

A lot had happened while I was gone. My mom died, as did several aunts and uncles and Sue's husband, Al. My sister Leigh-Anne had two kids; six years results in fully-formed children with personalities and quirks and questions about weird Uncle Steve from the desert.

In the desert I'd heard snippets of news from time to time, like the EFF chanting 'pay back the money' in parliament, or Trump coming to power. Al Qaeda were pleased about Trump, because it would make Muslims irate and recruitment would skyrocket. Lots of things were news to me, like the fact that Steve Jobs, Frank Sinatra and Casey Kasem died. The world moved on while I was gone, which reminded me of the *hadith* about how as the day of judgment approaches, the days will speed up. What I know more than anything is that sometimes we just have to slow down. We need to stop and become the calm.

Post-release, the South African Secret Service gave me rules and more rules; they were at war with DIRCO, who gave us other rules that contrasted with theirs. Then there were the Brits, the Ozzies and other secret service debriefs. I was flown to the UK to see MI5 and MI6, after much cloak-and-dagger James Bond subterfuge – *Take the 9am train from Clapham Junction down to Dorking, wear a blue scarf, walk past the post box and the statue of Robert the Bruce.* They'd never had a hostage come out of the desert with so much detail. I hold the Guinness World Record as the longest Al Qaeda-held prisoner, so I'm probably the best-informed on the subject of Al Qaeda in Mali. I was debriefing hard to everyone, but could only upload so much.

Getting my life back on track took time, from bank accounts to IDs, driver's licences and passports to tax documents for both South Africa and 'Britannia'. The UK government were helpful; South African, not so much.

One of the hardest things to get a grip on was time. I read the Canadian diplomat Robert Fowler's book. He was taken by AQIM for four months. One hundred and twenty-eight days. That's a picnic. What is six years? It's a doctor's degree. The penny really dropped when I was sitting at the British Embassy in Pretoria waiting to receive an emergency passport for my debriefing by MI5 and MI6. A young mother came in with her daughter, who was around 18. They were trying to get an emergency passport too. I sat there listening as they were filling out a form.

The mom said, 'Ah my *skat*, where were you in 2013?'

'Oh mom, I was in Standard Eight.'

'Okay and in 2015, what were you doing?'

'I was in Matric.'

I sat there listening to these dates and this person's life and thought,

The first date she spoke about I was already kidnapped. The last date she spoke about, I was still in the desert. She had gone through so many transitions in her life while I was sitting on a fucking sand dune.

I could talk about the desert, but I couldn't talk about anything else. I could talk about running from surveillance planes, digging a hole and slaughtering a goat, but as soon as somebody started on about rugby or the stock market or St Stithians building a pavilion next to the swimming pool, I was like, *huh*? That stuff went right over my head. My filter was still set to, 'Is somebody going to die?'

Getting on the plane home closed one door and opened another. My dad always said to me, 'We all get 24 hours in a day. We must take responsibility for what we do.' There were echoes of the Islamic teachings about what you do on Earth being entirely on you. I did not choose to get kidnapped, but once it happened I had to take responsibility and make the most of it. I had to control what I could and accept the rest. This was a skill I learned during six years as a prisoner with a boot above me. I had no choice. My time in the desert was the first phase of my rehab, my Sahara schooling. The second phase was my city schooling.

I had to get to grips with being Muslim or Christian, or being happy with something in between. I had to get to know my wife again and reconnect with my family and friends. In the beginning, I was an island. I wanted to be able to trust people again. What was it like to be normal in your 40s? My friend Rich Farber said, 'Don't compare yourself to us – we're more messed up than you are. Everyone is lost, chasing money.'

There was a lot I did not understand about the world. I didn't understand new vehicles. I hadn't heard of Uber or Airbnb. I joined a cycling group, and people thought I was pretty strange as I marvelled at this thing called Strava. Terminology had changed, as had the value of money. I remember being excited that mountain biking had become so popular; then I saw their prices and that silenced me. All I had in the desert was sand, sticks and stones, and now I was in a world where I was the weirdo because I did not know about a cycling app.

I was a giant sponge for the first six months, the camp wallflower again. The only thing I could relate to were my Saharan stories, so I started feeling like a one-trick pony at barbecues and dinner parties as conversation inevitably swung towards me and my shitty desert holiday. I didn't know how to be in the normal world. I desperately needed just to shoot the breeze with people, talk nonsense, listen to music. It wasn't a want, it was a need.

When I got home, I tried calling Radio 702 to talk to the science guy, but some questions they don't want on radio: 'Hi, I am the guy who was kidnapped. We used to count the seconds when we heard thunderstorms to work out that they were 20 kilometres away, but we'd also hear guys blowing themselves up and were told it was 200 kilometres away. How does that make sense?'

As time went by, I no longer wanted to talk about making grass huts and walking across sand dunes with Al Qaeda. I was not a specimen to be prodded and interrogated, nor did I want charity or 'ag, shame' vibes. I just wanted to be me, a guy from Johannesburg, who went to London and lived in the Sahara; a multi-faceted person who can talk about anything.

My memory was terrible. I struggled to hang on to things and had to hear them several times. My entire world had turned inside out. English words had become sounds while Arabic words were words. After being Lot for so long, even my name, 'Steve', was a sound. I found it easier to be alone at times.

In the desert I learned how to be myself again. In the city I had to learn how to interact with people. I had to learn how to laugh and joke and be easygoing again.

My dad and I took a drive to visit our farm in the Karoo. We ended up driving into Colesberg quite late. We went to the pub for a beer, and there was a big group of bikers there; huge Afrikaans guys whose 1300cc Suzuki motorbikes were lined up outside. We walked in, sat down at the bar, ordered drinks and started chatting to these guys about who they were, where they were from and what bikes they rode. I found it quite embarrassing, but my dad liked dropping the conversation bomb, 'This is my son, he rides bikes, he was kidnapped in Mali.'

One of the bikers, an absolute beast of a man, was drunk out of his skull. Despite his size, he seemed really gentle. When my dad dropped this comment, it went quiet in the pub and they all started to listen as I told my story. When we got to the end of the evening, the big guy came over to me in front of everybody and hugged me. He cried on my shoulder and said, 'I know what you've been through and I'm sorry. It's going to be okay.' And with that he disappeared out into the night.

The leader of the bikers tapped his temple and made a cuckoo sign. He explained that the big guy had been held prisoner in a bunker for three months during the Angola War. He'd been out for a long time, but he was still a mess. I'd probably been out of the desert for a month and a half.

My heart broke for this guy, and I realised how fortunate I was to be holding it together to the level I was, because of course I had PTSD. I went to a psychologist three times before things got too busy. The psychologist suggested that, because I was introspective and committed to understanding my situation right from the first year, I had started to get my head around my ordeal while I was still in the desert.

There were layers to my recovery. When I came out I thought I was fine, but three months later I looked back to how I was in August and realised I had been shaky. In January, I looked back at December and thought the same. In April I looked back at January and – same thing. It probably took me a year and a half to make proper progress, and to start to feel less like Lot and more like Steve again.

Original Steve, 18-year-old Steve, with the future in his hands.

Today, I still hear planes from far away long before anyone else does. Sometimes I am sure I can hear them at OR Tambo, 30 kilometres away.

Very rarely, when I'm listening to the radio in the car, somebody getting interviewed in Afrikaans will refer to the UK as 'Britannia', and that pronunciation, and the guttural similarity between an Arab and an Afrikaner saying the same word, will evoke a deep fear. In a split second I am transported back to the Edge of the Mountains, to a hazy spaghetti of confusion and terror, where I was helpless and on the brink of insanity.

Sometimes, I hear the blasts from mine dumps in Johannesburg and I am taken back to the shockwaves we felt in the desert when Abu Laith, said goodbye and with eyes set on *Jannah,* drove a Land Cruiser laden with explosives into a Malian army depot.

People ask if I will ever go back into banking. I joke with them and say that I would rather become a terrorist. It is not banking that I have a problem with; I have a problem with people being something that they aren't. It's like putting a round peg in a square hole; it just doesn't fit for me. I believe we need to be true to ourselves if we are going to be happy and make the most of our lives – after all, we each only get one shot at it. In Islam it says that if you do not use the gifts and talents that Allah has given you, then Allah, the Angels and the Prophets are all very angry with you.

I still think of *wudu* when I wash my face. I praise Allah and I call him God. I still appreciate many of the *hadiths* and the general outlook of Islam. Do I wish what happened to me to ever happen to anyone else? Hell no. I wish for all jihad to end.

When I hear of ISIS militants taking over towns in the north of Mozambique, South Africa's eastern neighbour, I wonder how long it is going to take for them to install Sharia law and turn their sights to Mzanzi. Years? Decades? Centuries? Millennia? This struggle, the wars of doctrine and dogma are as old as man. All I ask is that I'm left out of it.

Insha Allah.

CHAPTER THIRTY-SEVEN

Mom

'Just do what makes you happy' – Bev McGown

A lot of mates said my kidnapping showed people what was important in life and brought groups back together. So many friends came back into my life after I came home. One of them was Jacqui Schepers, who knew my mom back from when we were in Standard Eight. She contacted me from Australia.

'I am really sorry about your mom,' she said, 'but I truly believe that she passed away two months before you were released to go upstairs to kick someone's butt, because things were taking too long. And look, two months later you were released.'

My mom used to smoke. We pestered her for years to get off the cigarettes but she never did. Before I was kidnapped, a doctor gave her two years to live. Her health deteriorated until she eventually had to be put on a ventilator. I never saw her like that. My only experience with it came at my first Christmas post-desert.

In December 2017, Cath and I went to my dad's house to help with Christmas preparations. We got the Christmas tree out of the cupboard and put it up in the lounge. Just doing that reminded me of times when I was young, putting up decorations with my mom, my dad and my sister. I went down to my mom's room to look for the decorations; I opened up a drawer and came across her breathing equipment.

The pipes, the tubes and the mask completely flattened me. I wasn't expecting it. I had been told she had to do this to stay alive, but actually seeing the visual apparatus brought it home. As I removed the equipment from the drawer to inspect it, white powder fell from inside the mask. I assumed this was something they put inside it to ease up her chest. That really hit home. This was what she wore on her face, every day, just to breathe. It made me feel the six years' worth of pain my mom went through to stay alive.

My mom never left a message or note for me. I asked my sister about it. Leigh said, 'Let me tell you that mom loved you more than anything in the whole world. She lived to see you come out of the desert.'

While there was no note, she communicated in other ways. You could say one of her love languages was dealing with my admin. When I got back, I discovered that I had been blacklisted by my South African bank for disappearing for years. I sat up late one Wednesday night, going through documents in a lever-arch file. She'd filed them, month-by-month, right up to the end. The March/April bank statement had my mom's handwriting on it – writing I knew so well from my mom signing off on my homework in Grade 1. In that neat scrawl was packed so much love and care and generosity, all the things that made my mother such an amazing package.

This was a month before you died, I thought. *What were you doing, wasting your final days looking at my bank statements? Why didn't you throw these away and enjoy the last two months you had left? Instead you were here, doing this.*

When I told my sister about it, she said, 'That was exactly what she lived for, to be near you by helping you.'

When I turned the page and looked at the May/June statement, there was no more handwriting; that was the month she passed away. I could literally follow my mom through my bank statements to the end of her life.

Shortly after I got home, we escaped as a family to the Kruger National Park. There had been a lot of stress on us all, and this gave us a chance to unwind and get away from all the pressure and the journalists. As we were leaving the Kruger, we were down near the huge baobab tree en route to Tshokwane and we had my mom's ashes in a little urn. It was a special place for our family, one we had been to many times.

We all enjoyed birding as a family, and this waterhole had a lovely vista, with elephants and waterbuck coming down to drink. It was the kind of place my mom would want to be, so we decided to scatter her ashes there, overlooking the water. We thought, *A pond brings life*. There were lots of water birds, including my friends from the Sahara, the plovers.

We pulled up next to the dam and waited for other cars to drive away. I was driving my dad's Fortuner with my dad and Cath, my sister was following in another car with her husband Gregg and their kids.

Dad stepped out onto the grass and said a small prayer. Then he opened the urn and scattered my mom's ashes. When another vehicle started to come down the road, he climbed back in the car. I could see he was emotional, his eyes bright-red. He left the door open slightly for a breeze, put his hand on my shoulder and said, 'Your mother was an amazing lady.' Then he went quiet. I sat there looking at my dad, tears rolling down my cheeks from behind my sunglasses.

Being able to truly feel, deeply, is an absolute blessing. It shows you are alive, that you are in touch with what matters and that you embrace the full gamut of what life brings you. I learned that one should never shy away from those emotions. To be able to be emotional makes every part of being alive that much more special. The problem is when you don't feel anything, or when you put up walls to block out stress. That is when life becomes bland.

For quite some time I had this wall up around me about my mother. I wasn't allowing myself to engage in that conversation. On paper, the equation was simple: my mom died and it was very sad, because she wanted to be around to see me come home. That's what it is. The minute I tried to take it deeper, the wall was in the way.

My mom and I were very close, so I know she wouldn't want me to be angry about what she went through. I'm not even angry with Al Qaeda. A lot of good stuff came out of my kidnapping. I managed to figure out who I am and figure out what's important to me. I managed to give myself a reset, from being a money-obsessed taker who is never happy to someone who lives in the present and appreciates what he has, spends more time with people he loves and spends more time doing what he enjoys. My time in the desert helped me relearn how to live. I was given a second chance to rebuild my character based on what was important to me. My biggest fear is that, with time, I will start to forget my Saharan ways. I don't ever want that to happen.

Forget the murder, the terror and the boredom of the years spent in the sand: the most difficult part of this whole saga was my mom passing away. Her dying before I got home and having to suffer for so long – that is something I have not processed yet.

I like what Jacqui said, the idea of my old lady heading up there to sort things out. Because I never got to say goodbye, I still have some way to go to get closure, but I will get there.

Because I know myself now, and I know what to do.

Glossary

*Allahu akbar allahu akbar
Allahu akbar allahu akbar
Ash-hadu anla ilaha illah
Allah Ash-hadu anla ilaha
illah Allah Ash-hadu anna
muhammadar-rasulullah
Ash-hadu anna muhammadar-
rasulullah Hayya as-salah
Hayya as-salah Hayya al-
falah Hayya al-falah Allahu
akbar allahu akbar La ilaha
illa Allah* – The Adhan
(Call To Prayer)

adhan (call to prayer)

Allah hu Akbar (God is great)

amaliya (mission)

aya (verses of the Quraan)

bismillah (in the name
of God)

chai (tea)

dawah (spreading the word
of Islam)

dhabihah (animal slaughter)

dhuba (striped hyena)

dukhan (smoke)

Dunya (temporal world/
Earth)

emir (ruler)

faar (mice)

fakron (tortoise)

khateer (dangerous)

gelter (pond formed in *wadi*
after rains)

Haasi aghmar (the red well)

Haasi sheikh (the sheikh's
well)

habatoa soda (nigella sativa
oil)

halaal (permissible or lawful)

halaqa (circle)

harmoom (charcoal)

herassa (security detail)

Hassaniya (Arabic dialect)

hikma (wisdom)

imamah (scarf/turban)

Insha Allah (God willing)

Jannah (afterlife)

jasoos (spies)

jmal (camel)

kashiva (surveillance plane)

kamees (shirt)

korshi (Fennec foxes)

kuffar (non-believers)

lesa jayed (not good)

laurun (Monitor lizard)

makan (camp)

mauna (larder/kitchen)

misnuna (biting desert bug)

muhathin (person who does the call to prayer)

Mujahid (one engaged in jihad)

Mujahideen (plural of mujahid)

murtadeen (apostate)

Naar/Jahannam (hell)

Qaddarallahu wa maa sha'a fa'ala (Allah has ordained and as He willed, He has done)

Qamar abyad (big moon/white moon)

Quraan (holy book of Islam)

rahma (compassion)

raka (unit of prayer)

sakhen (hot)

sukr (sugar)

sabr (patience)

Salaam Alykum (Peace be upon you)

Salat al-'asr (prayers in the late part of the afternoon)

Salat al-fajr (dawn prayers, before sunrise)

Salat al-'isha (prayers between sunset and midnight)

Salat al-maghrib (prayers just after sunset)

Salat al-zuhr (midday prayers)

shibani (old person)

sujood (prostration to the ground)

sourat (chapters of the Quraan)

suruwal kameez (trouser and tunic combo)

thorban (porcupine)

Tuareg (tribe name)

Umma (the Muslim body)

virna (little cooker)

wadi (dry river bed)

wudu (washing before prayers)

zulzil (lizard)

Key events 2011–2017

2011

25 NOVEMBER 2011
Steve McGown captured by Al Qaeda in Timbuktu, Mali

2012

6 APRIL 2012
Steve converts to Islam

29 JUNE 2012
Al Qaeda and affiliates defeat the MNLA and take Timbuktu. Steve returns to the city, a prisoner

AUGUST 2012
Steve return to the city of Timbuktu as a prisoner

9 OCTOBER 2012
Malala Yousafzai is shot in the head by Taliban

2013

13 MARCH 2013
Cardinal Jorge Mario Bergoglio of Argentina becomes Pope Francis

5 MARCH 2013
'International Camp' as surviving Al Qaeda fighters, pushed into the desert by the French, meet en masse

FEBRUARY 2013
Johan attempts to escape and is caught

APRIL 15 2013
Boston Marathon Bombing

DECEMBER 5 2013
President Nelson Mandela dies

2014

17 JANUARY 2014
Deputy Emir Abu Laith blows himself up

8 MARCH 2014
Malaysian Airlines Flight MH370 vanishes

20 FEB–26 MARCH 2014
Russia annexes Crimea from the Ukraine

APRIL 2014
Football and Red Rover with Al Qaeda

17 JULY 2014
Malaysia Airlines Flight 17 (MH17) was shot down while flying over eastern Ukraine

2012–2016

26 DECEMBER 2013–9 JUNE 2016
Ebola outbreak in Sierra Leone, Guinea and Liberia

2015

7 JAN 2015
Al Qaeda attack and kill 10 journalists and 2 police officers in the Charlie Hebdo attack in Paris

5 APRIL 2015
ISIS style proof of life video

6 APRIL 2015
Sjaak Rijke is rescued by French forces

29 JULY 2015
After 54 years, Cuba and the United States establish full diplomatic relations

2016

23 JUNE 2016
Brexit: The UK votes to leave the European Union

DECEMBER 2016
Steve receives a four-month-old letter from South African government saying his mother is gravely ill

2017

20 JANUARY 2017
Donald Trump is inaugurated as the 45th President of the United States

23 JUNE 2017
Johan Gustafsson is released

21 JULY 2017
Steve begins his multi-day journey out of the desert

● LONDON

● TIMBUKTU

JOHANNESBURG ●

Depart London
13 October 2011

Arrive Johannesburg
30 July 2017

Acknowledgements

I would like to start by thanking the entire Daily Maverick team for all their efforts and hard work in creating this much-anticipated book.

My thanks must first and foremost go to Tudor Caradoc-Davies for being so effective and efficient throughout the process. He was able to accommodate my erratic work schedule during the Covid-19 months. Meeting with him regularly, even if only virtually, helped to develop a structure for me during these times. I want to thank him for listening so intently, for taking the time to understand the situation, for his Zoom punctuality, for his friendship, laughs and jokes. Tudor, thanks mate, for your hard work, dedication and creativity, and for the mammoth task of completing the book in four months. You really pulled the rabbit out of the hat. I'd also like to thank Tudor's wife Ingrid for putting up with him and looking after him while he wrote the book under huge time pressure.

I would like to thank Fran Beighton for believing in the story, for putting up with the boys' banter, for being so organised and steering the ship. Thank you for your reassurance during the difficult times; your guidance and encouragement were much appreciated.

Ingeborg Pelser, thank you for always being friendly, kind and a breath of fresh air. Your management of the process was critical for the publication of this book. You taught me a lot, and I thoroughly enjoyed working with you.

I thank editor Jacqui L'Ange for being so calm during the storm when the pressure was on. Despite the tractor and baboon issues, you managed to squeeze the overweight rabbit back into the hat by getting the book from 140,000 words down to the required 95,000!

I would like to thank Jane McDuff for steering us in the right direction and providing us with a good foundation in the unknown world of publishing; for her knowledge and years of experience in the publishing world and answering all our questions.

Thanks must also go to Sue Peiser, my mother-in-law, for introducing us to Daily Maverick and for her invaluable input.

On the legal front, thanks go to Keith Lister, who I have known for 30 years, for providing us with legal advice during the process. It helped having someone who had my best interests at heart.

Imtiaz Sooliman from Gift of the Givers played a pivotal role in my negotiations. I thank him for giving up his time to be interviewed, and for sharing his side of the story.

To my family: I thank my father Magoo and sister Leigh-Anne Quixley for answering all my 'black hole' questions, helping me make sense of the six years that I missed back here in the real world, as well as their input into the book and their unwavering support.

A special thanks to my wife, Cath, for all the cups of coffee and meals she prepared for me while I was dashing between Zoom calls. When I was overwhelmed, she stepped in and used her great writing and organisational skills to complete various tasks for me. I thank her for her bravery and honesty while writing up her stories, and having to relive the difficult memories that she wanted to put in the past.

Thank you to everybody who supported my family during my six years in captivity. There were many of you who always had them in your thoughts and prayers. My apologies for putting you through this.

Alhamdulillah (Praise be to God)